CW00370162

DUBLIN
STREETFINDER

Contents

Tourist and travel information 2

Key to map symbols 3

Key to map pages . . . . 4 - 5

Route planning map . . . . 6 - 7

Main Dublin maps . . . . 8 - 57

Central Dublin map . . . . 58 - 59

Guide to central Dublin . . . . . 60 - 79

Index to place names 80

Index to street names . . . . 80 - 96

Tourist and travel information

Air

Dublin Airport
Tel: 01 814 1111.
Web: www.dublin–airport.com
Frequent direct flights operate between Dublin and many airports in Britain, Europe and North America. Internal flights are available to Cork, Donegal, Galway, Kerry, Knock, Shannon & Sligo. Aer Arann **Tel: 0818 210210 (R of I), 0800 587 2324 (UK)** www.aerarannexpress.com & Aer Lingus **Tel: 01 886 8888 (R of I), 0845 084 4444 (UK)** www.aerlingus.com operate the internal routes. Other operators flying into Dublin are British Airways **Tel: 1890 626 747 (R of I), 0870 850 9850 (UK)** www.britishairways.com, Flybe **Tel: 1890 925 532 (R of I), 0871 700 0535 (UK)** www.flybe.com, British Midland **Tel: 01 407 3036 (R of I), 0870 6070 555 (UK)** www.flybmi.com & Ryanair **Tel: 01 609 7800 (R of I), 0871 246 0000 (UK)** www.ryanair.com.

The airport is 12km (8 miles) north of the city centre with Dublin Bus operating many services to and from the airport including the 'Airlink' express coach service operating between the airport, the central bus station in Store Street (Busáras) and the two mainline rail stations, Connolly and Heuston. It runs every 10 - 15 mins (15 - 20 mins on Sundays) between 05.45 and 23.30 from the airport and between 05.15 and 22.50 from O'Connell Street in the centre of Dublin. **Tel: 01 873 4222** www.dublinbus.ie. 'Aircoach' runs between the airport and Dublin City and South Dublin City stopping at major hotels. The 24 hour service operates every 10-20 minutes except from 24.00 and 05.00 when an hourly service operates. **Tel: 01 844 7118** www.aircoach.ie. 'Aerdart' is a bus service operating every 15 minutes between the airport and Howth Junction DART station.

Services at Dublin airport include Travel Information, Tourist Information and Bureau de Change

Passenger and vehicle ferries

Numerous modern ferries and high-speed services with drive-on drive-off facilities cross the Irish Sea to Dublin from Britain (Liverpool, Mostyn, Holyhead), the Isle of Man and France (Cherbourg).

Irish Ferries (Dublin–Holyhead). **Tel: 01 638 3333 / 0818 300 400** or from UK: **08705 17 17 17.**
Web: www.irishferries.com
Email: info@irishferries.ie

Norse Merchant Ferries (Dublin–Birkenhead). **Tel: 01 819 2999** or from UK: **0870 600 4321.**
Web: www.norsemerchant.com

P & O Irish Sea (Dublin–Liverpool).
Tel: 1800 409 049 or from UK: **0870 24 24 777.**
Web: www.poirishsea.com

Isle of Man Steam Packet Company/Sea Containers (Dublin–Douglas).
Tel: 1800 80 50 55 or from UK: **08705 523 523.**
Web: www.steam–packet.com

Stena Line
(Dún Laoghaire–Holyhead & Dublin–Holyhead).
Tel: 01 204 7777
or from UK: **08705 70 70 70.**
Web: www.stenaline.co.uk
Email: info.ie@stenaline.com

Dublin Port and Dún Laoghaire have bus and taxi services to the city centre although on busy sailings it may be prudent to pre-book a taxi. The ferry terminal at Dún Laoghaire is also linked to the city by the DART rail service with a 20 minute journey time.

Tourist information

Dublin Tourism Centre, Suffolk Street. **Tel: 01 605 7700.** Open: (July and August) Mon–Sat 09.00–19.00, (Sept–June) Mon–Sat 09.00–17.30. Open Sun & bank holidays 10.30–15.00; closed 25 & 26 Dec & 1 Jan.
Formerly St. Andrew's Church, the centre provides details of visitor attractions and events in the city as well as acting as a ticket and accommodation bureau. Transport and tour information, exchange facilities and a café are also on hand.
Other tourist information and reservation centres in Dublin (walk-in only) are located at:
Dublin Airport. Open: Mon–Sun 08.00–22.00. Open bank holidays except 25 & 26 Dec & 1 Jan.
Dún Laoghaire Ferry Terminal. Open: Mon–Sat 10.00–18.00, closed 13.00-14.00. Open bank holidays except 25 & 26 Dec & 1 Jan.

Baggott Street Bridge. Open: Mon–Fri 09.30–17.00, closed 12.00-12.30. Closed bank holidays.
For accommodation reservations in Dublin and Ireland contact Ireland Reservations. Tel from within Ireland: **1800 363 626**; from within UK: **008 002 580 2580.**

Official tourism website for Dublin:
Web: www.visitdublin.com
Email: information@dublintourism.ie
or reservations@dublintourism.ie

Irish Tourist Board Website:
Web: www.ireland.ie

Department of Environment, Heritage & Local Government:
Web: www.heritageireland.ie
Email: info@heritageireland.ie

Key to map symbols ❸

M1	Motorway / under construction	P	Car park
	Tunnelled motorway	Garda	Garda Síochána (police) station
N6	National primary road	i	Tourist information centre
N55	National secondary road	+	Church
R95	Regional road	▪ PO ▪ Lib	Public service building (appropriate name shown)
	Other road		Leisure / Tourism
	Track		Shopping
	Ferry		Administration / Law
	Administrative boundary		Health / Hospital
24	Postcode number		Education
	Postal boundary		Notable building
	Railway / Station		Built up area
JERVIS	Dublin Luas tramway / Station		Park / Garden / Sports ground / Public open space
	Bus / Coach station		Cemetery
	Lake / River		Golf course

```
0              ¼              ½ mile
0        0.25        0.5        0.75        1 km
```

Scale 1:15,840 4 inches (10.2cm) to 1 mile / 6.3cm to 1km

Published by Collins
An imprint of HarperCollins*Publishers*
77-85 Fulham Palace Road, Hammersmith, London W6 8JB

www.collins.co.uk

Copyright © HarperCollins*Publishers* Ltd 2005
Collins® is a registered trademark of HarperCollins*Publishers* Limited
Mapping generated from Collins Bartholomew digital databases

Based on Ordnance Survey Ireland by permission of the Government. © Government of Ireland.

Printed in Hong Kong
RI11894   NDB
e-mail: roadcheck@harpercollins.co.uk

Ward

Pinkeen

N3

Tolka

Kilbride ○ Coolquoy ○ Chapelmidway **S**

○ Ward ○ Skephubb

N2

○ Baytownpark

Killshane ○ St.
Margaret'

Dunboyne ○ Ballymacoll

○ Kilgraigue **Clonee**

Corduff **M50** Finglas

8 - 9 | **10 - 11**

Blanchardstown **6** Glasnevi

Rathleek

Clonsilla Castleknock

24 - 25 | **26 - 27**
Phoenix Park **N3**

Liffey **Leixlip** Toll

M4 **7** Palmerston

N4 **Lucan** Chapelizod | **34 - 35**

Celbridge **32 - 33**

Stacumny

Grand Canal

Coolfitch Clondalkin **40 - 41** | **42 - 43**
9 Crumlin

Hazelhatch Milltown

N7 **10** **N81**

Newcastle Kingswood **48 - 49** | **50 - 51**
Brownsbarn **11**

○ Ardclough Saggart **TALLAGHT** **12**

○ Athgoe **Rathcoole** **M50**

○ Oughterard Redgap ○

Friarstown ○ Rockbroo

N81

○ Porterstown Raheen ○

Brittas ○

○ Thornberry ○ **Kilteel** Cunard ○

○ Monaspick

○ **Rathmore**

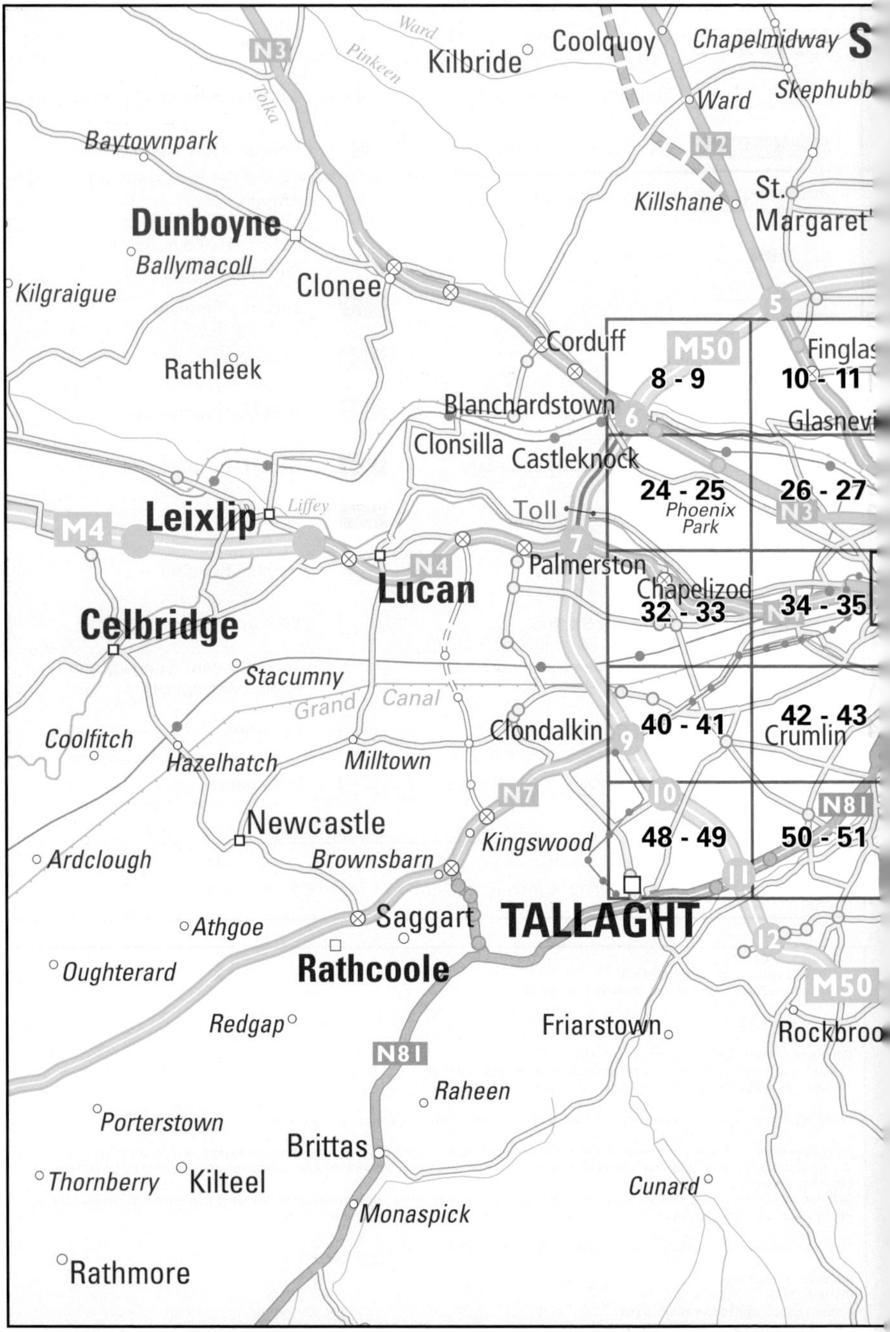

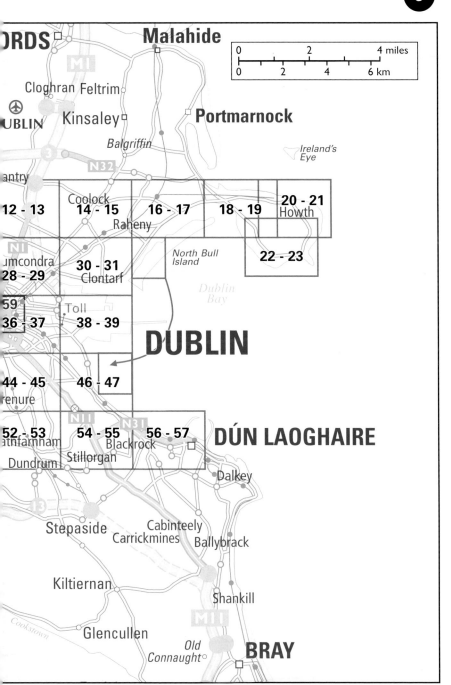

RDS

Malahide

Cloghran Feltrim

DUBLIN   Kinsaley

Portmarnock

Balgriffin

Ireland's Eye

antry

Coolock

12 - 13   **14 - 15**   **16 - 17**   **18 - 19**   **20 - 21**
Howth

Raheny

North Bull Island   **22 - 23**

umcondra   **30 - 31**
28 - 29   Clontarf

Dublin Bay

59   Toll
36 - 37   **38 - 39**

DUBLIN

44 - 45   **46 - 47**
enure

52 - 53   **54 - 55**   **56 - 57**   DÚN LAOGHAIRE
athfarnham   Blackrock
Dundrum   Stillorgan

Dalkey

Stepaside   Cabinteely
Carrickmines   Ballybrack

Kiltiernan

Shankill

Glencullen   Old
Connaught   **BRAY**

Cookstown

| 0 | | 2 | | 4 miles |
| 0 | 2 | 4 | 6 km | |

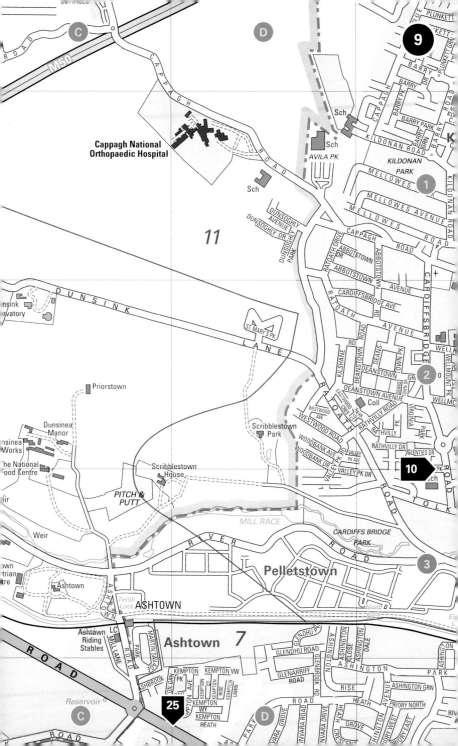

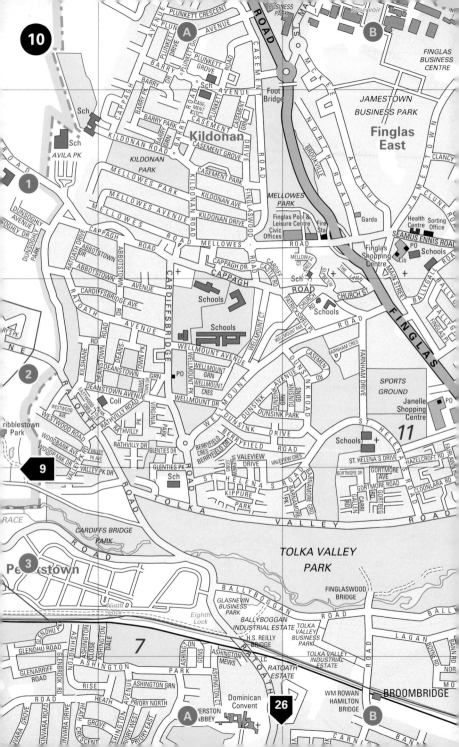

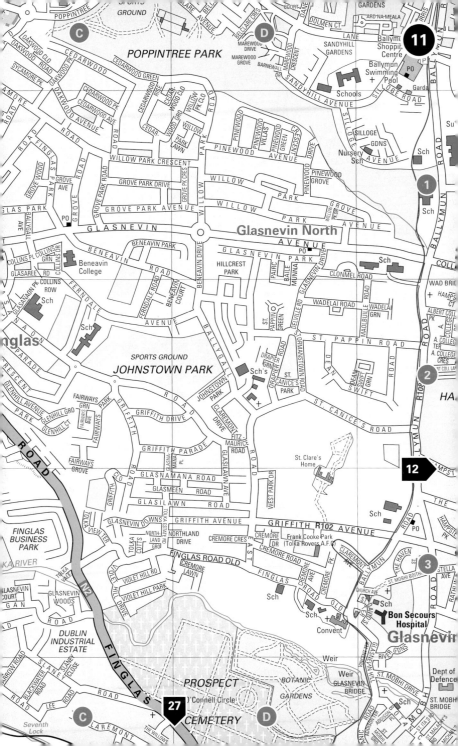

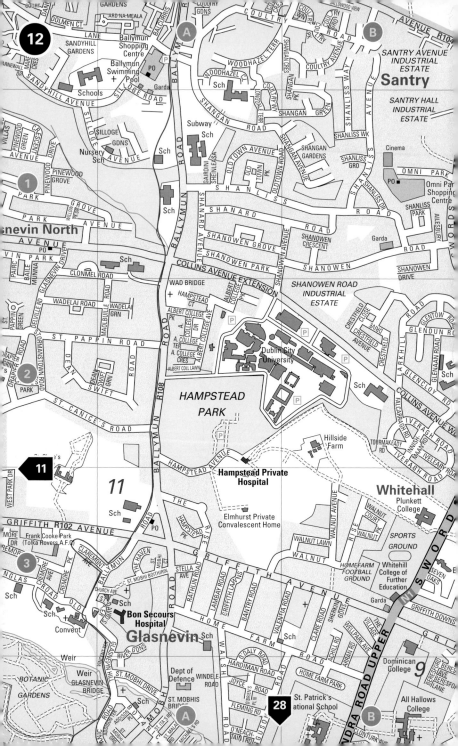

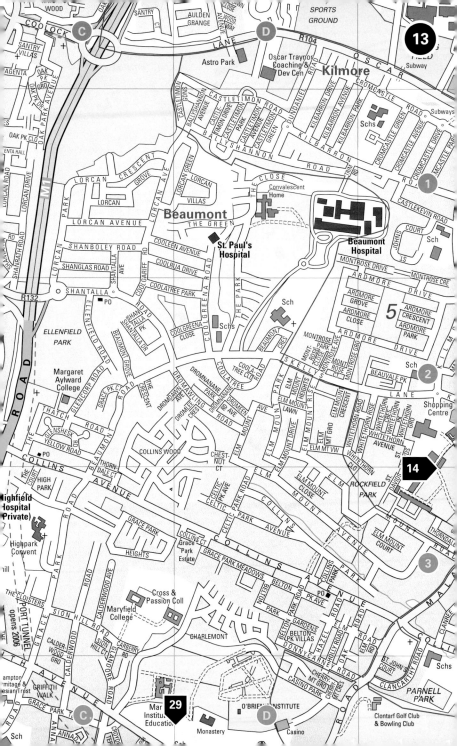

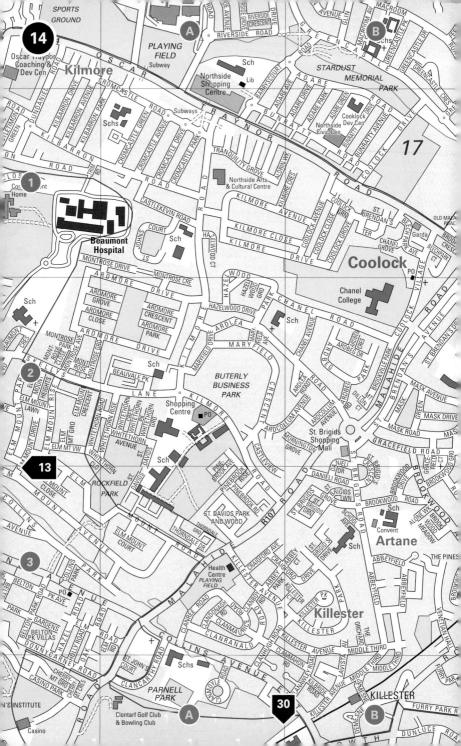

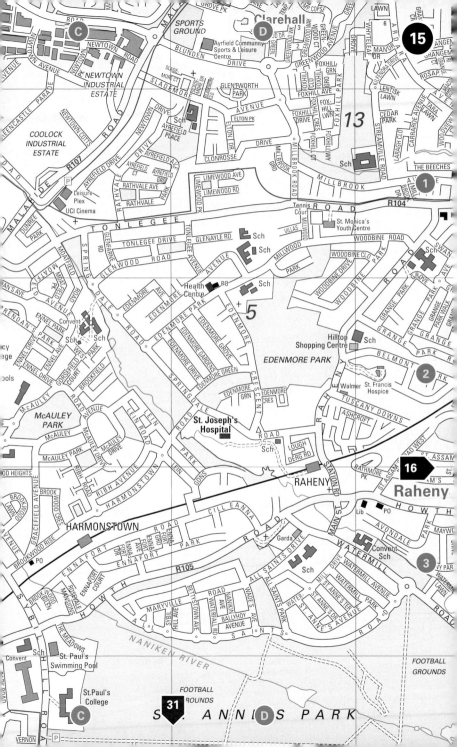

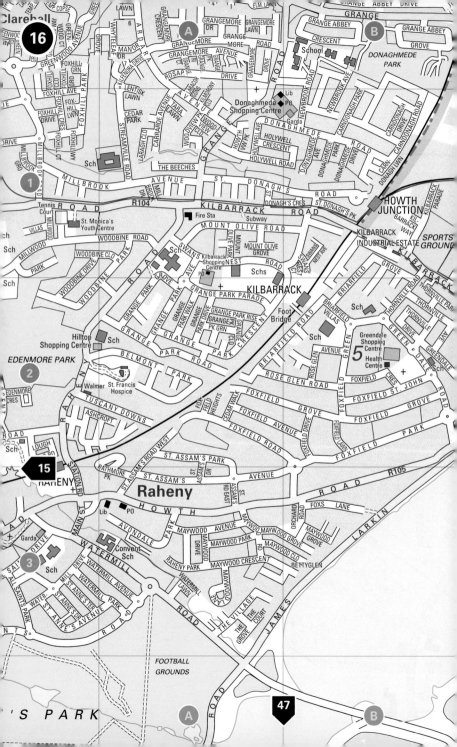

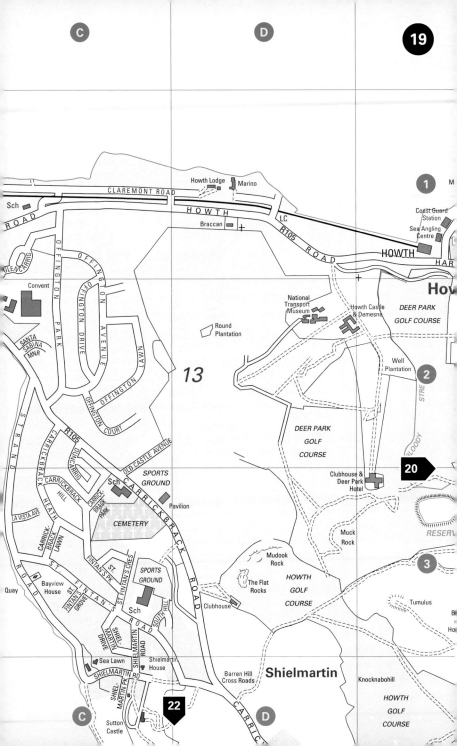

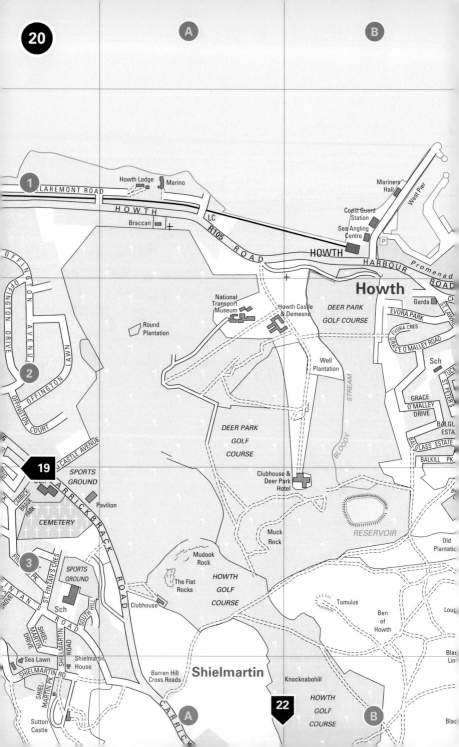

A   B

Claremont Road
Howth Lodge   Marino
HOWTH
LC
Braccan
R105 ROAD

Mariners Hall   West Pier
Coast Guard Station
Sea Angling Centre
HOWTH HARBOUR   Promenade ROAD

OFFINGTON DRIVE
OFFINGTON AVENUE

National Transport Museum
Round Plantation
Howth Castle & Demesne
DEER PARK GOLF COURSE
Howth

Garda
EVORA PARK
EVORA CRES
GRACE O'MALLEY ROAD

OFFINGTON COURT

Well Plantation

Sch
TUCK
ST PETER'S

BLOODY STREAM

GRACE O'MALLEY DRIVE

CASTLE AVENUE

SPORTS GROUND

19

CARRICK BRACK PARK
CARRICKBRACK ROAD

CEMETERY

Pavilion

DEER PARK GOLF COURSE

Clubhouse & Deer Park Hotel

RESERVOIR

BALGL ESTA
BALGLASS ESTATE
BALKILL PK

FINTAN PK

3

SPORTS GROUND

ST FINTAN'S CRES

Sch

FINTAN ROAD GROVE

SOUTH HILL ROAD

SHIEL MARTIN DRIVE

Sea Lawn

SHIELMARTIN RD

Shielmartin House

SHIEL MARTIN PK

SHIEL MARTIN CRES

Sutton Castle

Muck Rock

Mudook Rock

The Flat Rocks

Clubhouse

HOWTH GOLF COURSE

Barren Hill Cross Roads

Shielmartin

A

Knocknabohill

22

Tumulus

Ben of Howth

Old Plantatic

Lou

Blac
Lin

Blac

HOWTH GOLF COURSE

B

Blac

ghthouse

OWTH
RBOUR

East Pier

1

Martello
Tower

BALSCADDEN BAY

Health
Centre

ABBEY STREET

BALSCADDEN ROAD

P

Puck's Rocks

Lib

KILROCK ROAD

ASGARD PK

Kilrock

Nose
of
Howth

MAIN STREET

NASHVILLE PARK

13

NASHVILLE RD

CROSSTREES

THORMANBY

ASGARD
ROAD

CONBOOTER LANE

CLIFF WALK (Final Way)

2

THORMANBY

CANNON ROCK VIEW

Cannon Rock
Cottage

LAWNS

UPPER
CLIFF RD

DUNGRIFFAN ROAD

MARINERS
COVE

BALKILL

WOODCLIFF
HEIGHTS

CASANA VIEW

ROAD

Green
Ivy

GREYS LANE

Rookstown

THORMANBY
LODGE

3

ROAD

THORMANBY WOODS

Ashville

Highfield

Bearna

Piper's
Gut

WINDGATE

Oakley Park

lls

KITESTOWN ROAD

R105

NEW ROAD RISE

CLIFF WALK

Fox Hole

ROAD

WINDGATE ROAD

BAILEY GRN RD

The
Haven

K□CK ROAD

White
Water

Old Baily
Cottage

om Bed

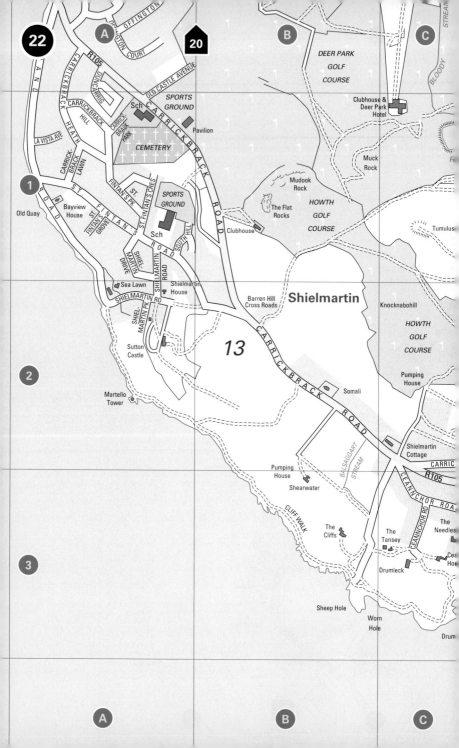

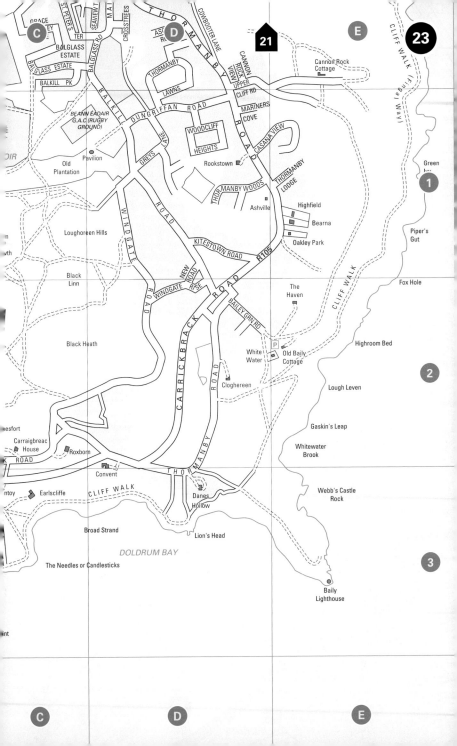

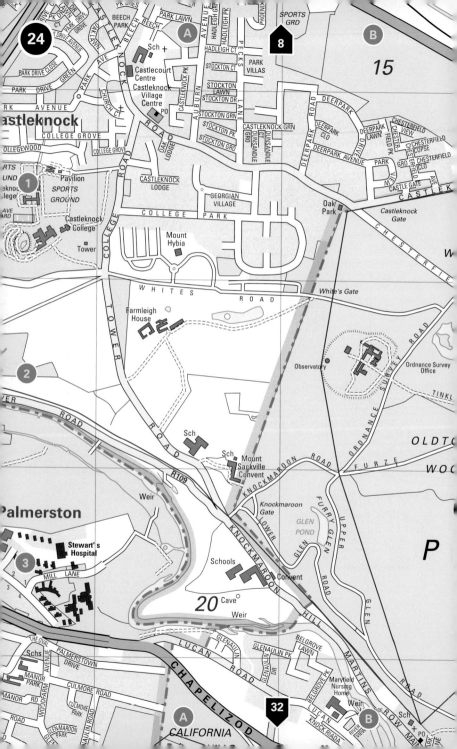

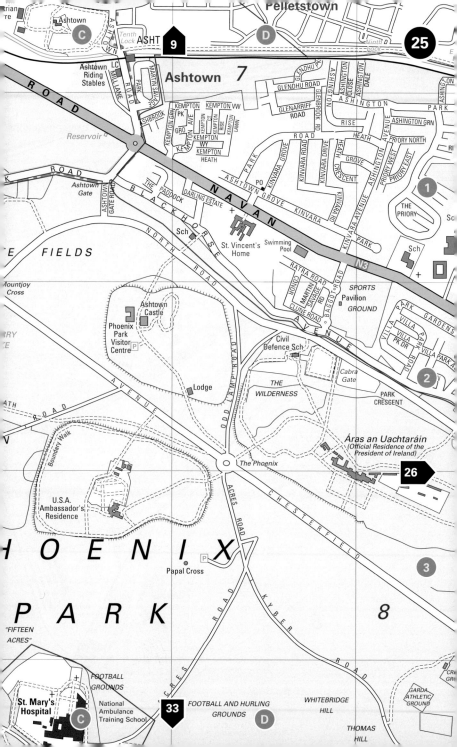

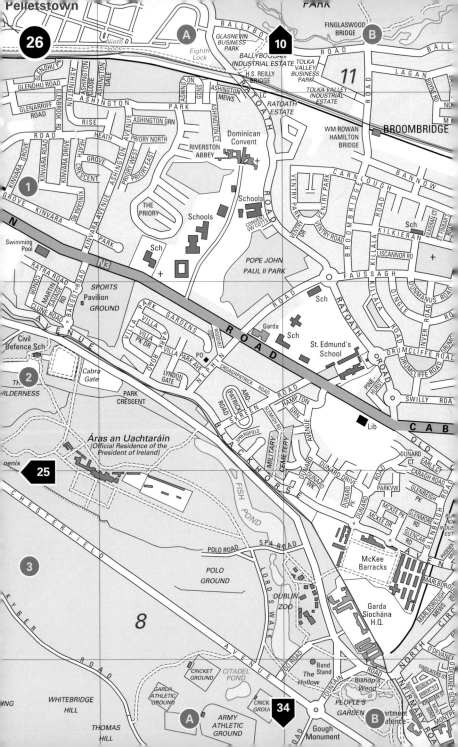

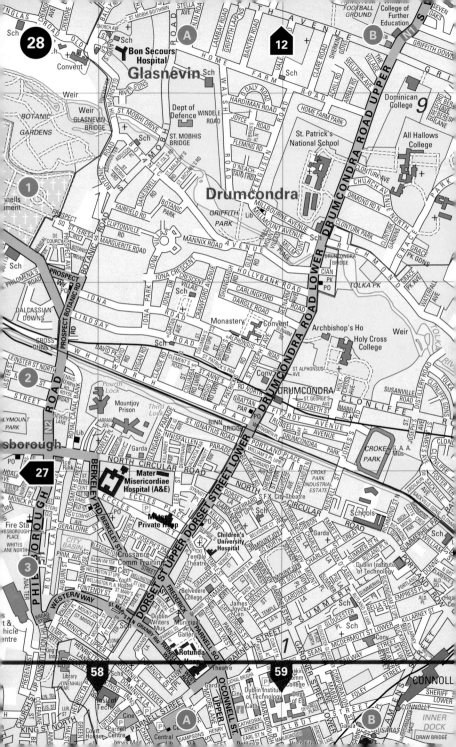

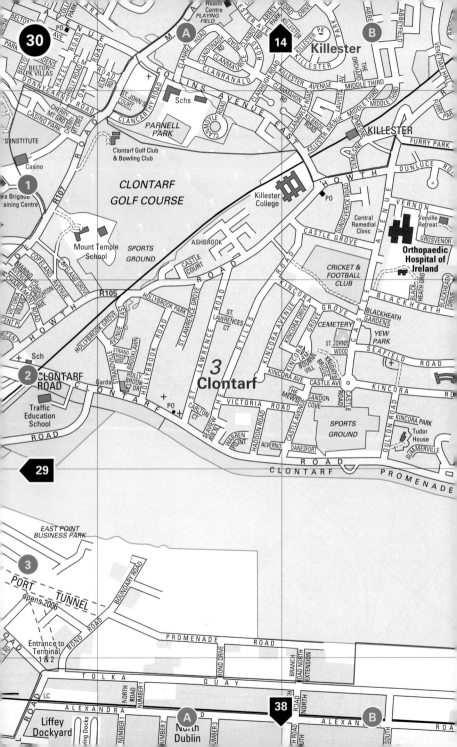

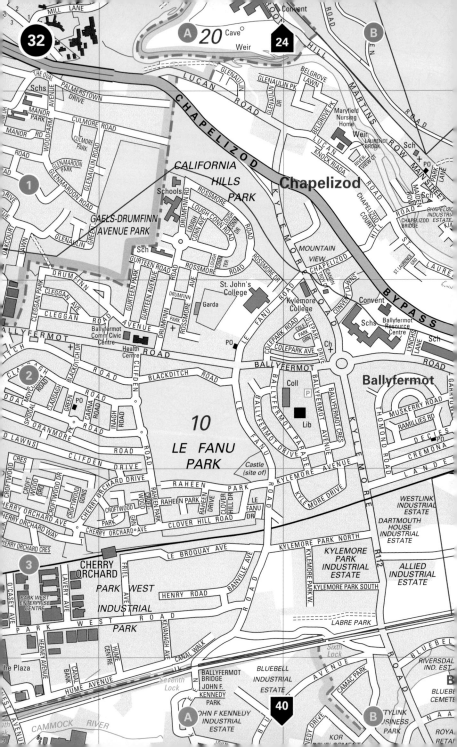

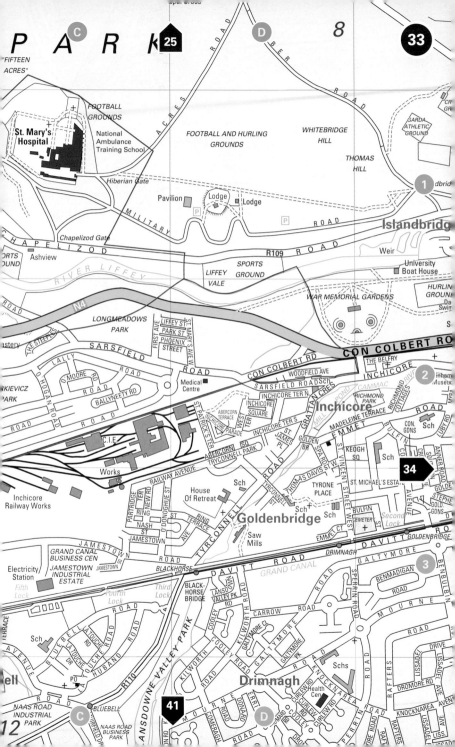

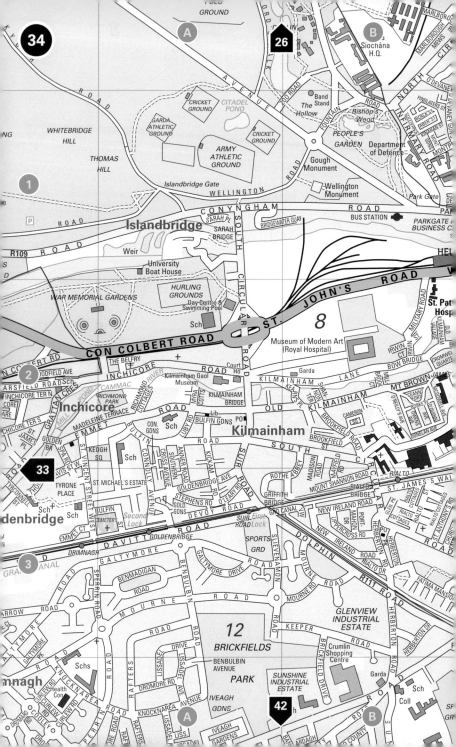

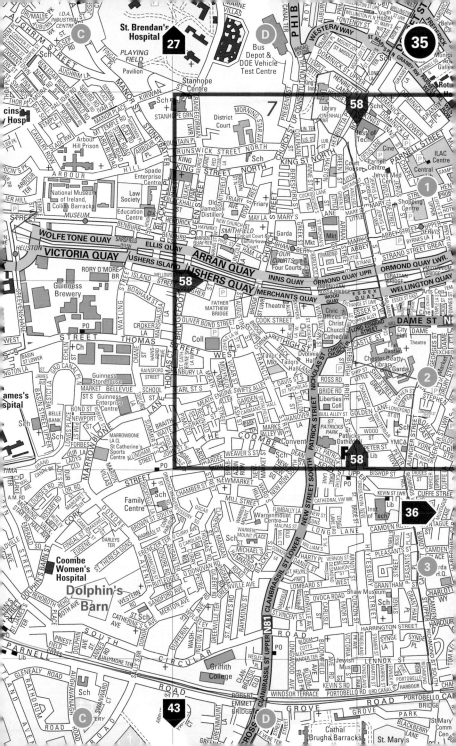

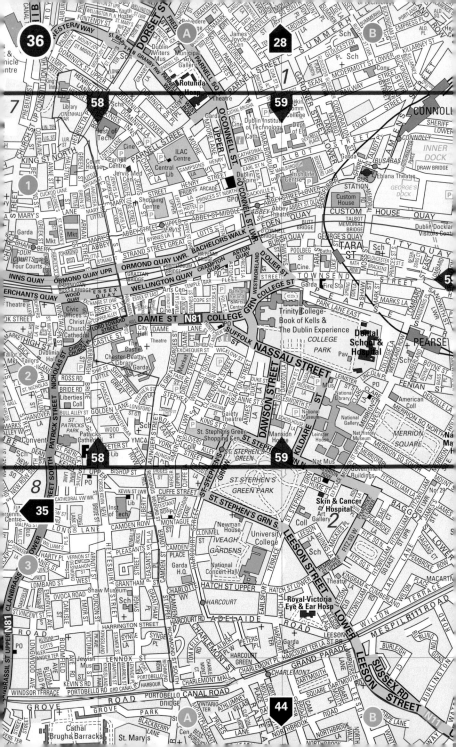

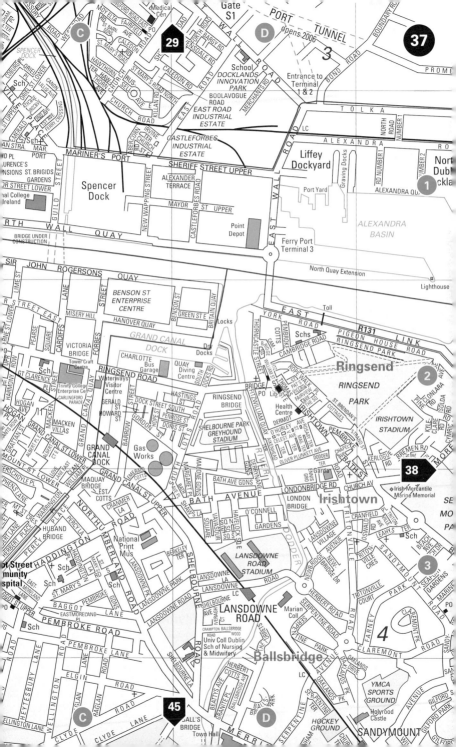

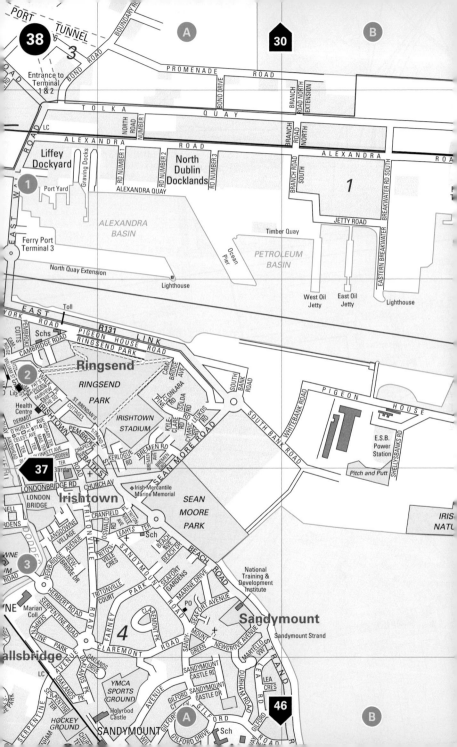

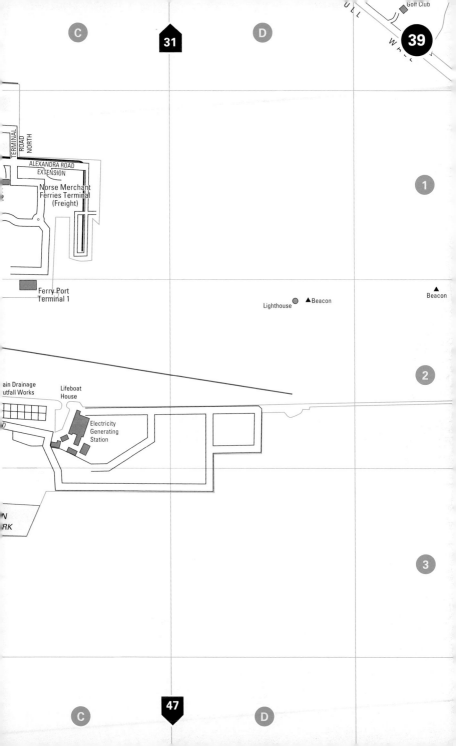

Golf Club

TERMINAL ROAD NORTH

ALEXANDRA ROAD EXTENSION

Norse Merchant Ferries Terminal (Freight)

Ferry Port Terminal 1

Lighthouse   ▲ Beacon

▲ Beacon

ain Drainage utfall Works

Lifeboat House

Electricity Generating Station

N RK

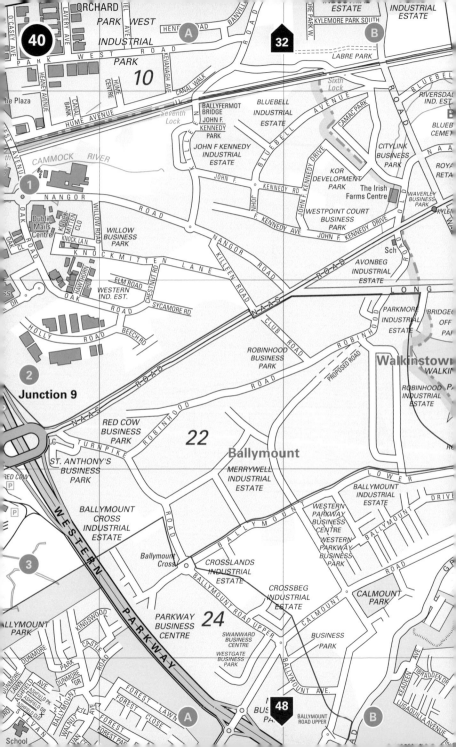

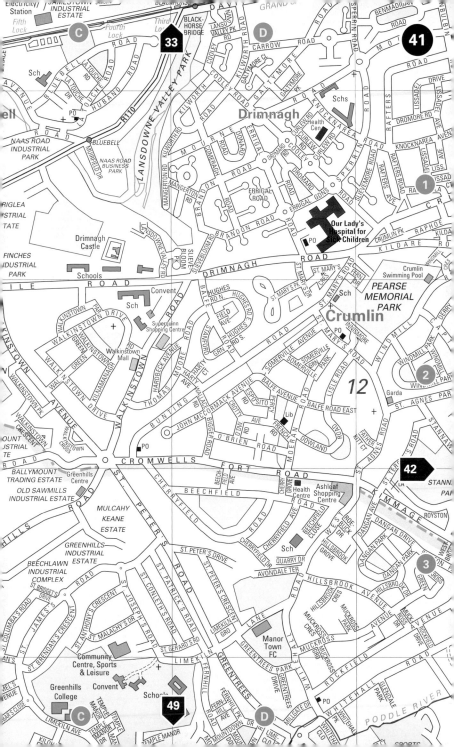

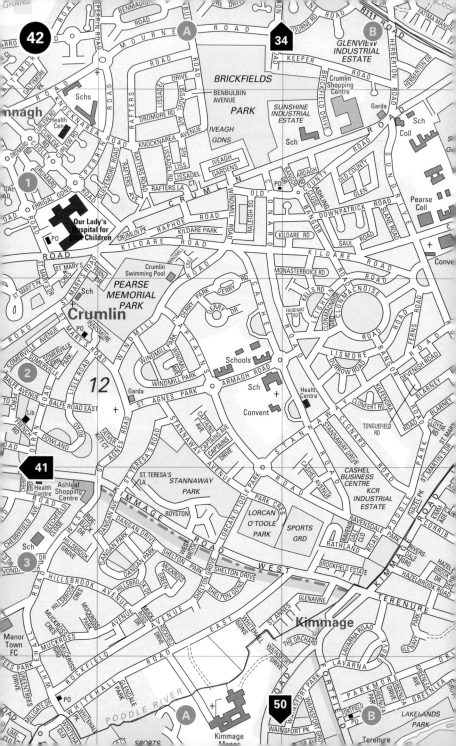

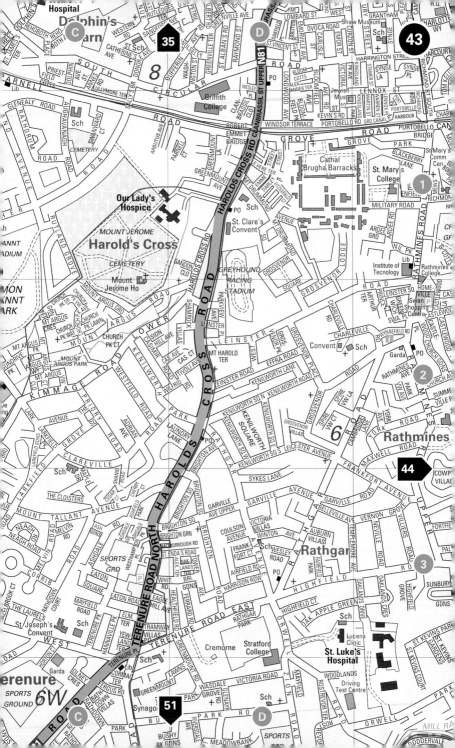

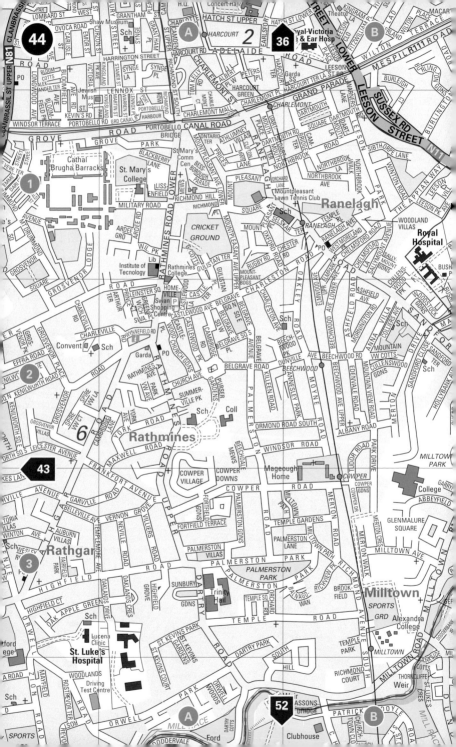

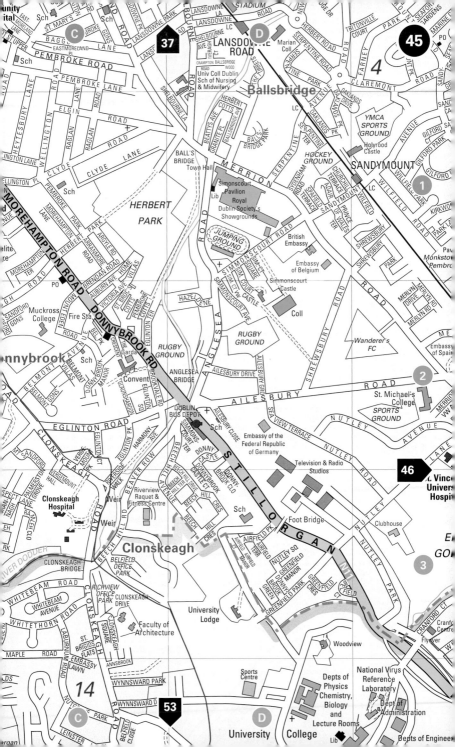

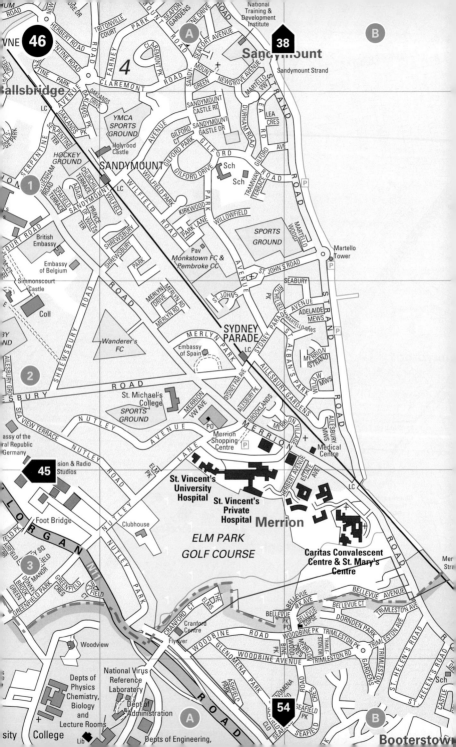

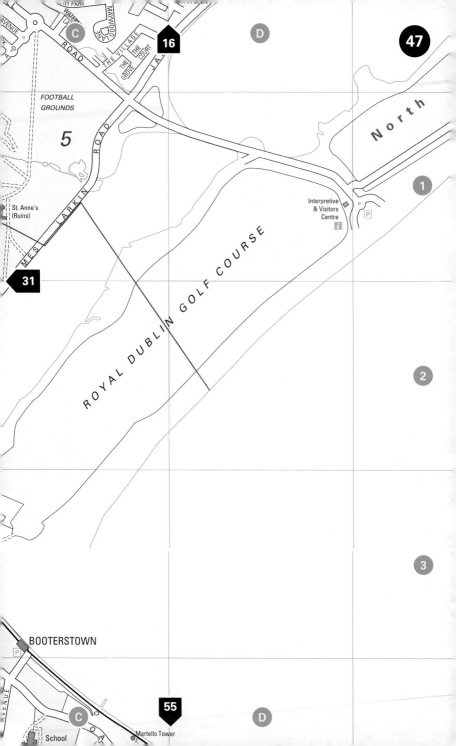

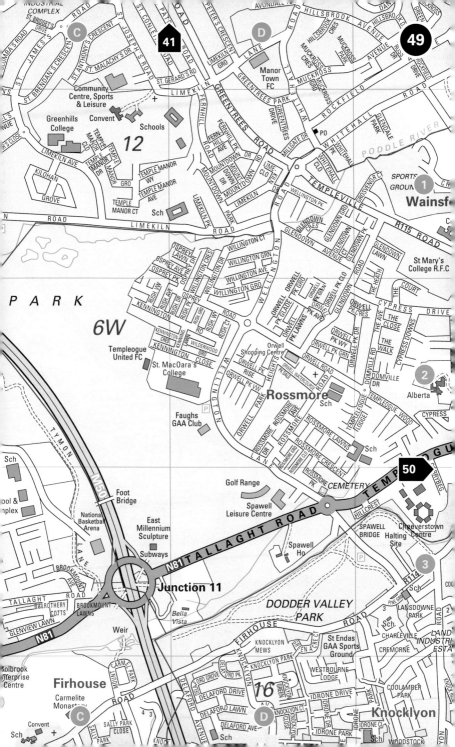

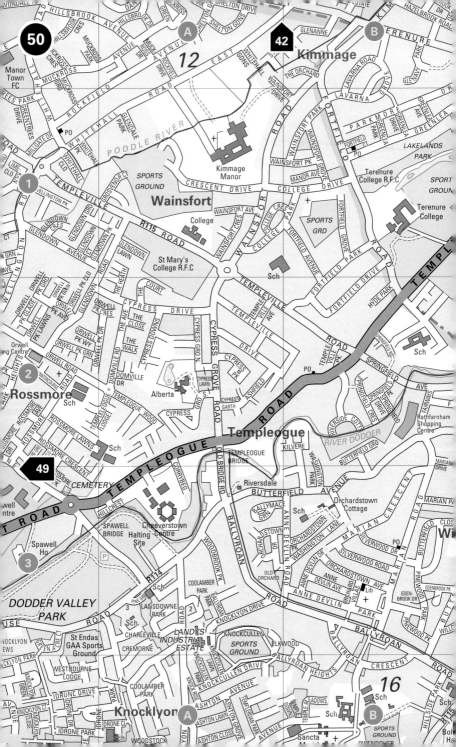

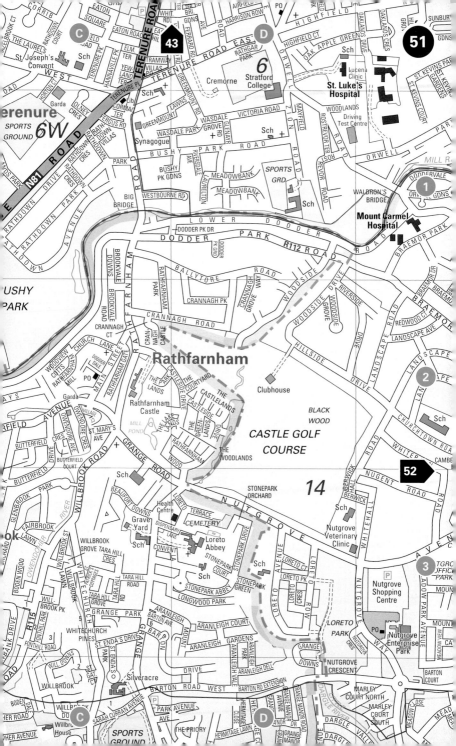

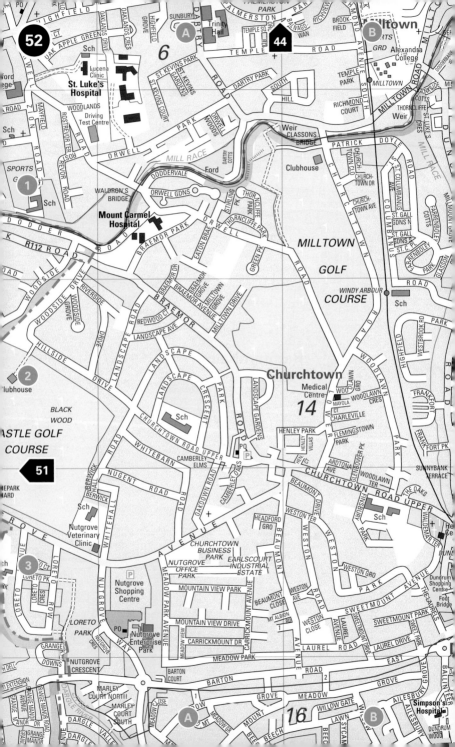

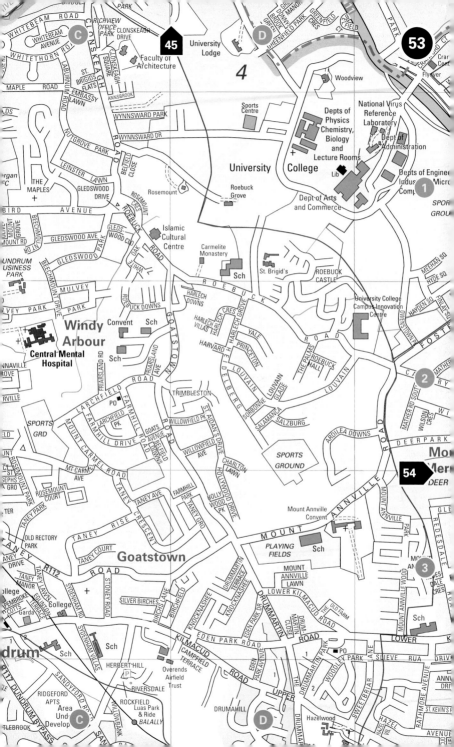

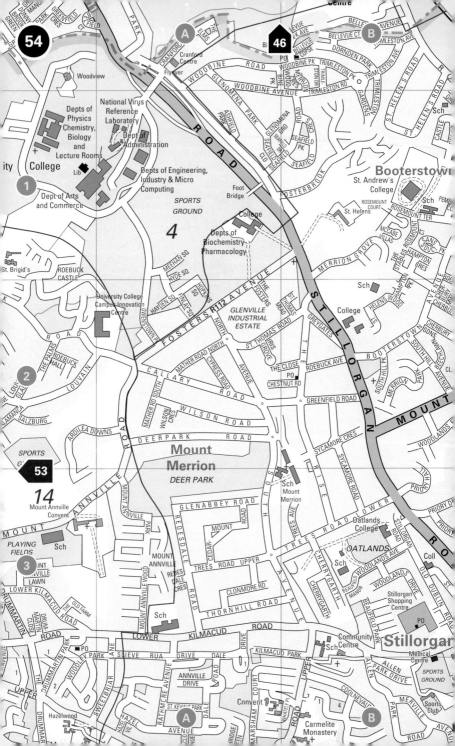

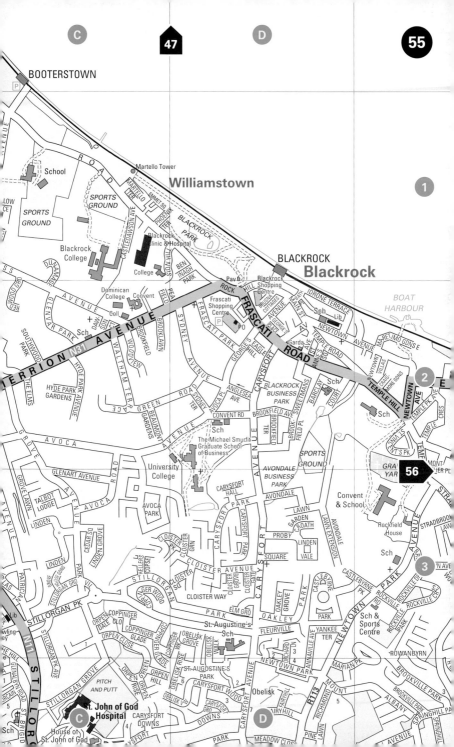

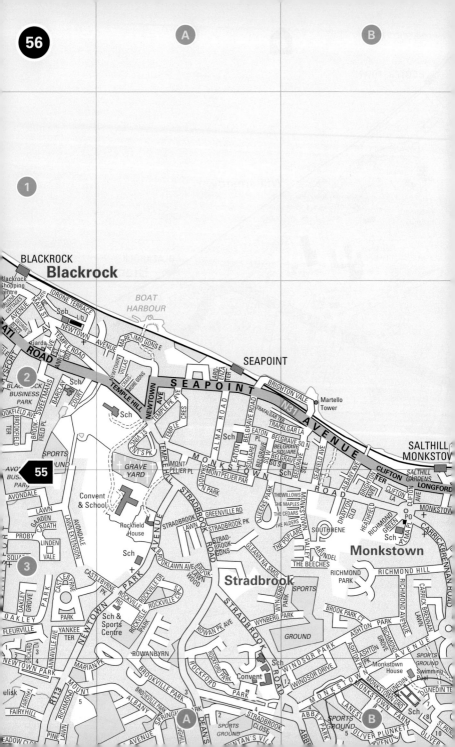

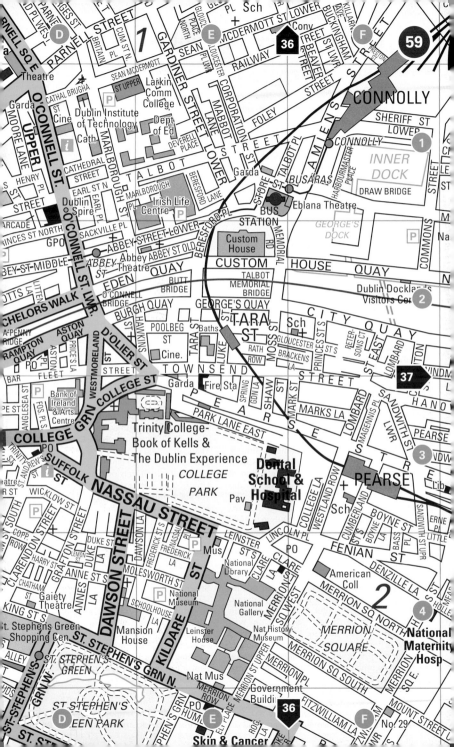

History

The ford over the River Liffey has been important since Celtic times and there was a thriving Christian community here from the 5thC, following their conversion by St Patrick in AD448. Marauding Vikings landed here in AD840, established a garrison port by the Dark Pool or Dubbh Linn, and within a few years had built a fortified town on the high ground above the estuary. Originally a base for raiding sorties, Dublin soon became a flourishing trading port as well, until Viking dominance was curtailed following a defeat by Brian Boru at the Battle of Clontarf in 1014.

Many of the Vikings had inter-married with the Irish and converted to Christianity but they were finally driven out by the Anglo-Normans under Strongbow, who took Dublin by storm and executed the Viking leader Hasculf. In 1170 Henry II arrived in Dublin, defeated Strongbow and received the submission of the Irish chieftains on the site of College Green. Henry granted the city by charter to the citizens of Bristol, thereby establishing English authority in Ireland.

The city and surrounding area, established as the seat of English government and protected by an enclosing wall and strategic castles, was known as The Pale. Frequently attacked during the 12thC and 13thC by the Irish clans based in the Wicklow Mountains, it was assaulted unsuccessfully by Edward Bruce in 1316. The city witnessed the crowning of Lambert Simnel, pretender to the English throne, in Christ Church in 1486. Unmoved by the rebellion of 'Silken' Thomas Fitzgerald in 1534, the inhabitants remained loyal to the English crown, supporting King Charles during the Civil Wars. Parliamentarians captured Dublin in 1647 and at this time the city was in decline. Following the Restoration of Charles I, however, Dublin underwent a great economic and architectural expansion.

By the end of the 17thC Dublin had become a flourishing commercial centre and during the following century the city was transformed into one of the most beautiful Georgian cities in Europe. The 'Wide Streets Commission' was established in 1757 and in 1773 the Paving Board was formed. New, elegantly spacious streets and squares were planned and palatial town houses built. In 1783 the Irish Parliament led by Henry Grattan was granted a short-lived autonomy but there was growing political unrest, which erupted in the unsuccessful uprising of 1798. Lord Edward Fitzgerald died of wounds sustained resisting arrest and in 1800 the detested Act of Union was established and the fortunes of the city began to wane.

With government now in London, few of the noblemen required their fine mansions and many returned to their country estates or left for London. Bitterness increased; in 1803 the Lord Chief Justice was assassinated and Robert Emmet, the leader of an abortive insurrection, was hanged. The newspaper The Nation was established by Charles Gavan Duffy in 1842, the heyday of the Repeal Movement. Daniel O'Connell was elected Lord Mayor in 1841 but only three years later he was interned in Richmond Gaol for campaigning for the repeal of the Union and the restoration of Grattan's 'Irish Parliament'. In 1873 the first great Home Rule Conference was held and in 1879 the Land League was formed, whose leaders, including Parnell and Davitt, were imprisoned as a consequence. In 1882 the new Chief Secretary, Lord Frederick Cavendish, and his Under-Secretary were assassinated in Phoenix Park by the Invincibles, a new terrorist organisation.

As the campaign for Home Rule gathered momentum, the Gaelic League, which started the Irish literary renaissance, was established by Douglas Hyde and Eóin MacNeill in 1893. Conceived as a means of reviving interest in the Irish language and traditional Irish life, the Gaelic League was also responsible for a remarkable literary revival resulting in the formation of the Abbey Theatre in 1904, where plays by J M Synge, Sean O'Casey and W B Yeats, amongst others, were performed.

In 1905 the Sinn Fein movement was formed, in 1909 the Irish Transport and General Workers Union was set up under the leadership of James Connolly, and in 1913 there was a massive strike, paralysing the city. The Irish Volunteers came into being in 1914, largely to combat the Ulster Volunteers who had been raised by Edward Carson in January 1913 to defend the right of Ulster to remain united with Great Britain. In 1916 the Irish Volunteers seized the General Post Office in Lower O'Connell Street as their headquarters and the Easter Rising had begun. It was quickly crushed, but so brutally that public conscience, clearly appalled, overwhelmingly elected Sinn Fein at the general election of December 1918 with Eamon de Valera as the new president.

Whilst the Dublin faction was openly in support of the guerrilla bands operating across the country, the Ulster Unionists set up their own provisional government, and the ambushes and assassinations which characterised the Anglo-Irish War, featuring the notorious Black and Tans, began in bloody

earnest. The war ended in the truce of July 1921. Despite the ratification of the Irish Free State in January 1922, a large and dissatisfied faction of leaders in the Irish movement took up arms against their former comrades and seized the Four Courts, which they held for two months. The subsequent shelling ordered by the new Dublin Government destroyed much of O'Connell Street but by the 1930s Dublin was emerging as a modern capital city and most of the public buildings had been restored.

Visiting Dublin

Passports
Citizens of the European Union need either a valid national identity card or passport to enter the Republic of Ireland. It is recommended that visitors from the UK bring a passport as a means of identification. Nationals of other countries require a passport and may require a visa. Enquiries should be made with a travel agent or Irish Embassy before travelling. The address of the Irish Embassy in London is 17 Grosvenor Place, SW1X 7HR.
Tel: 020 7235 2171 & (020 7225 7700 Passport/Visa)
Web: www.irlgov.ie

Banks
In February 2002 the Irish Punt (IEP) was withdrawn from circulation and the Euro (€) became the Irish unit of currency.
Banks open Monday–Friday from 10.00–16.00 and in Dublin most branches remain open until 17.00 on Thursdays. Major banks have 24 hour ATM machines which accept Plus and Cirrus symbols. Most credit cards, including all those with the Eurocard symbol, are widely accepted in shops, petrol stations, restaurants and hotels. Personal cheques from banks outside the Republic of Ireland are not accepted in the country without prior arrangement.

Bureaux de Change
Banks and Bureaux de Change generally offer the best exchange rates, although post offices, hotels, travel agents and some department stores offer exchange facilities.
There is a Bureau de Change at Dublin Airport and Dún Laoghaire ferry terminal. Dublin Airport also has a 24 hour Bank of Ireland foreign currency note exchanger and multi-currency Pass machines. Foreign exchange facilities are also to be found at the central bus station (Busárus) and Connolly railway station.

Language
English is spoken by everyone in Ireland. The country is officially bilingual with Irish (Gaelic) also spoken.

Customs and excise
The Republic of Ireland is a member of the European Union and, in accordance with EU regulations, travellers within the Community can import 90 litres of wine, 110 litres of duty paid beer and 800 cigarettes without question. Duty free sales of goods amongst European community members are now abolished. There are restrictions on taking certain food items into Ireland and checks should be made beforehand with the Irish Embassy or travel agent. Pets may not be brought into the country unless travelling from the UK, all other animals entering the country have to undergo quarantine.

Emergency
If you are involved in an emergency and require the services of the Police, Fire Brigade, Ambulance Service, or Coastguard, dial 999.

Medical treatment
Visitors to Ireland from European Community countries are entitled to free treatment by a general practitioner, medicines on prescription and treatment on a public ward in a hospital. British citizens need only show some form of identification such as a passport or driving licence to the doctor or hospital and request treatment under the EU health agreement. Visitors from other EU countries need to present form EIII (available from social security offices prior to departure). Health Insurance is recommended for visitors from outside the EU. No inoculations are required for travellers to Ireland.

Disabled visitors
The Irish Wheelchair association can offer advice and can arrange wheelchair hire. Tel: 01 818 6400 (Mon–Fri 09.00–17.00).
Web: www.iwa.ie
Irish Rail publishes a 'Guide for Mobility Impaired Passengers' which details the accessibility of all railway and DART stations. Obtainable at all manned stations or from the Access and Liaison officer, tel: 01 703 2634. Most of the Dublin Bus fleet is low floor easy access, and the buses run by Bus Éireann – Ireland's national bus company – are largely wheelchair accessible. Discounts on many ferry sailings from Britain are available to disabled drivers who wish to take their own car to Ireland. Drivers should contact the Disabled Drivers' Association or Motor Club in Britain to obtain the relevant form. This form should then be sent to the ferry company.

Phones
Most calls are dialled direct with cheaper call charge rates between 18.00 and 08.00 Mon–Fri

and all day Saturday, Sunday and bank holidays. The dialling code for Dublin is 01 and so for calls within Dublin omit 01 at the beginning of a number. To dial Dublin from abroad dial the access code for Ireland (00353) plus the area code for Dublin (01) but omit the zero. For directory enquiries, including Northern Ireland, dial 11811; for Great Britain or International numbers dial 11818. For operator assistance dial 10 (Ireland and UK) or 114 for the international operator. Card phones are cheaper than payphones and are widely available. Callcards are obtainable at post offices, newsagents and supermarkets. Mobile phones can be brought into Ireland but visitors need to ensure their phone company has a roaming agreement with the Irish network operators.

Transport

Driving

Driving is on the left-hand side of the road in Ireland as in the UK; at roundabouts give way to traffic from the right. All drivers and front seat passengers must wear seat belts, and rear belts if they are fitted. Children under twelve must have a suitable restraint. Helmets are compulsory for motorcyclists. The maximum speed limit is 97kph (60mph) outside urban areas and the motorway speed limit is 110kph (70mph). In urban areas the limit is usually 50kph (30mph). There are on-the-spot fines for speeding and drink driving laws are strict. Parking infringements are taken seriously and illegally parked cars in Dublin City are liable to be clamped or towed away to the Corporation pound with a recovery charge payable.

Distances and speed limits are now both measured in kilometres (speed limit signs changed on 20th January 2005). Place names are generally in English and Irish. Unleaded petrol and diesel are widely available. Recorded weather information is available for Dublin by calling the Meteorological Service Tel: 1550 123 854. There is a charge for this call.

Car hire

Car hire is readily available in Dublin, although in July and August there is a high demand and it is best to book in advance. You must have held a full licence for 2 years and be under 70 and over 23. Some companies make exceptions to this but charges may be higher. A full valid driving licence of your country of residence (which you must have held for at least two years without endorsements) must be presented at the time of hiring.

Most international car rental companies have offices in Dublin and cars can also be hired at the airport and Dún Laoghaire ferry terminal. The cost of hire will depend on the type of car and time of year and it is worthwhile shopping around. It is important, however, to check the insurance details and ensure Collision Damage Waiver is included. A deposit is usually payable at the time of booking or before you drive away. Fly-drive or rail-sail-drive packages arranged by travel agents or the air and ferry companies can be an economical and easy way of hiring a car.

Public transport

Dublin is linked with the cities and towns of Ireland by a network of rail and bus services overseen by Córas Iompair Éireann (CIE), which is Ireland's National Transport Authority. The CIE organises Iarnód Éireann (Irish Rail), Bus Éireann (Irish Bus) and Dublin Bus. Bus and rail timetables can be bought at most newsagents. Unlimited use period tickets are available for use on rail and/or bus services.

Bus and coach travel

Dublin Bus (Bus Átha Cliath) operates the public bus services in Dublin and the surrounding area. Pre-paid tickets can be bought for periods of time ranging from one day to one month and are good value for money. They can be bought at any of the many bus ticket agencies in the city, from the CIE information desk at Dublin Airport or at Dublin Bus head office at 59 O'Connell Street Upper. Many routes operate an exact fare only policy. Dublin Bus also operates late night services (Nitelink) to most suburban areas on Thursdays, Fridays and Saturdays, links to the ferry ports and railway stations, and also sightseeing tours.
Open Mon–Sat 09.00–19.00.
Tel: 01 872 0000 or 01 873 4222
Web: www.dublinbus.ie has details of routes, timetables, and special tickets.

National bus services between Dublin, Dublin Airport and other major cities and towns are provided by Irish Bus (Bus Éireann) and many private companies. Bus Éireann also operate combined bus and ferry services between Britain and Ireland.
Dublin Bus Station (Bus Áras), Store Street.
Tel: 01 836 6111
Web: www.buseireann.ie

Scheduled daily hop-on hop-off city sightseeing tours are operated by Gray Line, Guide Friday and City Sightseeing. Buses depart every 10-20 minutes from 09.30-17.30; also available are seasonal half and full day excursions further afield including to Newgrange and the Boyne Valley, Powerscourt Gardens, Glendalough and

Wicklow. 3 & 4 day trips to Kerry and Dingle are also available. Information and tickets from the Desk 1 at the Dublin Tourism Centre, Suffolk Street.
Tel: 01 605 7705
Web: www.irishcitytours.com
Email: info@irishcitytours.com

Taxis

Taxis are available at taxi ranks or by phoning one of the many radio-linked taxi companies. There are numerous taxi ranks including ones on O'Connell Street, Dame Street, and St. Stephen's Green West.
Taxi companies are listed in the Golden Pages classified telephone directory.

Rail travel

Dublin Connolly and Dublin Heuston are the two mainline railway stations and Irish Rail (Iarnród Éireann) operates an excellent service to most towns and cities in Ireland. Irish rail also operates the suburban rail network in Dublin and DART (Dublin Area Rapid Transit) with 26 stations between Howth on the north of Dublin Bay to Bray in the south.
Tel: 01 850 366222
Web: www.irishrail.ie

Bike hire

Tracks Bikes, Botanic Road, Glasnevin.
Tel: 01 850 0252

Irish Cycling Safaris, Belfield Bike Shop, University College Dublin.
Tel: 01 260 0749

Lost property

Enquire at the nearest police station or:
Dublin Airport. Open Mon–Fri 07.00-22.30.
Tel: 01 814 5555

Dublin Bus. Open Mon–Fri 08.45–17.00.
Tel: 01 703 1321

Irish Bus. Open Mon–Fri 09.00–17.00.
Tel: 01 703 2489

Irish Rail (Connolly Station). Open Mon–Fri 09.00–17.00. **Tel: 01 703 2358**

Irish Rail (Heuston Station). Open Mon–Fri 09.00–17.00. **Tel: 01 703 2102**

Places of interest

Arbour Hill Cemetery, Arbour Hill.
The leaders of the Easter Rising are buried here.

Bank of Ireland, College Green.
Designed by Sir Edward Lovett Pearce in 1729, it was later enlarged by James Gandon and Robert Parke between 1785–1794. Originally the Parliament House, the first of a series of great public buildings erected in 18thC Dublin, it was

taken over by the Bank of Ireland in 1804. A statue of Henry Grattan, leader of the Irish parliament of 1782, stands outside on the lawn of College Green. Two huge 18thC tapestries commemorating the Siege of Londonderry and the Battle of the Boyne hang in the oak-panelled chamber of the former House of Lords.
There are guided tours of the House of Lords on Tuesdays at 10.30, 11.30, and 13.45.
Admission free. Disabled access.
Tel: 01 671 1488

Bank of Ireland Arts Centre, Foster Place.
An arts centre which presents classical concerts and recitals and houses an interactive museum. The museum illustrates the history of the adjoining College Green buildings where many of the dramatic events of Irish history were played out in the Irish parliament. The museum also reflects the role played by the Bank of Ireland in the economic and social development of Ireland.
Open Tues-Fri 9.30–16.00, Sat 10.00-16.00.
Disabled access.
Tel: 01 671 1488

Belvedere House, North Great George's Street.
One of the best 18thC mansions in Dublin. Taken over by Jesuit Belvedere College in 1841; James Joyce went to school here between 1893–1898. Not open to the public.

Casino, off Malahide Road, Marino.
A miniature 18thC neo-classical masterpiece designed by Sir William Chambers and recently restored. Casino means 'small house'. It was built as a pleasure house beside Marino House (now demolished), Lord Charlemont's country residence, for the enormous sum of £60,000. It is a compact building, remarkably containing 16 rooms, with many interesting architectural features. The interior circular hall, ringed by columns, is crowned by a coffered dome. The graceful roof urns disguise chimneys while the columns conceal drainpipes.
Open Daily (May-Oct) 10.00-17.00 (18.00 Jun-Sept); (Nov-Apr) Sat & Sun 12.00-16.00 (17.00 Apr). Closed January. Access by guided tour only. Last tour leaves 45 mins before closing. Access to interior by stairway.
Tel: 01 833 1618

City Hall, Dame Street.
Completed in 1779, this fine building was designed as The Royal Exchange. Subsequent use included a prison and corn exchange before being taken over by the city in 1852. Presently used by Dublin City Council. It features a beautiful Corinthian coffered dome and portico.

The archives include the original charter of 1171 in which Henry II granted Dublin to the citizens of Bristol.

Open Mon-Sat 10.00-17.15, Sun 14.00-17.00.

Tel: 01 222 2204

Web: www.dublincity.ie/cityhall

Custom House Visitor Centre, Custom House Quay.

The Custom House, with a magnificent long river frontage, is an architectural masterpiece designed by James Gandon and completed in 1791. Exhibits relate to James Gandon and the history of the Custom House itself, with illustrations of how the building was restored after it was gutted by fire in 1921. The building is best viewed from the south bank of the River Liffey.

Open: Wed-Fri (Nov-16 Mar) & Mon–Fri (17 Mar-Nov) 10.00–12.30, Sat & Sun 14.00–17.00. Disabled access by prior arrangement.

Tel: 01 888 2538

Drimnagh Castle, Long Mile Road.

Ireland's only castle with a flooded moat. This Norman castle has a fully restored Great Hall, medieval undercroft and 17thC style formal garden.

Open (Apr–Sept) Wed, Sat, Sun 12.00–17.00; (Oct–March) Wed, Sun 12.00–17.00. Last tour 16.15. Open at other times by appointment.

Tel: 01 450 2530

Email: drimnaghcastle@eircom.net

Dublin Castle, off Dame Street.

The Castle was originally built between 1204–1228 as part of Dublin's defensive system. The Record Tower is the principal remnant of the 13thC Anglo-Norman fortress and has walls 5 metres (16ft) thick but what remains today is largely the result of 18thC and 19thC re-building. It now contains the Garda (Police) Museum. The 15thC Bermingham Tower was once the state prison where Red Hugh O'Donnell was interned in the 16thC; it was rebuilt in the 18thC. The State Apartments, Undercroft and ornate Chapel Royal are open to the public. The State Apartments, dating from the British Administration, were once the residence of the English Viceroys and are now used for Presidential Inaugurations and state receptions. Within these apartments are the magnificent throne room and St Patrick's Hall, 25 metres (82ft) long with a high panelled and decorated ceiling. In the undercroft can be seen the remains of a Viking fortress, part of the original moat, and part of the old city wall.

The Chester Beatty Library exhibits art treasures from around the world.

Open: Mon–Fri 10.00–17.00, Sat & Sun 14.00–17.00. Access by guided tour only. Disabled access/toilets.

Tel: 01 677 7129

Web: www.dublincastle.ie

Email: info@dublincastle.ie

Dublin Experience, Trinity College.

A film about the story of Dublin which is shown every hour in the Trinity College Arts Building.

Open daily from late May to late Sept 10.00–17.00. Last showing 17.00.

Tel: 01 608 1688

Dublin Writers Museum, Parnell Square.

Tracing the history of Irish literature from its earliest times to the 20thC, this museum is a celebration of this literary heritage. Writers and playwrights including Jonathan Swift, George Bernard Shaw, Oscar Wilde, W B Yeats, James Joyce and Samuel Beckett are brought to life through personal items, portraits, their books and letters. There is also a room dedicated to children's authors. The museum is housed in a restored 18thC Georgian mansion with decorative stained-glass windows and ornate plaster-work.

Open Mon–Sat 10.00–17.00 (18.00 Jun-Aug), Sun 11.00–17.00. Disabled access to ground floor. Last entry 45 mins before closing.

Tel: 01 872 2077

Email: writers@dublintourism.ie

Dvblinia, Christ Church, St. Michael's Hill.

A multi-media recreation of Dublin life in medieval times from the Anglo-Norman arrival in 1170 to the dissolution of the monasteries in 1540. There is a scale model of the medieval city, a life size reconstruction of a merchant's house, and numerous Viking and Norman artefacts from excavations at nearby Wood Quay. The building is the old Synod Hall and is linked to Christ Church Cathedral by an ornate Victorian pedestrian bridge.

Open Mon-Fri 10.00-17.00 (Oct-Mar 11.00-16.00); Sat & Sun 10.00-16.00. Disabled access.

Tel: 01 679 4611

Web: www.dublinia.ie

Email: marketing@dublinia.ie

Dublin Zoo, Phoenix Park.

The Zoo is well known for its captive-breeding programme and is committed to the conservation and protection of endangered species. The 'big cats', living in enclosures which simulate their natural habitats, include lions, tigers, jaguars and snow leopards. Attractive gardens surround two natural lakes where pelicans, flamingos, ducks and geese abound, while the islands in the lakes are home to chimps, gibbons, spider monkeys and orang-utans. A recent development 'Fringes of the

Arctic' has provided a state of the art enclosure for the polar bears and is home to wolves, arctic foxes and snowy owls. After the acquisition of more land, the zoo doubled in size in 2000 and an African Plains area has been developed providing greater space and freedom for giraffe, hippo, rhino and other African animals and birds. The city farm and pets' corner provide encounters with Irish domestic animals. Other attractions include a zoo train, discovery centre, and 'meet the keeper' programme.
Open: Mon–Sat 09.30–17.00, Sun 10.30–17.00. Last admission 16.00. Closes at dusk in winter.
Tel: 01 474 8900
Web: www.dublinzoo.ie
Email: info@dublinzoo.ie

Dunsink Observatory, Castleknock, Dublin 15.
Founded in 1783, it is one of the oldest observatories in the world and houses the astronomy section of the School of Cosmic Physics. Public open nights are held on the first and third Wednesdays of each month from October to March inclusive at 20.00. Requests for tickets for the open nights must be made by post to the Observatory.
Tel: 01 838 7911
Web: www.dunsink.dias.ie
Email: cwoods@dunsinkdias.ie

Four Courts, Inns Quay.
Originally designed by James Gandon in 1785, it was partially destroyed by a fire in 1922 in the struggle for Irish independence but restored again by 1932. The Four Courts has a 137 metre (450ft) river frontage and the building is fronted by a Corinthian portico with six columns. The square central block with circular hall is crowned by a copper-covered lantern-dome. Housed here are the Irish Law Courts and Law Library.
Tel: 01 888 6457/6460
Web: www.courts.ie
Email: schooltours@courts.ie

Fry Model Railway, Malahide Castle, Malahide.
Covering 233 square metres (2,500sq.ft) this is one of the world's largest working miniature railways and is a delight for children and adults alike. Besides the track, the railway has stations, bridges, trams, buses and barges and includes the Dublin landmarks of Heuston station and O'Connell Bridge. On display are the hand constructed models of Irish trains by Cyril Fry, draughtsman and railway engineer, who made them from the 1930s until his death in 1974. Perfectly engineered, the models represent the earliest trains to those of more modern times.

Situated in the grounds of Malahide Castle, 13km (8 miles) north of Dublin city centre.
Open (Apr-Sept) Mon-Sat 10.00-17.00, Sun & public holidays 14.00–18.00; Closed 13.00-14.00 and Oct-Mar.
Tel: 01 846 3779
Web: www.malahidecastle.com
Email: fryrailway@dublintourism.ie

GAA Museum, Croke Park.
The Gaelic Athletic Association (GAA) is Ireland's largest sporting and cultural organisation and is dedicated to promoting the games of hurling, Gaelic football, handball, rounders and camogie. The museum is at Croke Park, home of Irish hurling and football, and traces the history of Gaelic sports and their place in Irish culture right up to the present day. Interactive exhibits allow visitors the chance to try out the skills of the games for themselves. National trophies and sports equipment are also on display.
Open Mon-Sat 09.30-17.00, Sun 12.00-17.00. Last admission $1/2$ hour before closing. All groups must be pre-booked.
Tel: 01 819 2323
Web: www.gaa.ie/museum
Email: gaamuseum@crokepark.ie

Heraldic Museum, Kildare Street.
Part of the National Library of Ireland, the museum illustrates the uses of heraldry with displays of coat of arms and banners and a collection of heraldic glass, seals, stamps, and coins.
Open Mon-Wed 10.00-20.30; Thurs-Fri 10.00-16.30; Sat 10.00-12.30. Admission is free.
Tel: 01 603 0311
Email: herald@nli.ie

General Post Office, O'Connell Street.
Designed by Francis Johnston and completed in 1818. A century later the GPO became the headquarters of the 1916 Easter Rising and the Proclamation of the Irish Republic was read from the steps by Patrick Pearse. Bullet marks can still be seen on the pillars. Badly damaged in 1922 in the fight for independence, it was restored in 1929. A bronze sculpture, The Death of Cúchulainn by Oliver Sheppard, stands within the building.
Tel: 01 705 7000
Email: customer.service@anpost.ie

Guinness Storehouse, St. James's Gate.
The story of Guinness is told from its beginnings in 1759, how it is made and the advertising campaigns used to make it internationally famous. Housed in St James's Gate Brewery and spread over six floors, on the highest of which can be found the bar 'Gravity',

from which a 360° view of Dublin can be enjoyed. Open July-Aug 9.30-20.00; Sept-June 9.30-17.00. Disabled access.
Tel: 01 408 4800
Web: www.guinnessstorehouse.com
Email: guinness-storehouse@guinness.com

Ha'penny Bridge, Crampton Quay.
An elegant arching narrow cast-iron pedestrian bridge spanning the Liffey; it was first opened in 1816 and the name derives from the toll once charged.

Irish Jewish Museum, Walworth Road
Opened by President Herzog of Israel in 1985, exhibits relate to the Jewish community in Ireland including synagogue fittings and the reconstruction of a typical Dublin Jewish kitchen of 100 years ago.
Open (May–Sept) Sun, Tues, Thurs 11.00–15.30; (Oct–Apr) Sun 10.30–14.30. Admission is free.
Tel: 01 490 1857

Irish Museum of Modern Art, Military Road, Kilmainham.
Opened in the 17thC Royal Hospital building and grounds in 1991, the museum is an important institution for the collection of modern and contemporary art. A wide variety of work by major established 20thC figures and that of younger contemporary artists is presented in an ever changing programme of exhibitions, drawn from the museum's own collection and from public and private collections world-wide.
Open Tues-Sat 10.00–17.15, Sun & some bank holidays 12.00–17.15. Admission is free.
Tel: 01 612 9900
Web: www.modernart.ie
Email: info@imma.ie

James Joyce Centre, North Great George's Street.
A museum in a restored Georgian town house, built in 1784, devoted to the great novelist and run by members of his family. Dennis J Maginni, dancing master in Joyce's novel Ulysses, ran his dancing school from this house. The library contains editions of Joyce's work and that of other Irish writers as well as biographical and critical writing. There is a set of biographies of real Dublin people fictionalised in Ulysses, and also the door from the house occupied by the central character of the novel, Leopold Bloom and his wife Molly. The centre hosts readings, lectures and debates on all aspects of Joyce and his literature and conducts guided tours.
Open Tues–Sat 09.30–17.00.
Tel: 01 878 8547
Web: www.jamesjoyce.ie
Email: info@jamesjoyce.ie

James Joyce Museum, Sandycove.
The museum is housed in the Martello Tower which Joyce used as the setting for the opening chapter of Ulysses, his great work of fiction which immortalised Dublin. Joyce stayed here briefly in 1904 and the living room and view from the gun platform remains much as he described it in the novel. The museum collection includes personal possessions, letters, photographs, first editions and items that reflect the Dublin of Joyce. Situated 13km (8 miles) south of Dublin city centre, the tower was one of 15 defensive towers built along Dublin Bay in 1804 to withstand a threatened invasion from Napoleon.
Open (Mar–Oct) Mon–Sat 10.00–17.00, Sun 14.00–18.00. Closed 13.00–14.00.
Tel: 01 280 9265
Email: joycetower@dublintourism.ie

Kilmainham Gaol, Inchicore Road, Kilmainham.
Built as a gaol in 1796, Kilmainham is now dedicated to the Irish patriots imprisoned there from 1792–1924, including Emmet and his United Irishmen colleagues, the Fenians, the Invincibles and the Irish Volunteers of the Easter Rising. Patrick Pearse and James Connolly were executed in the prison yard and Eamon de Valera, later Prime Minister and then President of Ireland, was one of the last inmates. After its closure in 1924 Kilmainham re-opened as a museum in 1966. It is one of the largest unoccupied gaols in Europe with tiers of cells and overhead catwalks. Access is by guided tour only and features an exhibition and audio-visual show on the political and penal history of the gaol.
Open daily (May–Sept) 09.30–17.00; (Oct–Mar) Mon–Fri 09.30–16.00, Sun 10.00–17.00. Disabled toilets. Tours for visitors with special needs by prior arrangement.
Tel: 01 453 5984

King's Inns, Henrietta Street.
The Dublin Inns of Court is a glorious classical building, partly built to the plans of James Gandon at the end of the 19thC. The library was founded in 1787 and contains a large legal collection with about 100,000 books. The courtyard opens into Henrietta Street, where Dublin's earliest Georgian mansions remain.
Web: www.kingsinns.ie

Leinster House, Kildare Street.
Originally a handsome town mansion designed by Richard Castle for the Duke of Leinster in 1745; it has been a Parliament House since 1922. The Dáil Éireann (House of Representatives) and Seanad Éireann (Senate) sit here. The

house has two contrasting facades: an imposing formal side facing Kildare Street while from Merrion Square the building has more of the appearance of a country residence. Anybody wanting a tour of Irish Parliament must contact their respective embassy in Dublin where arrangements can be made. Advance notice is required.

Tel: 01 618 3000

Malahide Castle, Malahide.

Originally built in 1185, it was the seat of the Talbot family until 1973 when the last Lord Talbot died; the history of the family is detailed in the Great Hall alongside many family portraits. Malahide also has a large collection of Irish portrait paintings, mainly from the National Gallery, and is furnished with fine period furniture. Within the 100 hectares (250 acres) of parkland surrounding the castle is the Talbot Botanic Gardens, largely created by Lord Milo Talbot between 1948 and 1973. The grounds include walled gardens and a shrubbery with a collection of southern hemisphere plants. Malahide is situated 13km (8 miles) north of Dublin city centre.

Open Mon-Sat 10.00-17.00; Sundays & Bank Holidays 11.00-17.00 (18.00 Apr-Oct); Closed 13.00-14.00. Combined tickets with Fry Model Railway are available.

Tel: 01 846 2184

Web: www.malahidecastle.com
Email: malahidecastle@dublintourism.ie

Mansion House, Dawson Street.

Built in 1705, this Queen Anne style house has been the official residence of the Lord Mayor of Dublin since 1715. The first Irish parliament assembled here in 1919 to adopt Ireland's declaration of Independence and ratify the 1916 proclamation of the Irish Republic. Not open to the public.

National Museum of Ireland, Archaeology and History, Kildare Street.

Houses a fabulous collection of national antiquities including prehistoric gold ornaments, and outstanding examples of Celtic and medieval art. The 8thC Ardagh Chalice and Tara Brooch are amongst the treasures. The entire history of Ireland is reflected in the museum with 'The Road to Independence Exhibition' illustrating Irish history from 1916–1921. Additionally, there is an Ancient Egypt exhibition.

Open Tues-Sat 10.00–17.00, Sun 14.00–17.00. Admission is free. A Museumlink bus linking the 3 sites of the National Museum operates regularly throughout the day.

Tel: 01 677 7444

Web: www.museum.ie

National Museum of Ireland, Decorative Arts and History (Collins Barracks), Benburb Street.

Ireland's museum of decorative arts and economic, social, political and military history, based in the oldest military barracks in Europe. Major collections include Irish silver, Irish country furniture, costume jewellery and accessories. The work of museum restoration and conservation is explained and the Out of Storage gallery provides visitors with a view of artefacts in storage.

Open Tues-Sat 10.00–17.00; Sun 14.00–17.00. Admission is free. Full disabled access. A Museumlink bus linking the 3 sites of the National Museum operates regularly throughout the day.

Tel: 01 677 7444

Web: www.museum.ie

National Museum of Ireland, Natural History, Merrion Street.

First opened in 1857 and hardly changed since then, the museum houses a large collection of stuffed animals and the skeletons of mammals and birds from both Ireland and the rest of the world. The exhibits include three examples of the Irish Great Elk which became extinct over 10,000 years ago and the skeleton of a Basking Shark. Fascinating glass reproductions of marine specimens, known as the Blaschka Collection, are found on the upper gallery.

Open Tues-Sat 10.00–17.00; Sun 14.00–17.00. Admission is free. A Museumlink bus linking the 3 sites of the National Museum operates regularly throughout the day.

Tel: 01 677 7444

Web: www.museum.ie

National Print Museum, Haddington Road.

Situated in the former Garrison Chapel in Beggars Bush Barracks, the museum illustrates the development of printing from the advent of printing to the use of computer technology with a unique collection of implements and machines from Ireland's printing industry.

Open Mon–Fri 09.00–17.00, Sat & Sun and Bank Holidays 14.00–17.00.

Tel: 01 660 3770

National Sea Life Centre, Bray.

Features marine life from the seas around Ireland including stingrays, conger eels, and sharks; also freshwater fish from Irish rivers and streams. A touch pool gives children the opportunity to pick up small creatures such as starfish, crabs and sea anemones. By way of contrast is the fascinating 'Danger in the Depths' tank with many sea creatures from

around the world which have proved harmful or fatal to humans.

Open (May-Sept) Mon-Fri 10.00-18.00, Sat & Sun 10.00-18.30; (Oct-Apr) Mon-Fri 11.00-17.00, Sat & Sun 11.00-18.00.

Tel: 01 286 6939

National Transport Museum, Howth.

A collection of buses, trams, trucks, tractors and fire engines, some dating back to 1880, along with other memorabilia from the transport industry.

Open (Jun–Aug) Mon–Fri 10.00–17.00, Sat & Sun 14.00–17.00; (Sept-May) Sat & Sun only 14.00–17.00. Bank holidays 14.00–17.00.

Tel: 01 848 0831

Web: www.nationaltransportmuseum.org
Email: info@nationaltransportmuseum.org

National Wax Museum, Granby Row.

Over 300 life-size wax figures of well-known people and personalities from the past and present ranging from Eamon De Valera to Elvis Presley. Also a dimly lit Chamber of Horrors.

Open: Mon–Sat 10.00–17.30, Sun 12.00–17.30.

Tel: 01 872 6340

Newbridge House, Donabate.

Built in 1737 for Archbishop Charles Cobbe, and still the residence of his descendants, Newbridge has one of the most beautiful period manor house interiors in Ireland and is set within 142 hectares (350 acres) of parkland. A fully restored 18thC farm lies on the estate together with dairy, forge, tack room, and estate worker's house. Situated 19km (12 miles) north of Dublin.

Open (Apr–Sept) Tues–Sat 10.00–17.00, Sun & bank holidays 14.00–18.00; (Oct–Mar) Sat, Sun & bank holidays 14.00–17.00.

Tel: 01 843 6534

Newman House, St Stephen's Green.

Newman House is made up of two splendid Georgian mansions, No 85 and No 86, which were once part of the buildings of the Catholic University of Ireland and named after Cardinal Newman, the first rector of the university. They are now owned by University College Dublin. No 86 was built in 1765 for Richard Whaley MP with marvellous stucco by Robert West, the house has also been owned by the celebrated gambler Buck Whaley. The smaller house, No 85, was designed by Richard Castle in 1739 with beautiful plasterwork by the Swiss La Franchini brothers and includes the Apollo Room with a figure of the god above the mantle. Gerald Manley Hopkins was Professor of Classics here at the end of the 19thC and his study is on view. Also open to the public is a classroom furnished as it would have been when James Joyce was a

pupil here from 1899–1902. A guided tour explains the history and heritage of the house and how it was restored.

Open (Jun, Jul, Aug) Tues–Fri 12.00–17.00.

Tel: 01 716 7422

Number 29, Lower Fitzwilliam Street.

This elegant four-storey house has been restored and furnished exactly as it would have been between 1790–1820 by any well-to-do middle class family. Everything in the house is authentic with period items from the National Museum. The wallpaper was hand-made for Number 29 using 18thC methods. Among the rooms in the house are a kitchen, pantry, governess' room, nursery and boudoir.

Open Tues–Sat 10.00–17.00, Sun 14.00–17.00. Closed for about 2 weeks preceding Christmas.

Tel: 01 702 6165

Old Jameson Distillery, Bow Street, Smithfield Village.

The art of Irish Whiskey making shown through an audio-visual presentation, working models of the distilling process, and guided tour of the old distillery which was in use between 1780–1971.

Open daily 09.00–17.30 (tours only). Disabled access.

Tel: 01 807 2355

Pearse Museum, St. Enda's Park, Grange Road, Rathfarnham.

Housed in the former school run by nationalist Patrick Pearse from 1910–1916, it includes an audio-visual presentation and a nature study room with displays on Irish flora and fauna. Pearse was executed in 1916 for his part in the Easter Rising.

Open (Feb-Apr) 10.00-17.00; (May-Aug) 10.00-17.30; (Sept-Oct) 10.00-17.00; (Nov-Jan) 10.00-16.00; closed 13.00-14.00. Admission is free. Disabled access to ground floor/toilet.

Tel: 01 493 4208

Powerscourt Centre, South William Street.

A lively three storey centre of craft shops, galleries, boutiques and cafés, converted from Powerscourt Townhouse, a classical style mansion designed by Robert Mack and built between 1771–74. It features the original grand wooden staircase and finely detailed plasterwork.

Web: www.powerscourtcentre.com

Powerscourt House & Gardens, County Wicklow.

First laid out in the 1740s, the 18 hectare (45 acre) gardens, perhaps the finest in Ireland, include sweeping terraces cut into a steep hillside, statues and ornamental lakes. A

spectacular Italian style stairway leading down to the main lake was added in 1874. Secluded Japanese gardens with bamboo and walled gardens are also notable and there is a huge variety of trees and shrubs. The house suffered a serious fire in 1974 and is no longer lived in. Visitors may walk through the old ballroom, and an exhibition area illustrates the history of the construction of the house and there are models of some of the rooms as they would have been before the fire. The house dates back to the 18thC when in 1731 architect Richard Castle was commissioned by Richard Wingfield to transform the medieval Powerscourt Castle into a grand Pallladian style mansion; the castle walls were used to form the main structure and the central courtyard was converted into an entrance hall. Powerscourt is in the foothills of the Wicklow mountains, 19km (12 miles) south of Dublin.
Open daily 09.30–17.30.
Tel: 01 204 6000
Web: www.powerscourt.ie

Phoenix Park Visitor Centre, Phoenix Park.
The visitor centre illustrates the history and wildlife of the park with an audio-visual display, a variety of fascinating exhibits and temporary exhibitions. Adjoining the centre is a restored medieval tower house, Ashtown Castle. On Saturdays there are free guided tours to the Irish President's House which is situated in the Park.
Open: (Jun-Sept) 10.00-18.00; (Apr-May) 09.30-17.30; (Nov-Mar) Sat & Sun only 09.30-16.30. Last admission 45 minutes before closing. Toilet for people with disabilities.
Tel: 01 677 0095

Rathfarnham Castle, Rathfarnham.
Dating from around 1583, this castle has 18thC interiors by Sir William Chambers and James Stuart and is presented to visitors as a castle undergoing conservation. There is a toilet for people with disabilities but restricted access to the castle.
Open daily from May–Oct 09.30–17.00 (last tour 16.30).
Tel: 01 493 9462

Royal Hospital, Military Road, Kilmainham.
The Royal Hospital was built as a home for army pensioners and invalids by Charles I, and continued in use for almost 250 years. Designed by Sir William Robinson in 1684, it has a formal facade and large courtyard and bears similarities to Les Invalides in Paris and The Royal Hospital in Chelsea. The restored building has one of Dublin's finest interiors and houses

the Irish Museum of Modern Art in which there is an audio-visual presentation "The Story of the Royal Hospital Kilmainham". The grounds, including a formal garden, are open to the public.
Tel: 01 612 9900

Shaw Birthplace, Synge Street.
This delightful Victorian terrace home was the birthplace of one of Ireland's four Nobel prize-winners for literature, George Bernard Shaw. Restored to give the feeling that the Shaw family is still in residence, the home provides an insight into the domestic life of Victorian Dubliners.
Open (May–Sept) Mon–Fri 10.00–17.00, Sat & Sun 14.00–17.00. Closed 13.00–14.00.
Tel: 01 872 2077
Email: shawhouse@dublintourism.ie

Tara's Palace – Dolls House, Malahide.
The centrepiece of this museum is the one-twelfth size scale model house reflecting the splendour of 18thC Irish mansions. Conceived by Ronald and Doreen McDonnell in 1980, it was ten years in the making. Irish craftsmen paid meticulous attention to detail, with unique miniature furniture and paintings adorning the walls. The museum also has rare pieces of porcelain, miniature glass and silver. Dolls houses of the 18thC and 19thC are displayed, together with dolls and antique toys.
Open (Apr–Sept) Mon–Sat 10.00–17.00, Sun and bank holidays 14.00–18.00; (Oct–Mar) Sat, Sun and bank holidays 14.00–17.00. Closed all year 13.00–14.00.
Tel: 01 846 3779

Temple Bar
Named after a 17thC landowner, Sir William Temple, this charming neighbourhood is Dublin's cultural quarter. With its narrow cobbled streets running close to the Liffey, Temple Bar is full of character and home to many artists and musicians. The area has been regenerated in recent years and boasts a wide variety of cultural venues and events and an eclectic mix of studios, galleries, shops, markets and eating-places. Modern architecture now blends with the historic. Many free open-air events take place in summer at Meeting House Square and Temple Bar Square, including circus acts, concerts and the outdoor screening of films. Temple Bar is bounded by the south quays of the Liffey, Dame Street, Westmoreland Street and Fishamble Street.
Temple Bar Information Centre, 12 Essex Street East.
Tel: 01 677 2255
Web: www.temple–bar.ie
Email: info@templebar.ie

The Chimney, Smithfield Village.
Originally built in 1895, this 53 metre (175ft) chimney which belonged to the Jameson Whiskey Distillery now provides a 360 degree panoramic viewpoint over the city. A glass walled lift takes visitors up the side of the chimney to two viewing galleries at the top.
Open daily 10.00–17.30.
Tel: 01 817 3800

Trinity College, College Green.
The original Elizabethan college was founded in 1592 but the present building was largely built between 1755–1759. The cruciform complex surrounding cobbled quadrangles and peaceful gardens has an impressive 91 metre (300ft) Palladian facade designed by Henry Keene and John Sanderford. One of the most notable features within the main college square is the 30 metre (98ft) Campanile or bell tower built in 1853 by Sir Charles Lanyon. The oldest surviving part of the college is the red brick apartment building from 1700 known as The Rubrics. Originally a Protestant College, Catholics did not start entering Trinity until the 1970s. The Library has over a million books and a magnificent collection of early illuminated manuscripts, including the famous Book of Kells; areas open to the public include the Colonnades, the Treasury, and the Long Room Library. Edmund Burke, Oliver Goldsmith and Samuel Beckett are among famous former Trinity College students.
Web: www.tcd.ie

Waterways Visitor Centre, Grand Canal Quay.
A modern centre built on piers over the Grand Canal, housing an exhibition about Ireland's inland waterways. Working models of various engineering features are displayed and there is an interactive multimedia presentation.
Open (Jun–Sept) daily 09.30–17.00; (Oct–May) Wed–Sun 12.30–17.00. Last admission 45 minutes before closing. Access to ground floor for people with disabilities.
Tel: 01 677 7510

Cathedrals and churches

Augustinian Church, Thomas Street.
Designed by E W Pugin and G C Ashlin in 1862, it has a mountainous exterior with lofty side aisles to the nave and a 49 metre (160ft) high tower crowned by a spire.

Christ Church Cathedral, Christchurch Place.
The Cathedral was established by Strongbow and Archbishop Laurence O'Toole in 1173 on the site of the cathedral founded around 1030 by the Norse King Sitric Silkenbeard. Lambert Simnel, pretender to the English throne, was crowned here as Edward VI in 1487. It was extensively restored between 1871–78 by George Edmund Street and is one of the best examples in Ireland of early Gothic architecture. The medieval crypt is one of the oldest and largest in Ireland.
Open Mon-Fri 09.45-17.00, Sat & Sun 10.00-17.00.
Tel: 01 677 8099
Web: www.cccdub.ie
Email: welcome@cccdub.ie

Franciscan Church, (Adam and Eve's)
Merchants Quay.
Designed by Patrick Byrne in 1830.

St. Ann's Church, Dawson Street.
Designed by Isaac Wells in 1720 with a Romanesque-style facade added by Sir Thomas Deane in 1868. Much of the colourful stained glass dates back to the mid 19thC. Wooden shelves behind the altar were once used to take bread for distribution to the poor. Music recitals are held in the church.
Tel: 01 676 7727

St. Audoen's Church, High Street.
Dublin's only surviving medieval parish church, with a 12thC font and portal. The bell tower, restored in the 19thC, has three 15thC bells. The guild chapel has an exhibition on the importance of the church in the life of the medieval city. Dublin's only surviving city gate, known as St. Audoen's Arch, stands nearby.
Open Jun–Sept 09.30 (10.15 on Sun)–16.45. Toilet for people with disabilities and church partly accessible.
Tel: 01 677 0088

St. Audoen's RC Church, High Street.
Designed by Patrick Byrne in 1841–47, it has a monumental, cliff-like exterior with a huge Corinthian portico added by Stephen Ashlin in 1898.

St. George's, Temple Street.
This neo-classical church was designed by Francis Johnston in 1802 and has a 61 metre (200ft) high steeple modelled on St. Martin-in-the-Fields, London.

St. Mary's Church, Mary Street.
A handsome galleried church designed by Thomas Burgh in 1627. Wolfe Tone, leader of the United Irishmen, was baptised here in 1763 and Sean O'Casey in 1880.

St. Mary's Abbey, Meetinghouse Lane.
Established originally as a Benedictine foundation in 1139, it became Cistercian eight years later. Until the 16thC it was one of the largest and most important monasteries in

Ireland. The remains include a fine vaulted Chapter House of 1190 and there is an interesting exhibition about the history of the abbey.
Open mid June–mid Sept, Wed and Sun 10.00–17.00. Last admission 45 minutes before closing.
Tel: 01 872 1490

St. Mary's Pro-Cathedral, Marlborough Street.

A Greek Doric style building with the interior modelled on the Church of St. Philippe de Roule in Paris, designed by John Sweetman and built between 1815–1825. St. Mary's is Dublin's most important Catholic Church and is used on State occasions. Tenor John McCormack was once a member of the Palestrina choir that sings a Latin mass every Sunday at 11.00.
Open Mon-Fri 07.30-18.45, Sat 07.30-19.15, Sun 09.00-13.45 and 17.30-19.45.
Tel: 01 874 5441
Web: www.procathedral.ie

St. Michan's Church, Church Street.

Founded in 1095 as a Viking parish church, largely rebuilt in 1685 and restored in 1828. Famous for the 17thC mummified bodies in the crypt which are preserved with skin and hair because of the dry atmosphere created by the limestone walls. Handel is thought to have played on the organ which dates from 1724.
Open (March/April–Oct) Mon–Fri 10.00–12.45 and 14.00-16.45; (Nov–March) Mon–Fri 12.30–15.30; all Saturdays 10.00–12.45. Vaults closed on Sundays.
Tel: 01 872 4154

St. Patrick's Cathedral, St. Patrick's Close.

The National Cathedral of the Church of Ireland, it was built in the late 12thC on the site of the pre-Norman parish church of St. Patrick. It gained and lost cathedral status more than once in its chequered history and Cromwellian soldiers stabled horses here in the Civil War. Architect John Semple added a spire in 1749 and St. Patrick's was fully restored in the 19thC with finance from the Guinness family. The massive west tower houses the largest ringing peel of bells in Ireland. The cathedral is full of memorial brasses, busts and monuments to famous Irishmen. Jonathan Swift was Dean here from 1713–1745; there are memorials to Swift and his beloved Stella (Esther Johnson) and Swift's pulpit contains his writing table and chair, and portrait.
Usually open daily 09.00–17.00. Wheelchair access by arrangement.
Tel: 01 453 9472
Web: www.stpatrickscathedral.ie
Email: admin@stpatrickscathedral.ie

St. Saviour's, Dominick Street.

Designed by J J McCarthy in 1858, this extravagant French style Gothic edifice has a bold west door under a triangular hood, crowned by a large rose window.

St. Stephen's (Pepper Canister), Mount Street Crescent.

This handsome neo-classical church, designed by John Bowden in 1824, has a Greek style portico.

St. Werburgh's Church, Werburgh Street.

Originally the site of an Anglo-Norman foundation, the present church was built in 1715–19 and rebuilt in 1759 following a fire. St. Werburgh's was the Chapel Royal until 1790. Lord Edward Fitzgerald, one of the leaders of the 1798 rebellion, is buried in the vaults.

Whitefriar Street Carmelite Church, Aungier Street.

19thC church standing on the site of a 16thC Carmelite Priory. The remains of Saint Valentine are buried here and there is a 15thC oak statue of the Virgin and Child, thought to be the only surviving Pre-reformation statue of its kind.
Tel: 01 475 8821

Libraries

Central Catholic Library, Merrion Square.

Of religious and general interest, with a large Irish section.
Open Mon–Fri 11.00–18.00, Sat 11.00–17.30.
Tel: 01 676 1264
Web: www.catholiclibrary.ie

Central Library, Ilac Centre.

Tel: 01 873 4333.
Enquiries about other Dublin City Public Libraries (lending, reference and special collections).
Tel: 01 674 4800
Web: www.iol.ie/dublincitylibrary
Email: dublinpubliclibraries@dublincity.ie

Chester Beatty Library, Dublin Castle, Dame Street.

Reopened in 2000 in a purpose designed home in the Clock Tower building of Dublin Castle, the library is a treasure of manuscripts, books, prints and textiles collected by American scholar Sir Alfred Chester Beatty. It has some of the rarest original manuscripts still in existence. The collection reflects the art of manuscript production and printing from many parts of the world and from early to modern times with picture scrolls, jade books and woodblock prints from the Far East, around 4,000 Islamic manuscripts, and fine books, bindings and

manuscripts from Western Europe. With many Early Christian papyri, the library is a major resource for the study of the Old and New Testaments.

Open Mon-Fri 10.00–17.00, Sat 11.00–17.00, Sun 13.00–17.00. Oct-Apr closed Mondays. Admission is free.

Tel: 01 407 0750

Web: www.cbl.ie

Email: info@cbl.ie

Genealogical Office, Kildare Street.

Part of the National Library, the genealogical office offers a service to assist in the task of tracing family history, familiarising people with the relevant records and procedures.

Open Mon–Fri 10.00–17.00, Sat 10.00–12.30.

Tel: 01 603 0200

Gilbert Library, Pearse Street.

Books and manuscripts relating to Dublin which were accumulated by 19thC Dublin historian Sir John T Gilbert and now in the care of Dublin Corporation. The collection includes rare early Dublin newspapers, 18thC bindings, Irish Almanacs, manuscripts of the municipal records of the City of Dublin and the records of the Dublin guilds.

Tel: 01 674 4800

Goethe Institute Library, Merrion Square.

German cultural information centre and library.

Open Tues-Thurs 12.00–20.00, Fri 10.00-14.30, Sat 10.00-13.30.

Tel: 01 661 1155

Irish Architectural Archive, Merrion Square.

Open Tues–Fri 10.00-17.00.

Tel: 01 663 3040

Marsh's Library, St Patrick's Close.

Given to the city by Archbishop Narcissus Marsh and opened in 1701, this is Ireland's oldest public library containing many rare books still in their original carved bookcases. The building was designed by Sir William Robinson who was also the architect of the Royal Hospital, Kilmainham. To prevent the theft of rare books readers were locked in wire cages and three of these cages survive.

Open Mon-Fri 10.00-17.00 (closed 13.00-14.00); Sat 10.30-13.00; closed Tuesdays.

Tel: 01 454 3511

Web: www.marshlibrary.ie

Email: keeper@marshlibrary.ie

National Library of Ireland, Kildare Street.

Offers over half a million books, a vast collection of maps, prints and manuscripts and an invaluable collection of Irish newspapers and periodicals. The impressive Victorian building has been home to the Library since 1890, and there is a large domed reading room. Holds temporary exhibitions on Irish writers and books.

Open: Mon–Wed 10.00–21.00, Thurs–Fri 10.00–17.00, Sat 10.00–13.00.

Tel: 01 603 0200

Web: www.nli.ie

Email: info@nli.ie

National Photographic Archive, Meeting House Square.

Only established in 1998, it has over 600,000 photographs recording people, political events, and scenes of Irish cities, towns and countryside. Images from the collection are always on view. There is also a reading room and darkrooms.

Open: Mon–Fri 10.00–17.00. Sat 10.00-14.00 (exhibition only) Admission is free. Disabled access/toilet.

Tel: 01 603 0374

Web: www.nli.ie/fr_arch.htm

Email: photoarchive@nli.ie

Royal Irish Academy Library, Dawson Street.

One of the largest collections of ancient Irish manuscripts in the country with one usually on display together with a small exhibition. Access may be restricted depending on Royal Academy meetings and large groups need to make a prior arrangement to visit.

Open Mon–Fri 10.00–17.00. Admission is free.

Tel: 01 676 2570

Trinity College Library, College Green.

The oldest and most famous of Dublin's libraries dating from the late 16thC. Entitled to receive a copy of every book published in Ireland, the library also contains an extensive collection of Irish manuscripts including the Book of Kells, a beautifully illuminated copy of the gospels written on vellum in Latin around the year AD800. The Book of Kells is now bound in four volumes and two are always on display in the Treasury, one open at a major ornamental page and the other to show two pages of script. An exhibition explains how the Book of Kells and other manuscripts such as the Book of Durrow (AD675) and Book of Armagh (AD807) were created and illustrates monastic life in the 8thC. The impressive Old Library or Long Room Library is lined with marble busts of scholars and is nearly 64 metres (210ft) long. It rises two storeys with a high barrel vaulted ceiling and contains over 200,000 of the college's books.

Open Mon–Sat 09.30–17.00; Sun 09.30–16.30 (Jun–Sept), Sun 12.00–16.30 (May–Oct). Last admission 30 minutes before closing.
Tel: 01 608 2308
Web:www.tcd.ie

Arts centres, galleries and concert halls

Douglas Hyde Gallery, Trinity College.
Showing mainly temporary exhibitions of contemporary art.
Tel: 01 608 1116
Web: www.douglashydegallery.com
Email: dhgallery@tcd.ie

Gallery of Photography, Meeting House Square.
Exhibitions of contemporary photography. Roof terrace has views over the square.
Tel: 01 671 4654
Web: www.irish-photography.com
Email: gallery@irish–photography.com

Hugh Lane Municipal Gallery of Modern Art, Parnell Square North.
19thC and 20thC paintings, mainly Impressionist works, bequeathed by Sir Hugh Lane who was drowned in the Lusitania in 1915, form the nucleus of this collection. The Lane Collection is split with the Tate Gallery in London; each half is alternated between the galleries every 5 years. There is an extensive range of Irish and international paintings, sculpture and stained glass and the acquisition of contemporary work is ongoing. Included is the London studio of Dublin-born artist Francis Bacon, which was carefully dismantled and reconstructed here. Regular 'Sundays at Noon' Concerts are held at the gallery (apart from July and August) with everything from early music to commissioned new works; the music is often arranged to complement one of the temporary exhibitions. The classical building which houses the gallery, Charlemont House, was designed by William Chambers in 1763 for James Caulfield, later 1st Earl Charlemont. It was reconstructed in 1929 to house the Lane Collection and opened in 1933.
Open Tues–Thurs 09.30–18.00, Fri & Sat 09.30–17.00, Sun 11.00–17.00. Admission free except for special exhibitions. Disabled access.
Tel: 01 874 1903
Web: www.hughlane.ie
Email: info@hughlane.ie

National Concert Hall, Earlsfort Terrace.
Home of the National Symphony Orchestra of Ireland, but also a venue for international artists and orchestras, jazz, contemporary and traditional Irish music. The classical building was designed for the Great Exhibition of 1865, then became the centrepiece of University College Dublin before opening as Ireland's National Concert Hall in 1981.
Booking office open Mon–Sat 10.00–19.00. Disabled access/toilet.
Tel: 01 417 0000
Web: www.nch.ie (online booking)
Email:info@nch.ie

National Gallery of Ireland, Merrion Square.
Paintings by illustrious 20thC European artists such as Morrisot, Bonnard, Picasso and Monet hang in the National Gallery as well as the work of Old Masters including Titian, Caravaggio, Rembrandt and Vermeer. There is the National Collection of Irish art, a room dedicated to the work of Jack B Yeats, English paintings, and over 250 sculptures. William Dargan organised the 1853 Dublin Exhibition on this site and used the proceeds to found the collection; his statue stands on the lawn.
Open Mon–Sat 09.30–17.30, Thurs 09.30-20.30, Sun 12.00–17.30. Admission free. Disabled access/toilet.
Tel: 01 661 5133
Web: www.nationalgallery.ie
Email: info@ngi.ie

Royal Dublin Society, Ballsbridge.
Venue for large events including craft and antiques fairs and Ideal Homes exhibitions.
Tel: 01 668 0866
Web: www.rds.ie

Royal Hibernian Academy Gallagher Gallery, Ely Place.
Showing both traditional and innovative work from both Irish and international artists.
Tel: 01 661 2558
Web: www.royalhibernianacademy.com
Email: www.rhagallery@eircom.net

Solomon Gallery, Powerscourt Centre.
One of Ireland's leading contemporary art galleries, situated in an 18thC Georgian townhouse.
Open Mon–Sat 10.00–17.30. Admission free.
Tel: 01 679 4237
Web: www.solomongallery.com
Email: info@solomongallery.com

Temple Bar Gallery and Studios, Temple Bar.
A large complex with studios and exhibition spaces.
Tel: 01 671 0073
Web: www.templebargallery.com
Email: info@templebargallery.com

Temple Bar Music Centre, Curved Street.
Live music venue with recording and rehearsal studios.
Tel: 01 677 0647
Web: www.tbmc.ie
Email: info@tbmc.ie

Taylor Galleries, Kildare Street.
Contemporary art gallery, mainly Irish, with the emphasis on painting and sculpture.
Tel: 01 676 6055

The Ark, Eustace Street.
A cultural centre for children with a child-size theatre.
Tel: 01 670 7788
Web: www.ark.ie
Email: boxoffice@ark.ie

Parks and gardens

Garden of Remembrance, Parnell
Square East.
The Garden of Remembrance, opened in 1966, is dedicated to all those who died in the cause of Irish Freedom. There is a sculpture by Oisín Kelly representing the Irish legend, "Children of Lir".
Open (Oct-Mar) 09.30-1600, (Apr-Sept) 08.30-18.00.
Tel: 01 874 3074 (garden) or 01 647 2498 (head office)

Iveagh Gardens, Clonmel Street.
Designed by Ninian Niven in 1863, this is one of the least known and most tranquil of Dublin's parks. Features include a rustic grotto, cascade, fountains, maze, archery grounds, wilderness and woodlands.
Opening according to daylight hours.
Tel: 01 475 7816

Marlay Park, Rathfarnham.
This large park situated at the foot of the Dublin Mountains contains areas of woodland, a large pond, nature trail and model railway.

National Botanic Gardens, Glasnevin.
Established in 1795, these magnificent gardens occupy an area of 20 hectares (49 acres) and contain a fabulous collection of plants, shrubs and trees. Many of the plants come from tropical Africa and South America and are housed in large Victorian glasshouses. Features include a rose garden, rockery and wall plants, herbaceous borders, vegetable garden and arboretum.
Open Summer Mon-Sat 09.00-18.00, Sun 10.00-18.00; Winter Mon-Sat 10.00-16.30, Sun 10.00-16.30. Shorter opening hours for glasshouses. Admission is free. Toilet for people with disabilities, and gardens largely accessible.
Tel: 01 857 0909

Phoenix Park
Phoenix Park, covering over 712 hectares (1,760 acres), is Europe's largest enclosed city park. Its name is thought to derive from the Irish meaning "clear water" and a spring does rise in the park. Enclosed by an 11km (7 mile) long stone wall, the park was laid out in the mid 18thC and was the scene of the Phoenix Park murders in 1882, when the Chief Secretary and the Under-Secretary for Ireland were assassinated. A more recent event was when the Pope celebrated mass in the park in front of 1 million people; a 27 metre (90ft) steel cross marks the spot. The park includes a number of buildings, the most important of which is Áras an Uachtaráin; the Viceroy's Lodge built in 1751 but later becoming the official house of the President of Ireland when Dr Douglas Hyde moved there in 1938. Other important buildings are the American ambassador's residence and the Ordnance Survey Office. A 60 metre (205 ft) high obelisk, erected in 1817, is a memorial to the Dublin-born Duke of Wellington. The People's Garden by the main entrance on Parkgate Street is laid out with ornamental planting in ribbon borders, much as it would have been in Victorian times. Dublin Zoo is in the south-east corner. The open space covered by playing fields and paths, known as Fifteen Acres but actually covering more than 200, was used in the 18thC as a duelling ground. Phoenix Park is open to the public at all times but the People's Gardens usually close at sunset.

St. Anne's Park, Dollymount.
Once part of the Guinness family estate, the park covers over 110 hectares (270 acres) and is wooded with oak, pine, beech, chestnut and lime. There is a lovely rose garden, opened in 1975.

St. Enda's Park, Grange Road,
Rathfarnham.
The park surrounds the Pearse Museum and includes a walled garden, riverside walks and waterfall. Open daily from 10.00, closing time varies according to daylight hours. Limited access for people with disabilities.

St. Stephen's Green
In the heart of the city, St Stephen's Green was originally an open common but was enclosed in 1663. Opened to the general public in 1877, it is laid out as a public park with flowerbeds, an ornamental pond and several sculptures. There is a garden for the visually impaired and there are summer lunchtime concerts.
Open daily 08.00 (Sun & bank Holidays 10.00); closes according to daylight hours.
Tel: 01 475 7816

War Memorial Garden, South Circular Road, Islandbridge.
Dedicated to the memory of the Irish soldiers who died in the First World War, these gardens include a sunken rose garden and herbaceous borders. They were designed by Sir Edward Lutyens. The names of the 49,400 soldiers who died between 1914–1918 are contained in the granite bookrooms in the gardens, access to which is only by arrangement with the management.
Open Mon–Fri 08.00, Sat & Sun 10.00; closes according to daylight hours.
Tel: 01 677 0236 (gardens)
Tel: 01 647 2498 (head office)

Theatres

Abbey Theatre, Lower Abbey Street.
Ireland's National Theatre, founded by Lady Gregory and W B Yeats in 1904. The Abbey quickly became world renowned, staging plays by J M Synge and Sean O'Casey, and played a significant role in the renaissance of Irish culture. It also provoked controversy in Dublin and even riots. The present theatre was built in 1966 to replace the previous building which had been destroyed by fire. The Abbey stages classic Irish plays, while the Peacock theatre downstairs presents new and experimental drama.
Tel: 01 878 7222
Web: www.abbeytheatre.ie

Andrews Lane Theatre and Studio, Andrews Lane.
A wide variety of works shown both in the theatre and studio.
Tel: 01 679 5720
Web: www.andrewslane.com

Civic Theatre, Tallaght.
New theatre staging everything from drama to variety shows
Tel: 01 462 7477
Web: www.civictheatre.ie

Focus Theatre, Pembroke Place, Pembroke Street.
Small theatre presenting the classics and new writing.
Tel: 01 676 3071

Gaiety Theatre, South King Street.
Restored Victorian building and Dublin's oldest theatre, founded in 1837. Drama, opera (Opera Ireland have two seasons a year), ballet, musicals, pantomime, comedy.
Tel: 01 677 1717
Web: www.gaietytheatre.net

Gate Theatre, Cavendish Row.
Modern Irish and classical drama, also international plays. Founded in 1928.
Tel: 01 874 4045
Web: www.gate-theatre.ie

Lambert Puppet Theatre, Clifton Lane, Monkstown.
Tel: 01 280 0974
Web: www.lambertpuppettheatre.com

Olympia Theatre, Dame Street.
Comedy, drama, pantomime, musicals, concerts.
Tel: 0818 719330

Peacock Theatre, Lower Abbey Street.
New and experimental work.
Tel: 01 878 7222

Project Arts Centre, 39 East Essex Street.
Moved in 2000 into new custom designed building with performance and gallery space; generally innovative new work and everything from drama and visual arts to talks and events.
Tel: 01 881 9613
Web: www.project.ie
Email: info@project.ie

Samuel Beckett Theatre, Trinity College.
Trinity College School of Drama theatre with a variety of student productions during term and touring companies at other times. Venue for Festival Fringe events.
Tel: 01 608 2461

The Point, North Wall Quay.
Theatre and concert venue including ballet.
Tel: 01 836 3633

Sugar Club, Lower Leeson Street.
Multimedia theatre with wide range of entertainment; drama, film, cabaret, comedy, music, events.
Tel: 01 678 7188
Web: www.thesugarclub.com

The Dublin Theatre Festival, held at many venues throughout the city, runs for two weeks every October.
Tel: 01 677 8439, Box office 01 677 8899
Web: www.dublintheatrefestival.com

The Fringe Festival which presents theatre, dance and the visual arts is held for three weeks, commencing in September.
Tel: 01 872 9433
Web: www.fringefest.com

Cinemas

Most cinemas offer cheaper seats before 5pm.
IMC, Dún Laoghaire,
Tel: 01 280 7777. 12 screens.

Irish Film Institute, Eustace Street,
Art house with 2 screens and restaurant
converted from old Quaker meeting house.
New Irish films and film seasons. The Irish Film
Archive, library and special events.
Tel: 01 679 3477.
Web: www.irishfilm.ie
Email: info@irishfilm.ie

Omniplex, Santry, **Tel: 01 842 8844.** 11 screens.

Ormonde Cinema, Stillorgan,
Tel: 01 278 0000. 7 screens.

Savoy Cinema, O'Connell Street Upper,
Tel: 01 874 6000. 6 screens.

Screen Cinema, D'Olier Street,
Tel: 01 672 5500. 3 screens.

Ster Century, Liffey Valley Shopping Centre,
Fonthill Road
Tel: 01 605 5700. 14 screens.

UCI Cinema, Blanchardstown,
Tel: 01 8222 624. 9 screens.

UCI Cinema, Coolock,
Tel: 01 848 5122. 10 screens.

UCI Cinema, Tallaght,
Tel: 01 459 8400. 12 screens.

UGC Cinemas, Parnell Street,
Tel: 01 872 8444. 17 screens.
The largest cinema in Ireland.

Shopping

Opening hours are generally 09.00–18.00
Mon–Sat. Many city centre shops and shopping
centres remain open until 20.00 or 21.00 on
Thursdays and Fridays and open 12.00–18.00 on
Sundays.
The main city centre shopping areas are around
Grafton Street and Nassau Street to the south of
the Liffey and around Henry Street (off
O'Connell Street) to the north of the river. Both
Grafton Street and Henry Street are pedestrianised.
Many up-market and international designer stores
can be found in Grafton Street, while shops
around Henry Street are generally less
expensive. The Temple Bar area has a number
of craft and specialist shops.

Department stores

Arnotts, Henry Street, **Tel: 01 872 1111.**

Brown Thomas, Grafton Street,
Tel: 01 605 6666.

Clery and Co, O'Connell Street Lower,
Tel: 01 878 6000.

Debenhams, Jervis Centre, **Tel: 01 878 1222.**

Dunnes Stores, Henry Street, **Tel: 01 671 4629.**

Guiney & Co, Talbot Street, **Tel: 01 878 8835.**

Marks & Spencers, Grafton Street,
Tel: 01 679 7855.

Penneys Stores, Mary Street, **Tel: 01 872 7788.**

Roches Stores, Henry Street, **Tel:01 873 0044.**

Shopping centres

Dún Laoghaire Shopping Centre, Marine Road,
Tel: 01 280 2981.

Ilac Centre, Henry Street, **Tel: 01 704 1460.**

Irish Life Shopping Mall, Abbey Street,
Tel: 01 704 1452.

Jervis Shopping Centre, Jervis Street,
Tel: 01 878 1323.

Powerscourt Centre, South William Street,
Tel: 01 679 4144.

St. Stephen's Green Centre, Tel: 01 478 0888.
There are also shopping centres at Clondalkin
(Liffey Valley), Blanchardstown, and Tallaght on
the outskirts of Dublin.

Markets

Blackrock, Sat, Sun & bank holidays 11.00–17.30
(bric-a-brac, china and antiques).
Tel: 01 283 3522

George's Street Market Arcade (second hand
clothes, jewellery, records).
Tel: 01 280 8683

Liberty Market (clothes, fabrics, household
goods), Meath Street.
Tel: 01 280 8683

Moore Street Market, Mon–Sat (flower, fruit and
vegetables), off Henry Street.

St. Michan's Street Vegetable Market (fruit,
vegetables, fish and flowers).

Temple Bar Square. Food market is open every
Saturday from 09.30–18.00 selling organic fruit
and vegetables, bread, cheeses, oysters, and
smoked fish. Book Market is open on Saturdays
from 09.30.
Tel: 01 677 2255

Sport and leisure

International sports venues:
Athletics – Croke Park.
Tel: 01 836 3222

Gaelic Football and Hurling – Croke Park.
Tel 01 836 3222

Rugby and Soccer – Lansdowne Road,
Ballsbridge.
Tel: 01 668 4601

Golf (18-hole golf clubs):
Balcarrick Golf Club, Donabate, 16km (10m)
north of city centre.
Tel: 01 843 6957

Ballinascorney, 13km (8m) south west of city centre.
Tel: 01 451 6430

Beaverstown Golf Club, Donabate, 16km (10m) north of city centre.
Tel: 01 843 6439

Blanchardstown Golf Centre, Mulhuddart, 13km (8m) north west of city centre.
Tel: 01 821 2054

Castle Golf Club, Rathfarnham, 6km (4m) south of city centre.
Tel: 01 490 4207

Citywest Golf Resort, Saggart, 16km (10m) south west of city centre.
Tel: 01 401 0500

Corballis Golf Links, Donabate,16km (10m) north of city centre.
Tel: 01 843 6583
Web: www.golfdublin.com
Email: corballislinks@golfdublin.com

Deerpark Hotel and Golf Courses, Howth, 14km (9 m) north east of city centre.
Tel: 01 832 2624
Web: www.deerpark–hotel.ie
Email: sales@deerpark.iol.ie

Druids Glen, Newmountkennedy, 32km (2m) south east of city centre.
Tel: 01 287 3600
Web: www.druidsglen.ie
Email: info@druidsglen.ie

Edmondstown, Rathfarnham,   11km (7m) south of city centre.
Tel: 01 493 1082
Email: info@edmondstowngolfclub.ie

Elmgreen Golf Centre, Castleknock, 8km (5m) north west of city centre.
Tel: 01 820 0797
Web: www.golfdublin.com
Email: elmgreen@golfdublin.com

Elm Park, Donnybrook, 5km(3m) south of city centre.
Tel: 01 269 3438
Email: office@elmparkgolfclub.ie

Forrest Little Golf Club, Cloghean, 9km (6m) north of city centre, near to airport.
Tel: 01 840 1183

Grange Castle, Clondalkin, 8km (5m) south west of city centre.
Tel: 01 464 1043
Web: www.grange-castle.com

Grange Golf Club, Rathfarnham, 6km (4m) south of city centre.
Tel: 01 493 2889

Hermitage Golf Club, Lucan, 11km (7m) west of city centre.
Tel: 01 626 8491

Howth Golf Club, Sutton, 14km (9m) north east of city centre.
Tel: 01 832 3055
Web: www.howthgolfclub.ie
Email: manager@howthgolfclub.ie

Island, Corballis, Donabate, 14km (9m) north of city centre.
Tel: 01 843 6462
Web: www.theislandgolfclub.com
Email: info@theislandgolfclub.com

Luttrellstown Castle, Castleknock, 10 km (6 m) west of city centre.
Tel: 01 808 9988
Email: golf@luttrellstown.ie

Malahide Golf Club, 13km (8m) north of city centre. **Tel: 01 846 1611**
Web: www.malahidegolfclub.ie
Email: malgc@clubi.ie

Portmarnock Golf Club, 11km (7m) north east of city centre.
Tel: 01 846 2968
Web: www.portmarnockgolfclub.ie
Email: emer@portmarnockgolfclub.ie

Portmarnock Hotel and Golf Links, 11km (7m) north east of city centre.
Tel: 01 846 1800
Email: golfres@portmarnock.com

Royal Dublin Golf Club, Dollymount, 5km (3m) north east of city centre.
Tel: 01 833 6346
Web: www.theroyaldublingolfclub.com
Email: info@theroyaldublingolfclub.com

St. Anne's Golf Club, Dollymount, 5km (3m) north east of city centre.
Tel: 01 833 6471
Web: www.stanneslinksgolf.com
Email: info@stanneslinksgolf.com

St. Margaret's Golf Club, 11km (7m) north of city centre.
Tel: 01 864 0400
Web: www.stmargaretsgolf.com
Email: info@stmargaretsgolf.com

Swords Open Golf Course, 13km (8m) north of city centre.
Tel: 01 840 9819/890 1030

Greyhound racing

Greyhound racing is one of Ireland's leading spectator sports. Meetings are held at:

Shelbourne Park Stadium, Ringsend, (Wed, Thurs, Sat at 20.00).
Tel: 01 668 3502
Web: www.shelbournepark.com

Harold's Cross Stadium, (Mon, Tues & Fri at 20.00).
Tel: 01 497 1081

Horse racing

There are two racecourses on the outskirts of Dublin:

Leopardstown.
10km (6 miles) south of Dublin. National Hunt and Flat racing with 22 meetings including 4 day Christmas National Hunt Festival.
Tel: 01 289 3607
Web: www.leopardstown.com
Email: info@leopardstown.com

Fairyhouse.
19km (12 miles) north west of Dublin. Home of the Irish Grand National.
Tel: 01 825 6167
Web: www.fairyhouseracecourse.ie
Email: info@fairyhouseracecourse.ie

Sailing

The Irish Sailing Association, Dún Laoghaire, for information on sailing, windsurfing and powerboating in the Dublin area and elsewhere in Ireland.
Tel: 01 280 0239
Web: www.sailing.ie

Sports centres

Aughrim Street, Tel: 01 838 8085

Glin Road, Coolock, **Tel: 01 847 8177**

Swimming pools

Ballymun, Town Centre, **Tel: 01 842 1368**

Coolock, Northside Shopping Centre, **Tel: 01 847 7743**

Crumlin, Windmill Road, **Tel: 01 455 5792**

Finglas, Mellowes Road, **Tel: 01 864 2584**

Markievicz Pool, Townsend Street, **Tel: 01 672 9121**

Rathmines, Lower Rathmines Road, **Tel: 01 496 1275**

Sean, McDermott Street, **Tel: 01 872 0752**

Help and advice

Embassies

Apostolic Nunciature, Navan Road. Tel: 01 838 0577

Argentina, Ailesbury Drive. Tel: 01 269 1546

Australia, Fitzwilton House, Wilton Terrace. Tel: 01 676 1517

Austria, Ailesbury Road. Tel: 01 269 4577

Belgium, Shrewsbury Road. Tel: 01 269 2082

Brazil, Harcourt Street. Tel: 01 475 6000

Britain, Merrion Road. Tel: 01 205 3700

Bulgaria, Burlington Road. Tel: 01 660 3293

Canada, St. Stephen's Green. Tel: 01 478 1988

China, Ailesbury Road. Tel: 01 269 1707

Czech Republic, Northumberland Road. Tel: 01 668 1135

Denmark, St. Stephen's Green. Tel: 01 475 6404

Egypt, Clyde Road. Tel: 01 660 6566

Finland, St. Stephen's Green. Tel: 01 478 1344

France, Ailesbury Road. Tel: 01 260 1666

Germany, Trimleston Avenue. Tel: 01 269 3011

Greece, Pembroke Street Upper. Tel: 01 676 7254

Hungary, Fitzwilliam Place. Tel: 01 661 2902

India, Leeson Park. Tel: 01 497 0843

Iran, Mount Merrion Avenue. Tel: 01 288 0252

Israel, Pembroke Road. Tel: 01 668 0303

Italy, Northumberland Road. Tel: 01 660 1744

Japan, Merrion Centre. Tel: 01 202 8300

Korea, Clyde Road. Tel: 01 660 8800

Mexico, Ailesbury Road. Tel: 01 260 0699

Morocco, Raglan Road. Tel: 01 660 9449

Netherlands, Merrion Road. Tel: 01 269 3444

Nigeria, Leeson Park. Tel: 01 660 4366

Norway, Molesworth Street. Tel: 01 662 1800

Poland, Ailesbury Road. Tel: 01 283 0855

Portugal, Knocksinna Road. Tel: 01 289 4416

Romania, Ailesbury Road. Tel: 01 269 2852

Russian Federation, Orwell Road. Tel: 01 492 3492

Slovakia, Clyde Road. Tel: 01 660 0008

South Africa, Earlsfort Terrace. Tel: 01 661 5553

Spain, Merlyn Park. Tel: 01 269 1640

Sweden, Dawson Street. Tel: 01 671 5822

Switzerland, Ailesbury Road. Tel: 01 269 2515

Turkey, Clyde Road. Tel: 01 668 5240

USA, Elgin Road. Tel: 01 668 8777

Health centres and pharmacies

Grafton Street Centre, Open Mon, Tues & Thurs 08.30-18.15, Wed 09.30-18.15, Fri 08.30-17.45.
Tel: 01 671 2122

Mercer's Medical Centre, Stephen Street Lower, Open: Mon–Thurs 09.00–17.30, Fri 09.00–16.30.
Tel: 01 402 2300

O'Connell's Late Night Pharmacy, O'Connell Street Lower, Open daily Mon-Fri 07.30-22.00, Sat 08.00-22.00, Sun 10.00–22.00.
Tel: 01 873 0427

Garda Síochána (Police)

City centre Garda stations:
Pearse Street station, Tel: 01 666 9000

Store Street station, Tel: 01 666 8000

Dublin Metropolitan Area Headquarters, Harcourt Square,
Tel: 01 666 6666

Greater Dublin Area Headquarters, Phoenix Park,
Tel: 01 666 0000

Dún Laoghaire station, Tel: 01 666 5000
Web: www.garda.ie

Post Offices
General Post Office, O'Connell Street. Open Mon–Sat 08.00-20.00.
Tel: 01 705 8833
Web: www.anpost.ie

Post offices are usually open Mon–Fri 09.00–17.30 (closed 13.00–14.15) and from 09.00–13.00 on Saturdays.

Welfare organisations
Citizens Information Centre (Comhairle), 13a O'Connell Street Upper.
Tel: 01 809 0633

Samaritans, 112 Marlborough Street.
Tel: 01 872 7700 or callsave 1850 609 090
Web: www.samaritans.org

Social Welfare Services, Store Street.
Tel: 01 874 8444

Tourist Victim Support Service, Garda Headquarters, Harcourt Square.
All referrals must go through the Garda.
Open: Mon–Sat 10.00–18.00, Sun 12.00–18.00.
Tel: 01 478 5295
Web: www.victimsupport.ie/tourist.html
Email: info@touristvictimsupport.ie

Hospitals

Baggot Street Community Hospital, Upper Baggot Street. **Tel: 01 668 1577**

Beaumont, Beaumont Road. **Tel: 01 809 3000**

Blackrock Clinic (private), Rock Road.
Tel: 01 283 2222

Bon Secours Private Hospital, Glasnevin.
Tel: 01 837 5111

Cappagh National Orthopaedic, Cappagh Road.
Tel: 01 834 1211

Central Mental Hospital, Dundrum.
Tel: 01 298 9266

Clonskeagh Hospital, Clonskeagh.
Tel: 01 268 0500

Coombe Women's Hospital, Dolphin's Barn Street. **Tel: 01 408 5200**

Dental Hospital, Lincoln Place, **Tel: 01 612 7200**

James Connolly Memorial Hospital, Blanchardstown. **Tel: 01 646 5000**

Mater Misericordiae, Eccles Street.
Tel: 01 803 2000

Mater Private, Eccles Street. **Tel: 01 885 8888**

Mount Carmel, Braemor Park. **Tel: 01 492 2211**

National Maternity, Holles Street.
Tel: 01 661 0277

Orthopaedic Hospital of Ireland, Clontarf.
Tel: 01 833 8167

Our Lady's Hospital for Sick Children, Crumlin.
Tel: 01 409 6100

Rotunda Hospital, Parnell Square.
Tel: 01 873 0700

Royal Hospital, Donnybrook. **Tel: 01 406 6600**

Royal Victoria Eye and Ear, Adelaide Road.
Tel: 01 678 5500

St. Brendan's, Rathdown Road. **Tel: 01 838 5844**

St. James's, James's Street, **Tel: 01 410 3000**

St. Luke's, Rathgar. **Tel: 01 406 5000**

St. Mary's Hospital, Phoenix Park.
Tel: 01 677 8132

St. Michael's, George's Street Lower,
Dún Laoghaire. **Tel: 01 280 6901**

St. Patrick's, James's Street.
Tel: 01 249 3200

St. Vincent's, Convent Avenue, Richmond Road.
Tel: 01 884 2400

St. Vincent's (private), Herbert Avenue.
Tel: 01 260 9200

St. Vincent's University Hospital, Elm Park.
Tel: 01 269 4533

Skin and Cancer Hospital, Hume Street.
Tel: 01 676 6935

Artane	14 B3	Donnybrook	45 C2	Irishtown	37 D3	Rathmines	44 A2
Ashtown	9 C3	Drimnagh	41 D1	Islandbridge	34 A1	Ringsend	37 D2
Ballsbridge	45 D1	Drumcondra	28 A1	Kilbarrack	17 C2	Rossmore	49 D2
Ballyfermot	32 B2	Dundrum	53 C3	Kildonan	10 A1	Sandymount	38 A3
Ballymount	40 A2	Dún Laoghaire		Killester	14 B3	Shielmartin	22 B2
Beaumont	13 C1	(Dunleary)	57 C3	Kilmainham	34 A2	Stillorgan	54 B3
Blackrock	55 D1	Dunleary		Kimmage	42 B3	Stradbrook	56 A3
Bluebell	40 B1	(Dún Laoghaire)	57 C3	Marino	29 C2	Sutton	18 A1
Booterstown	54 B1	Finglas	11 C2	Merrion	46 A3	Templeogue	50 A2
Cabra	27 C2	Finglas East	10 B1	Milltown	44 B3	Terenure	51 C1
Chapelizod	32 B1	Glasnevin	12 A3	Monkstown	56 B3	Wainsfort	50 A1
Churchtown	52 A2	Glasnevin North	11 D1	Mount Merrion	54 A2	Walkinstown	40 B2
Clonskeagh	45 C3	Goatstown	53 C3	Pelletstown	9 D3	Whitehall	12 B3
Clontarf	30 A2	Goldenbridge	33 D3	Phibsborough	27 D2	Willbrook	50 B3
Coolock	14 B1	Greenhills	48 B1	Raheny	16 A3	Williamstown	55 D1
Crumlin	41 D2	Harold's Cross	43 C1	Ranelagh	44 B1	Windy Arbour	53 C2
Dollymount	31 D2	Howth	20 B2	Rathfarnham	51 C2		
Dolphin's Barn	35 C3	Inchicore	33 D2	Rathgar	43 D3		

Index to street names

General abbreviations

All	Alley	Dr	Drive	Junct	Junction	S	South		
Av	Avenue	Dws	Dwellings	La	Lane	Sch	School		
Ave	Avenue	E	East	Lo	Lodge	Sq	Square		
Bk	Bank	Ex	Exchange	Lwr	Lower	St.	Saint		
Bldgs	Buildings	Ext	Extension	Mans	Mansions	St	Street		
Boul	Boulevard	Fld	Field	Mkt	Market	Sta	Station		
Br	Bridge	Flds	Fields	Ms	Mews	Ter	Terrace		
Bri	Bridge	Fm	Farm	Mt	Mount	Vil	Villa, Villas		
Cem	Cemetery	Gdn	Garden	N	North	Vw	View		
Cen	Central,	Gdns	Gardens	No	Numbers	W	West		
	Centre	Gra	Grange	Par	Parade	Wd	Wood		
Cl	Close	Grd	Ground	Pas	Passage	Wds	Woods		
Clo	Close	Grn	Green	Pk	Park	Wk	Walk		
Coll	College	Gro	Grove	Pl	Place	Yd	Yard		
Cotts	Cottages	Ho	House	Prom	Promenade				
Cres	Crescent	Hosp	Hospital	Rd	Road				
Ct	Court	Hts	Heights	Ri	Rise				

District abbreviations

Abb.	Abberley	Clond.	Clondalkin	Grey.	Greystones	Manor.	Manorfields
B'brack	Ballybrack	Clons.	Clonsilla	Jobs.	Jobstown	Mulh.	Mulhuddart
B'mun	Ballymun	Collins.	Collinstown	Kill.	Killiney	Palm.	Palmerston
Bald.	Baldoyle	Cool.	Coolmine	Kilsh.	Kilshane	Port.	Portmarnock
Balg.	Balgriffin	Corn.	Cornelscourt	Kilt.	Kiltipper	Sally.	Sallynoggin
Black.	Blackrock	D.L.	Dún Laoghaire	Kins.	Kinsaley	Sandy.	Sandyford
Boot.	Booterstown	Deans Gra	Deans Grange	Leix.	Leixlip	Shank.	Shankill
Cabin.	Cabinteely	Dunb.	Dunboyne	Leo.	Leopardstown	Still.	Stillorgan
Carp.	Carpenterstown	Fox.	Foxrock	Lou.V.	Louisa Valley	Will.	Willbrook
Carrick.	Carrickmines	G'geary	Glenageary	Lough.	Loughlinstown		
Castle.	Castleknock	Gra M.	Grange Manor	Mala.	Malahide		

Some streets are not named on the map due to insufficient space. In some of these cases the nearest street that does appear on the map is listed in *italics*. In other cases they are indicated on the map by a number which is listed here in **bold**.

A

Abbey Cotts 1
  off Abbey St Upr — 58 C2
Abbey Ct 5 — 14 B3
Abbeyfield 5 — 14 B3
Abbeyfield 6 — 44 B3
Abbey Pk 5 — 14 A3
Abbey Pk 13 — 17 C1
Abbey St 13 — 21 C2
Abbey St Lwr 1 — 59 D2
Abbey St Mid 1 — 59 D2
Abbey St Old 1 — 59 E2
Abbey St Sta 1 — 59 D2
Abbey St Upr 1 — 58 C2
Abbotsford Av
  (Ascal Bhaile An
  Abba) 11 — 9 D1
Abbotsford Dr 11 — 9 D1
Abbotstown Rd 11 — 10 A1
Abercorn Rd 3 — 37 C1
Abercorn Sq 8 — 33 D2
Abercorn Ter 7 — 27 C3
Abercorn Ter 8 — 33 D2
Aberdeen St 7 — 34 B1
Achill Rd 9 — 28 B1
Acres Rd 8 — 25 D3
Adair 4 — 45 D1
Adam Ct 2
  off Grafton St — 59 D4
Adare Av 17 — 14 A1
Adare Dr 17 — 14 A1
Adare Grn 17 — 14 B1
Adare Pk 17 — 14 B1
Addison Pl 9 — 28 A1
Addison Rd 3 — 29 C2
Addison Ter 9 — 28 A1
Adelaide Ms 4 — 46 B2
Adelaide Rd 2 — 36 A3
Adelaide St D.L. — 57 D3
Adelaide Ter 8
  off Brookfield St — 34 B2
Adrian Av 6W — 43 C2
Aideen Av 6W — 42 B3
Aideen Dr 6W — 42 B3
Aideen Pk 6W — 42 B3
Aikenhead Ter 4 — 37 D2
Ailesbury 9 — 12 B1
Ailesbury Cl 4 — 45 D2
Ailesbury Dr 4 — 45 D2
Ailesbury Gdns 4 — 46 A2
Ailesbury Gro 4 — 45 D2
Ailesbury Ms 4 — 46 B2
Ailesbury Pk 4 — 46 A2
Ailesbury Rd 4 — 45 D2
Airfield Ct 4 — 45 D3
Airfield Manor 4 — 45 D3
Airfield Pk 4 — 45 D3
Airfield Rd 6 — 43 D3
Airfield Ter 4 — 45 D3
Airton Cl 24 — 48 A3
Albany Av Black. — 56 B3
Albany Rd 6 — 44 B2
Albert Coll Av 9 — 12 A2
Albert Coll Cres 9 — 12 A2
Albert Coll Dr 9 — 12 A2
Albert Coll Lawn 9 — 12 A2
Albert Coll Pk 9 — 12 A2
Albert Coll Ter 9 — 12 A2
Albert Ct E 2 — 37 C2
Albert Pl E
  off Inchicore Rd — 34 A2
Albert Pl E 2 — 37 C2
Albert Pl W 2 — 36 A3
Albert Ter 8
  off Albert Pl W — 36 A3
Albert Vil 4
  off Morehampton Rd — 45 C1
Albion St
  off Inchicore Rd — 34 A2
Aldborough Par 1 — 29 C3
Aldborough Pl 1 — 28 B3
Aldborough Sq 1 — 28 B3
Alden Dr 13 — 16 B1
Alden Pk 13 — 17 C1
Alden Rd 13 — 16 B1
Alders, The D.L. — 56 A3
Aldrin Wk 5 — 14 A1
Alexander Ter 1 — 37 C1
Alexander Ter 8 — 35 D3
Alexandra Quay 1 — 38 A1
Alexandra Rd 1 — 37 D1
Alexandra Rd
  Extension 1 — 39 C1

Alexandra Ter 3
  off Clontarf Rd — 31 C3
Alexandra Ter 6 — 43 D3
Alexandra Ter
  (Dundrum) 14 — 52 B3
Alfie Byrne Rd 3 — 29 D3
All Hallows La 9
  *off Drumcondra
  Rd Upr* — 28 B1
Allied Ind Est 10 — 32 B3
Allingham St 8 — 35 C2
All Saints Dr 5 — 15 D3
All Saints Pk 5 — 15 C3
All Saints Rd 5 — 15 C3
Alma Pl Black. — 56 B3
Alma Rd Black. — 56 A2
Almeida Av 8
  off Brookfield St — 34 B2
Almeida Ter 8
  off Brookfield St — 34 B2
Alone Wk 5 — 14 B3
Altona Ter 7 — 27 C3
Alverno 3 — 30 A2
Amiens St 1 — 59 F1
Anglesea Av Black. — 55 D2
Anglesea Br 4 — 45 D2
Anglesea Fruit Mkt 7
  off Green St Little — 58 B2
Anglesea La D.L. — 57 D3
Anglesea Rd 4 — 45 D2
Anglesea Row 7 — 58 B2
Anglesea St 2 — 59 D3
Annadale Av 3 — 29 C3
Annadale Cres 9 — 29 C1
Annadale Dr 9 — 29 C1
Annaly Rd 7 — 27 C2
Annamoe Dr 7 — 27 C2
Annamoe Par 7 — 27 C3
Annamoe Pk 7 — 27 C3
Annamoe Rd 7 — 27 C2
Annamoe Ter 7 — 27 C3
Anna Vil 6 — 44 B2
Annaville Gro 14 — 53 C2
Annaville Ter 14
  off Annaville Gro — 53 C2
Anne Devlin Av 14 — 50 B3
Anne Devlin Dr 14 — 50 B3
Anne Devlin Pk 14 — 50 B3
Anne Devlin Rd 14 — 50 B3
Anner Rd 8 — 34 A2
Annes La 2 — 59 D4
Annesley Av 3 — 29 C3
Annesley Br 3 — 29 C3
Annesley Br Rd 3 — 29 C2
Annesley Pk 6 — 44 B2
Annesley Pl 3 — 29 C2
Anne St N 7 — 58 B1
Anne St S 2 — 59 D4
Annsbrook 14 — 53 C1
Appian Way, The 6 — 44 B1
Aranleigh Ct 14 — 51 D3
Aranleigh Gdns 14 — 51 D3
Aranleigh Mt 14 — 51 C3
Aranleigh Pk 14 — 51 D3
Aranleigh Vale 14 — 51 C3
Arbour Hill 7 — 35 C1
Arbour Pl 7 — 35 C1
Arbour Ter 7 — 35 C1
Arbutus Av 12 — 43 C1
Arbutus Pl 8 — 35 D3
Arcade 1 — 59 D2
Ardagh Rd 12 — 42 B1
Ardbeg Cres 5 — 14 B2
Ardbeg Dr 5 — 14 B2
Ardbeg Pk 5 — 14 B2
Ardbeg Rd 5 — 14 B2
Ardcollum Av 5 — 14 A2
Ardee Gro 6 — 44 A1
Ardee Rd 6 — 44 A1
Ardee Row 8 — 58 A4
Ardee St 8 — 58 A4
Ardenza Pk Black.
  off Seapoint Av — 56 A2
Ardenza Ter Black. — 56 A2
Ardilaun Rd 3 — 28 B3
Ardilea Downs 14 — 53 D2
Ardlea Rd 5 — 14 A2
Ardmore Av 7 — 27 C3
Ardmore Cl 5 — 13 D2
Ardmore Cres 5 — 14 A2
Ardmore Dr 5 — 13 D2
Ardmore Gro 5 — 13 D2
Ardmore Pk 5 — 14 A2

Ardpatrick Rd 7 — 26 A2
Ard Ri Pl 7
  off Ard Ri Rd — 35 C1
Ard Ri Rd 7 — 35 C1
Ardtona Av 14 — 52 B2
Argyle Rd 4 — 45 C1
Arklow St 7 — 27 C3
Armagh Rd 12 — 42 A2
Armstrong St 6
  off Harolds Cross Rd — 43 D1
Arnott St 8 — 35 D3
Arranmore Av 7 — 28 A2
Arranmore Rd 4 — 45 C1
Arran Quay 7 — 58 A2
Arran Quay Ter 7 — 58 A2
Arran Rd 9 — 28 B1
Arran St E 7 — 58 B2
Arran St W 7 — 58 A2
Arundel Black. — 56 B3
Ascal An Charrain Chno
  (Nutgrove Av) 14 — 51 D3
Ascal Bhaile An Abba
  (Abbotstown Av) 11 — 9 D1
Ascal Bhaile Thuaidh
  (Ballyhoy Av) 5 — 15 D3
Ascal Dun Eanna
  (Ennafort Av) 5 — 15 C3
Ascal Measc
  (Mask Av) 5 — 14 B2
Ascal Phairc An Bhailtini
  (Villa Pk Av) 7 — 26 A2
Ascal Ratabhachta
  (Ratoath Av) 11 — 9 D2
Asgard Pk 13 — 21 C2
Asgard Rd 13 — 21 C2
Ash, The 15 — 8 A3
Ashbrook 3 — 30 A1
Ashbrook 7 — 25 C1
Ashcroft 5 — 15 D2
Ashdale Av 6W — 43 C3
Ashdale Gdns 6W — 43 C3
Ashdale Pk 6W — 43 C3
Ashdale Rd 6W — 43 C3
Ashfield
  (Templeogue) 6W — 50 A2
Ashfield Av 6 — 44 B2
Ashfield Cl 6W
  off Ashfield — 50 A2
Ashfield Pk
  (Templeogue) 6W
  off Ashfield — 50 A2
Ashfield Pk
  (Terenure) 6W — 43 C3
Ashfield Pk Boot. — 54 A1
Ashfield Rd
  (Ranelagh) 6 — 44 B2
Ashford Cotts 7
  off Ashford St — 27 C3
Ashford Pl 7
  off Ashford St — 27 C3
Ashford St 7 — 27 C3
Ashgrove Ter 1 16 — 53 C3
Ashington Av 7 — 26 A1
Ashington Cl 7 — 9 D3
Ashington Ct 7 — 26 A1
Ashington Dale 7 — 10 A3
Ashington Gdns 7 — 26 A1
Ashington Grn 7 — 26 A1
Ashington Ms 7 — 10 A3
Ashington Pk 7 — 25 D1
Ashington Ri 7 — 9 D3
Ashleaf Shop Cen 12 — 41 D3
Ashling Cl 12 — 42 A2
Ash St 8 — 58 A4
Ashton Pk Black. — 56 B3
Ashtown Gate Rd 8 — 25 C1
Ashtown Gro 7 — 25 D1
Ashtown Rd 15 — 9 C3
Ashtown Sta 15 — 9 C3
Aston Pl 2 — 59 D2
Aston Quay 2 — 59 D2
Athlumney Vil 6 — 44 A1
Auburn Av 4 — 45 C2
Auburn Av 15 — 24 A1
Auburn Cl 15
  off Auburn Dr — 8 A3
Auburn Dr 15 — 8 A3
Auburn Grn 15
  off Auburn Dr — 8 A3
Auburn Rd 4
  off Auburn Av — 45 C2
Auburn St 7 — 27 D3
Auburn Vil 6 — 43 D3

Auburn Wk 7 — 27 C3
Aughavanagh Rd 12 — 43 C1
Aughrim La 7 — 27 C3
Aughrim Pl 7 — 27 C3
Aughrim St 7 — 27 C3
Aughrim Vil 7
  off Aughrim St — 27 C3
Aungier Pl 2 — 58 C4
Aungier St 2 — 58 C4
Austins Cotts 3
  off Annesley Pl — 29 C3
Ave Maria Rd 8 — 35 C3
Avenue, The 6W — 50 A2
Avenue Rd 8 — 35 D3
Avila Pk 11 — 9 D1
Avoca Av Black. — 55 C3
Avoca Pk Black. — 55 C3
Avoca Pl Black. — 55 D2
Avoca Rd Black. — 55 C3
Avonbeg Ind Est 12 — 40 B1
Avondale Av 7 — 27 D3
Avondale Business Pk
  Black. — 55 D2
Avondale Lawn Black. — 55 D3
Avondale Lawn Extension
  Black. — 55 D2
Avondale Pk 5 — 16 A3
Avondale Rd 7 — 27 D3
Avondale Ter 12 — 41 D3
Ayrefield Av 13 — 15 C1
Ayrefield Ct 13 — 15 C1
Ayrefield Dr 13 — 15 C1
Ayrefield Gro 13 — 15 C1
Ayrefield Pl 13 — 15 C1

B

Bachelors Wk 1 — 59 D2
Back La 8 — 58 B3
Baggot Cl 2
  off Baggot St Lwr — 36 B3
Baggot Ct 2 — 36 B3
Baggot La 4 — 37 C3
Baggot Rd 7 — 25 D2
Baggot St Lwr 2 — 36 B3
Baggot St Upr 4 — 37 C3
Baggot Ter 7
  off Blackhorse Av — 25 D2
Bailey Grn Rd 13 — 23 D2
Baldoyle Ind Est 13 — 17 C1
Baldoyle Rd 13 — 18 A1
Balfe Av 12 — 41 D2
Balfe Rd 12 — 41 D2
Balfe Rd E 12 — 41 D2
Balfe St 2
  off Chatham St — 59 D4
Balglass Est 13 — 20 B2
Balglass Rd 13 — 21 C2
Balkill Pk 13 — 20 B2
Balkill Rd 13 — 21 C3
Ball's Br 4 — 45 D1
Ballsbridge Av 4 — 45 D1
Ballsbridge Pk 4 — 45 D1
Ballsbridge Ter 4
  off Ballsbridge Av — 45 D1
Ballsbridge Wd 4 — 37 D3
Ballyboggan Ind Est 11 — 10 A3
Ballyboggan Rd 11 — 10 B3
Ballybough Av 3
  off Spring Gdn St — 29 C3
Ballybough Br 3 — 29 C2
Ballybough Ct 3
  off Spring Gdn St — 29 C3
Ballybough Rd 3 — 28 B3
Ballyfermot Av 10 — 32 B2
Ballyfermot Cres 10 — 32 B2
Ballyfermot Dr 10 — 32 B2
Ballyfermot Par 10 — 32 A2
Ballyfermot Rd (Bothar
  Baile Thormod) — 32 A2
Ballygall Av 11 — 11 C1
Ballygall Cres 11 — 11 D2
Ballygall Par 11 — 11 D2
Ballygall Pl 11 — 11 D2
Ballygall Rd E 11 — 11 D2
Ballygall Rd W 11 — 10 B2
Ballyhoy Av (Ascal
  Bhaile Thuaidh) 5 — 15 D3

Ballymace Grn 14 50 A3
Ballymount Av 12 48 B1
Ballymount Av 24 48 B1
Ballymount Cross 24 40 A3
Ballymount Dr 12 40 B3
Ballymount Ind Est 12 40 B3
Ballymount Lwr Rd 12 40 A3
Ballymount Rd
  Ind Est 12 40 B2
Ballymount Rd Upr 24 40 A3
Ballymount Trd Est 12 41 C3
Ballymun Rd 9 12 A3
Ballyneety Rd 10 33 C2
Ballyroan Ct 1 16 50 A3
Ballyroan Cres 16 50 B3
Ballyroan Pk 16 50 A3
Ballyroan Rd 16 50 A3
Ballyshannon Av 5 13 D1
Ballyshannon Rd 5 13 D1
Ballytore Rd 14 51 D1
Balnagowan 6 44 B3
Balrothery Cotts 24 49 C3
Balrothery Est 24 48 B3
Balscadden Rd 13 21 C2
Bancroft Av 24 48 A3
Bancroft Cl 24 48 B3
Bancroft Gro 24 48 B3
Bancroft Pk 24 48 A3
Bancroft Rd 24 48 B3
Bangor Dr 12 42 B1
Bangor Rd 12 42 B1
Bankside Cotts 14 52 B1
Bannow Rd 7 26 B1
Bann Rd 11 10 B3
Bantry Rd 9 12 A3
Banville Av 10 32 A3
Barclay Ct Black. 55 D2
Bargy Rd 3 29 D3
Barnamore Cres 11
  off Barnamore Gro 10 B3
Barnamore Gro 11 10 B3
Barnamore Pk 11 10 B3
Barrett St D.L. 57 C3
Barrow Rd 11 27 C1
Barrow Sta 4 37 C2
Barrow St 4 37 C2
Barry Grn 11 10 A1
Barry Pk 11 10 A1
Barry Rd 11 10 A1
Barryscourt Rd 17 14 A1
Barton Av 14 51 C3
Barton Dr 14 51 C3
Basin St Lwr 8 35 C2
Basin St Upr 8 35 C2
Basin Vw Ter 7 27 D3
Bass Pl 2 59 F4
Bath Av 4 37 D3
Bath Av Gdns 4 37 D3
Bath Av Pl 4 37 D3
Bath La 1 28 A3
Bath Pl Black. 55 D2
Bath St 4 37 D2
Baymount Pk 3 31 D1
Bayside Boul N 13 17 C1
Bayside Boul S 13 17 C1
Bayside Pk 13 17 C1
Bayside Sq E 13 17 C1
Bayside Sq N 13 17 C1
Bayside Sq S 13 17 C1
Bayside Sq W 13 17 C1
Bayside Sta 13 17 D1
Bayside Wk 13 17 C1
Bayview 4
  off Pembroke St 37 D2
Bayview Av 3 29 C3
Beach Av 4 38 A3
Beach Dr 4 38 A3
Beach Rd 4 38 A3
Beach Vw 13 17 C2
Beaconsfield Ct 8
  off The Belfry 34 A2
Beattys Av 4 45 D1
Beaufield Manor Still. 54 D3
Beaufield Pk Still. 54 B3
Beaufort Downs 14 51 C3
Beaumont Av 14 52 A3
Beaumont Cl 14 52 A3

Beaumont Cres 9 13 D2
Beaumont Dr 14 52 B3
Beaumont Gdns Black. 55 C2
Beaumont Gro 9 13 C2
Beaumont Rd 9 13 C2
Beaver Row 4 45 C3
Beaver St 1 28 B3
Bedford Row 2
  off Temple Bar 59 D3
Beechdale Ms 6 44 A2
Beeches, The 13 16 A1
Beeches, The 6 14 51 C3
Beeches, The Black. 56 B3
Beechfield Av 12 41 D3
Beechfield Cl 12 41 D3
Beechfield Rd 12 41 D3
Beech Gro Boot. 54 B1
Beech Hill 4
  off Beech Hill Rd 45 C3
Beech Hill Av 4 45 D2
Beech Hill Cres 4 45 D2
Beech Hill Dr 4 45 D2
Beech Hill Rd 4 45 C3
Beech Hill Ter 4 45 D3
Beech Hill Vil 4
  off Beech Hill Ter 45 D3
Beechlawn Boot. 54 B2
Beechlawn Ind
  Complex 12 41 C3
Beechmount Dr 14 53 C1
Beech Pk 15 8 A3
Beech Pk Av 5 14 B1
Beech Pk Av 15 8 A3
Beechpark Ct 5 14 B1
Beech Pk Cres 15 8 A3
Beech Pk Lawn 15 8 A3
Beech Rd 12 40 A2
Beechwood Av Lwr 6 44 B2
Beechwood Av Upr 6 44 B2
Beechwood Pk 6 44 A2
Beechwood Rd 6 44 B2
Beechwood Sta 6 44 B2
Belfield Cl 14 53 C1
Belfield Ct 4 45 D3
Belfield Downs 14 53 C2
Belfield Office Pk 4 45 C3
Belfry, The 8 34 A2
Belgrave Av 6 44 A2
Belgrave Pl 6 44 A2
Belgrave Rd 6 44 A2
Belgrave Rd Black. 56 A2
Belgrave Sq E 6 44 A2
Belgrave Sq E Black. 56 B3
Belgrave Sq N 6 44 A2
Belgrave Sq N Black. 56 A2
Belgrave Sq S 6 44 A2
Belgrave Sq S Black. 56 A2
Belgrave Sq W 6 44 A2
Belgrave Sq W Black. 56 A2
Belgrave Ter Black.
  off Belgrave Rd 56 A2
Belgrove Lawn 20 24 B3
Belgrove Pk 20 32 B1
Belgrove Rd 3 30 B2
Bella Av 1
  off Bella St 28 B3
Bella St 1 28 B3
Belle Bk 8 35 C2
Belleville Av 6 43 D3
Bellevue 8 35 C2
Bellevue Av Boot. 46 B3
Bellevue Copse Boot. 46 B3
Bellevue Ct Boot. 46 B3
Bellevue Pk Boot. 46 A3
Bellevue Pk Av Boot. 46 B3
Bellmans Wk 1
  off Ferrymans
  Crossing 37 C1
Belmont Av 4 45 C2
Belmont Ct 4
  off Belmont Av 45 C2
Belmont Gdns 4 45 C2
Belmont Pk 4 45 C2
Belmont Pk 5 16 A2
Belmont Vil 4 45 C2
Belton Av 9 13 D3
Belton Pk Gdns 9 13 D3
Belton Pk Rd 9 13 D3
Belton Pk Vil 9 13 D3
Belvidere Av 3 28 A3
Belvidere Ct 1 28 A3
Belvidere Pl 1 28 A3

Belvidere Rd 1 28 A2
Belview Bldgs 8
  off School St 35 C2
Benbulbin Av 12 42 A1
Benbulbin Rd 12 34 A3
Benburb St 7 35 C1
Beneavin Ct 11 11 C2
Beneavin Dr 11 11 D2
Beneavin Pk 11 11 C1
Beneavin Rd 11 11 C1
Ben Edar Rd 7 27 C3
Bengal Ter 9 27 D1
Ben Inagh Pk Boot. 55 D1
Benmadigan Rd 12 34 A3
Benson St 2 37 D2
Benson St Enterprise
  Cen 2 37 C2
Beresford 9 28 A1
Beresford Av 9 28 B1
Beresford La 9 28 B1
Beresford La 3 28 B1
Beresford Pl 1 59 E2
Beresford St 7 58 B1
Berkeley Rd 7 27 D2
Berkeley St 7 28 A3
Berkeley Ter 4 37 C3
Berryfield Cres 11 10 A2
Berryfield Dr 11 10 A2
Berryfield Rd 11 10 A2
Berwick 14 51 D3
Berwick Hall 14 51 D3
Berystede 6
  off Leeson Pk 44 B1
Bessborough Av 3 29 C3
Bessborough Par 6 44 A1
Bethesda Pl 1
  off Dorset St Upr 28 A3
Bettyglen 5 16 B3
Bettystown Av 5 15 D3
Big Br 6W 51 C1
Bigger Rd 12 41 D2
Binn Eadair Vw 13 18 A1
Binns Br 7 28 A2
Birchfield 14 53 D3
Birchs La 14 53 C3
Birchview 24 48 A2
Birchview Cl 24 48 A2
Birchview Ct 24
  off Treepark Rd 48 A2
Birchview Dr 24 48 A2
Birchview Hts 24
  off Birchview Dr 48 A2
Birchview Lawn 24
  off Birchview Av 48 A2
Birchview Ri 24
  off Birchview Dr 48 A2
Bird Av 14 53 C1
Bishop St 8 36 A3
Blackberry La 6 44 A1
Blackditch Rd 10 32 A2
Blackhall Par 7 58 A2
Blackhall Pl 7 35 C1
Blackhall St 7 35 C1
Blackheath Av 3 30 B2
Blackheath Gro 3 30 B2
Blackheath Dr 3 30 B2
Blackheath Gdns 3 30 B2
Blackheath Gro 3 30 B2
Blackheath Pk 3 30 B2
Blackhorse Av 7 26 A2
Blackhorse Br 12 33 D3
Blackhorse Gro 7 26 B3
Blackhorse Ind Est 7 26 B3
Blackhorse Sta 12 33 D3
Blackpitts 8 35 D3
Blackrock Business Pk
  Black. 55 D2
Blackrock Shop Cen
  Black. 55 D1
Blackrock Sta Black. 55 D1
Black St 7 34 B1
Blackwater Rd 11 27 C1
Blarney Pk 12 42 B2
Blessington Ct 7
  off Blessington St 28 A3
Blessington St 7 27 D3
Bloom Cotts 8 35 D3
Bloomfield Av
  (Donnybrook) 4 44 B1
Bloomfield Av 8 35 D3
Bloomfield Pk 8 43 D1
Bluebell Av 12 32 B3
Bluebell Ind Est 12 40 A1

Bluebell Rd 12 41 C1
Bluebell Sta 12 41 C1
Blythe Av 3
  off Church Rd 37 C1
Boden Wd 14 51 C3
Bolton St 1 58 B1
Bond Dr 3 38 A1
Bond Rd 3 29 D3
Bond St 8 35 C2
Bonham St 8 35 C2
Boolavogue Rd 3 37 D1
Booterstown Av Boot. 54 B1
Booterstown Pk Boot. 55 D1
Booterstown Sta Boot. 47 C3
Botanic Av 9 28 A1
Botanic Gdns 11 27 D1
Botanic Ms 9 27 D1
Botanic Pk 9 28 A1
Botanic Rd 9 27 D2
Botanic Vil 9
  off Botanic Rd 28 A1
Bothar An Easa
  (Watermill Rd) 5 15 D3
Bothar Baile Thormod
  (Ballyfermot Rd) 10 32 A2
Bothar Chille Na Manac
  (Walkinstown Rd) 12 41 C2
Bothar Coilbeard
  (Con Colbert Rd) 8 34 A2
Bothar Coilbeard
  (Con Colbert Rd) 10 33 D2
Bothar Dhroichead
  Chiarduibh
  (Cardiffsbridge Rd) 11 10 A1
Bothar Drom Finn
  (Drumfinn Rd) 10 32 A2
Bothar Loch Con
  (Lough Conn Rd) 10 32 A1
Bothar Phairc An Bhailtini
  (Villa Pk Rd) 7 26 A2
Bothar Raitleann
  (Rathland Rd) 12 42 B3
Boundary Rd 3 30 A3
Bow Br 8 34 B2
Bow La E 2 58 C4
Bow La W 8 34 B2
Bow St 7 58 A2
Boyne La 2 59 F4
Boyne Rd 11 10 B3
Boyne St 2 59 F3
Brabazon Row 8 35 D3
Brabazon Sq 8
  off Gray St 58 A4
Brabazon St 8
  off The Coombe 58 A4
Brackens La 2 59 E2
Braemor Av 14 52 A2
Braemor Dr 14 52 A2
Braemor Gro 14 52 A2
Braemor Pk 14 52 A1
Braemor Rd 14 52 A2
Brainborough Ter 8
  off South Circular Rd 35 C3
Braithwaite St 8 35 C2
Branch Rd N 1 38 B1
Branch Rd N
  Extension 1 38 B1
Branch Rd S 1 38 B1
Brandon Rd 12 41 D1
Breakwater Rd S 1 38 B1
Bregia Rd 7 27 C2
Bremen Av 4 38 A2
Bremen Gro 4 38 A2
Bremen Rd 4 38 A2
Brendan Behan Ct 1
  off Russell St 28 B3
Brendan Rd 4 45 C2
Brian Av 3 29 C2
Brian Boru Av 3 31 C3
Brian Boru St 3 31 C2
Brian Rd 3 29 C2
Brian Ter 3 29 C2
Briarfield Gro 5 16 B2
Briarfield Rd 5 16 A2
Briarfield Vil 5 16 B2
Brickfield Dr 12 34 B3
Brickfield La 8 35 C3
Bride Rd 8 58 B4
Bride St 8 58 B4
Bridgecourt Office
  Pk 12 40 B2
Bridgefoot St 8 58 A3
Bridge St 4 37 D2

Name	Page	Grid
Bridge St Lwr *8*	58	A3
Bridge St Upr *8*	58	A3
Bridgewater Quay *8*	34	A1
Brighton Av *3*	29	D2
Brighton Av *6*	43	D3
Brighton Av *Black.*	56	B3
Brighton Gdns *6*	43	D3
Brighton Grn *6*	43	C3
Brighton Rd *6*	43	D3
Brighton Sq *6*	43	D3
Brighton Vale *Black.*	56	A2
Britain Pl *1*	28	A3
Britain Quay *2*	37	D2
Broadstone *7*	27	D3
Broadstone Av *7* off Phibsborough Rd	27	D3
Brookfield *5*	15	C2
Brookfield *6*	44	B3
Brookfield *Black.*	55	C2
Brookfield Av *Black.*	55	D2
Brookfield Est *12*	42	B3
Brookfield Pl *Black.*	55	D2
Brookfield Rd *8*	34	B2
Brookfield St *8*	34	B2
Brookfield Ter *Black.*	55	D2
Brooklands *4*	46	A2
Brooklawn *3*	30	A2
Brooklawn *Black.*	55	C2
Brooklawn Av *D.L.*	56	A3
Brooklawn Wd *D.L.*	56	A3
Brookmount Av *24*	49	C3
Brookmount Lawns *24* off Tallaght Rd	49	C3
Brook Pk Ct *Black.*	56	B3
Brookvale Downs *51*	51	C1
Brookvale Rd *4*	45	C2
Brookvale Rd *14*	51	C2
Brookville *11*	10	B1
Brookville Cres *5*	14	B1
Brookville Pk (Artane) *5*	14	B2
Brookville Pk (Coolock) *5*	15	C1
Brookwood Av *5*	14	B3
Brookwood Cres *5*	15	C3
Brookwood Dr *5*	14	B3
Brookwood Glen *5*	15	C3
Brookwood Gro *5*	14	B3
Brookwood Hts *5*	14	B3
Brookwood Lawn *5*	15	C3
Brookwood Meadow *5*	14	B3
Brookwood Pk *5*	14	B3
Brookwood Ri *5*	15	C3
Brookwood Rd *5*	14	B3
Broombridge Rd *7*	26	B1
Broombridge Sta *7*	26	B1
Broomhill Business Pk *24*	48	A2
Broomhill Rd *24*	48	A2
Broom Hill Ter *24*	48	A2
Brown St N *7*	58	A1
Brown St S *8*	35	C3
Brunswick Pl *2* off Pearse St	37	C2
Brunswick St N *7*	58	A1
Brusna Cotts *Black.*	55	D2
Buckingham St Lwr *1*	28	B3
Buckingham St Upr *1*	28	B3
Bulfin Gdns *8*	34	A2
Bulfin Rd *8*	34	A2
Bulfin St *8*	34	A3
Bull All St *8*	58	B4
Bunratty Av *17*	14	B1
Bunratty Dr *17*	14	B1
Bunratty Rd *17*	14	A1
Bunting Rd *12*	41	C2
Burgess La *7* off Haymarket	58	A2
Burgh Quay *2*	59	D2
Burke Pl *8*	34	B2
Burleigh Ct *4*	36	B3
Burlington Gdns *4*	36	B3
Burlington Rd *4*	44	B1
Burris Ct *8* off School Ho La W	58	B3
Burrowfield Rd *13*	18	A1
Burrow Rd *13*	18	B1
Busáras Sta *1*	59	F1
Bushfield Av *4*	45	C2
Bushfield Pl *4*	44	B2
Bushfield Ter *4*	44	B2
Bushy Pk Gdns *6*	51	C1
Bushy Pk Rd *6*	51	C1
Buterly Business Pk *5*	14	A2
Butt Br *1*	59	E2
Butterfield Av *14*	50	B2
Butterfield Cl *14*	50	B3
Butterfield Ct *14*	51	C2
Butterfield Cres *14*	51	C2
Butterfield Dr *14*	51	C3
Butterfield Gro *14*	50	B2
Butterfield Meadow *14*	50	B3
Butterfield Orchard *14*	51	C3
Butterfield Pk *14*	50	B3
Byrnes La *1*	58	C2

C

Name	Page	Grid
Cabra Dr *7*	27	C2
Cabra Gro *7*	27	C2
Cabra Pk *7*	27	D2
Cabra Rd *7*	26	B2
Cadogan Rd *3*	29	C2
Calderwood Av *9*	13	C3
Calderwood Gro *9*	13	C3
Calderwood Rd *9*	29	C1
Caledon Rd *3*	29	C3
Callary Rd *Still.*	54	A2
Calmount Rd *12*	40	B3
Camac Pk *12*	40	B1
Camac Ter *8* off Bow Br	34	B2
Camberley Elms *14*	52	A2
Camberley Oaks *14*	52	A3
Cambridge Av *4*	38	A2
Cambridge La *6*	43	D2
Cambridge Rd *8*	37	D2
Cambridge Rd (Rathmines) *6*	44	A2
Cambridge Sq *4*	37	D2
Cambridge Ter *6*	44	B1
Cambridge Vil *6* off Belgrave Rd	44	A2
Camden Lock *4* off South Docks Rd	37	D2
Camden Mkt *2* off Camden St Lwr	36	A3
Camden Pl *2*	36	A3
Camden Row *8*	36	A3
Camden St Lwr *2*	36	A3
Camden St Upr *2*	36	A3
Cameron Sq *8*	34	B2
Cameron St *8*	35	C3
Campbell's Ct *7* off Little Britain St	58	B1
Campbells Row *1* off Portland St N	28	B3
Canal Rd *6*	44	A1
Canal Ter *12*	33	C3
Canal Wk *10*	32	A3
Cannon Rock Vw *13*	21	C2
Canon Lillis Av *1*	29	C3
Canon Mooney Gdns *4* off Cambridge Rd	37	D2
Canon Troy Ct *20*	32	B1
Capel St *1*	58	C1
Cappagh Av *11*	10	A1
Cappagh Dr *11*	10	A1
Cappagh Rd *11*	10	A1
Captains Av *12*	42	A2
Captains Dr *12*	42	A2
Captains Rd *12*	42	A2
Caragh Rd *7*	26	B3
Carberry Rd *9*	13	C3
Cardiff Br *7* off Phibsborough Rd	27	D3
Cardiff Castle Rd *11*	10	A1
Cardiffsbridge Av *11*	9	D2
Cardiffsbridge Gro *11* off Cappagh Rd	10	A1
Cardiffsbridge Rd (Bothar Dhroichead Chiarduibh) *11*	10	A1
Cardiffs La *2*	37	C2
Cards La *2* off Townsend St	59	E3
Carleton Rd *3*	29	D2
Carlingford Par *2*	37	C2
Carlingford Pl *2* off Carlingford Par	37	C2
Carlingford Rd *9*	28	A2
Carlisle Av *4*	45	C1
Carlisle St *8*	35	D3
Carlton Ct *3*	30	A2
Carlton Ms *4* off Shelbourne Av	37	D3
Carmans Hall *8*	58	A4
Carndonagh Dr *13*	16	B1
Carndonagh Lawn *13*	16	B1
Carndonagh Pk *13*	16	B1
Carndonagh Rd *13*	16	B1
Carnew St *7*	27	C3
Carnlough Rd *7*	26	B2
Caroline Row *4* off Bridge St	37	D2
Carraroe Av *13*	16	A1
Carrickbrack Heath *13*	19	C2
Carrickbrack Hill *13*	19	C3
Carrickbrack Lawn *13*	19	C3
Carrickbrack Pk *13*	19	C3
Carrickbrack Rd *13*	19	C3
Carrick Brennan Lawn *Black.*	56	B3
Carrickbrennan Rd *Black.*	56	B3
Carrickmount Av *14*	52	A3
Carrickmount Dr *14*	52	A3
Carrick Ter *8*	34	B3
Carrigallen Dr *11* off Carrigallen Rd	10	B3
Carrigallen Pk *11* off Carrigallen Rd	10	B3
Carrigallen Rd *11*	10	B3
Carriglea Ind Est *12*	41	C1
Carrow Rd *12*	33	D3
Carysfort Av *Black.*	55	D2
Carysfort Hall *Black.*	55	D3
Carysfort Pk *Black.*	55	D3
Casana Vw *13*	21	C3
Casement Cl *11*	10	A1
Casement Dr *11*	10	A1
Casement Grn *11*	10	A1
Casement Gro *11*	10	A1
Casement Pk *11*	10	A1
Casement Rd (Finglas S) *11*	10	B2
Casement Rd (Finglas W) *11*	10	A1
Cashel Av *12*	42	A3
Cashel Business Cen *12*	42	B3
Cashel Rd *12*	42	A2
Casimir Av *6W*	43	C2
Casimir Ct *6W*	43	D2
Casimir Rd *6W*	43	C2
Casino Pk *3*	29	D1
Casino Rd *3*	29	C1
Castilla Pk *3*	31	C2
Castle Av *3*	30	B2
Castlebyrne Pk *Black.*	55	D3
Castle Ct *3*	30	A1
Castle Ct *Boot.*	54	B1
Castledawson Av *Boot.*	55	C1
Castle Elms *17*	14	B1
Castleforbes Ind Est *3*	37	D1
Castleforbes Rd *1*	37	D1
Castle Gate *15*	24	A1
Castle Gro *3*	30	B1
Castlekevin Rd *5*	14	A1
Castleknock Grn *15*	24	A1
Castleknock Lo *15*	24	A1
Castleknock Pines Lwr *15*	8	A3
Castleknock Pines Upr *15*	8	A3
Castleknock Rd *15*	24	B1
Castleknock Village Cen *15*	24	A1
Castlelands, The *14*	51	D2
Castle Lawns Est *24*	48	B3
Castle Mkt *2* off Drury St	58	C4
Castle Pk *24*	48	B3
Castle Pk *Black.*	56	B3
Castle Pk Est *24*	48	B3
Castle Rd *3*	30	B2
Castleside Dr *14*	51	D2
Castle St *2*	58	B3
Castletimon Av *5*	13	D1
Castletimon Dr *5*	13	D1
Castletimon Gdns *5*	13	D1
Castletimon Grn *5*	13	D1
Castletimon Pk *5*	13	D1
Castletimon Rd *5*	13	D1
Castletymon Ct *24*	48	B3
Castleview *5*	14	A2
Castlewood Av *6*	44	A2
Castlewood Cl *6* off Castlewood Av	44	A2
Castlewood La *6*	44	A2
Castlewood Pk *6*	44	A2
Castlewood Pl *6*	44	A2
Castlewood Ter *6*	44	A2
Cathal Brugha St *1*	59	D1
Cathedral La *8*	35	D3
Cathedral St *1*	59	D1
Cathedral Vw Ct *8* off Cathedral Vw Wk	35	D3
Cathedral Vw Wk *8*	35	D3
Catherines La *7* off Church St Upr	58	B1
Catherine St *8* off Ash St	58	A4
Cavalry Row *7*	35	C1
Cavendish Row *1* off Parnell St	28	A3
Ceannchor Rd *13*	22	C3
Ceannt Fort *8*	34	B2
Cecil Av *3*	29	D2
Cecilia St *2* off Temple La S	58	C3
Cedar Ct *6W*	43	C3
Cedar Hall *6* off Prospect La	45	C3
Cedarmount Rd *Still.*	54	A3
Cedar Pk *13*	16	A1
Cedars, The *D.L.*	56	A3
Cedar Sq *Black.*	55	C3
Cedar Wk *5*	16	A2
Cedarwood Av *11*	11	C1
Cedarwood Cl *11*	11	C1
Cedarwood Gro *11*	11	C1
Cedarwood Pk *11*	11	C1
Cedarwood Ri *11*	11	C1
Ceide Dun Eanna (Ennafort Dr) *5*	15	C3
Ceide Gleannaluinn (Glenaulin Dr) *20*	32	A1
Ceide Phairc An Bhailtini (Villa Pk Dr) *7*	26	A2
Celestine Av *4*	37	D3
Celtic Pk Av *9*	13	D3
Celtic Pk Rd *9*	13	D3
Chamber St *8*	35	D3
Chancery La *8*	58	C4
Chancery Pl *7*	58	B2
Chancery St *7*	58	B2
Chanel Av *5*	14	B2
Chanel Gro *5*	14	B1
Chanel Rd *5*	14	A2
Chapel Av *4*	37	D2
Chapelizod Bypass *20*	32	A1
Chapelizod Ct *20*	32	A1
Chapelizod Hill Rd *20*	32	A1
Chapelizod Ind Est *10*	32	B1
Chapelizod Rd *8*	33	C1
Chapelizod Rd *20*	33	C1
Chapel La *1*	58	C1
Charlemont *9*	13	D3
Charlemont Av *D.L.*	57	D3
Charlemont Ct *2*	44	A1
Charlemont Gdns *2* off Charlemont St	36	A3
Charlemont Mall *2*	44	A1
Charlemont Par *3*	29	C3
Charlemont Pl *2*	44	A1
Charlemont Rd *3*	29	D2
Charlemont Sq *2* off Charlemont St	36	A3
Charlemont Sta *6*	44	A1
Charlemont St *2*	36	A3
Charles La *1*	28	B3
Charles St Gt *1*	28	B3
Charles St W *7*	58	B2
Charleston Av *6*	44	A2
Charleston Rd *6*	44	A2
Charleville *14*	52	B2
Charleville *16*	50	A3
Charleville Av *3*	29	C3
Charleville Mall *1*	28	B3
Charleville Rd *6*	43	D2
Charleville Rd *7*	27	C2
Charleville Sq *14*	50	B2
Charlotte Quay *4*	37	C2
Charlotte Way *2*	36	A3
Charlton Lawn *14*	53	D2
Chatham Row *2* off William St S	59	D4

Chatham St *2* 59 D4
Chaworth Ter *8*
  off Hanbury La 58 A3
Cheaters La *2*
  off Redmonds Hill 36 A3
Cheeverstown Cen *6W* 50 A3
Chelmsford La *6* 44 B1
Chelmsford Rd *6* 44 B1
Chelsea Gdns *3* 31 C2
Cheltenham Pl *6*
  off Portobello Br 44 A1
Cherbury Ct *Boot.* 54 B2
Cherbury Gdns *Boot.* 54 B2
Cherbury Ms *Boot.* 54 B2
Cherry Ct *6W* 43 C3
Cherryfield Av *6* 44 B2
Cherryfield Av *12* 41 D3
Cherryfield Dr *12* 41 D3
Cherryfield Rd *12* 41 C3
Cherrygarth *Still.* 54 B3
Cherry Gro *12* 41 D3
Cherrymount Cres *3* 29 D1
Cherrymount Gro *3* 29 D1
Cherrymount Pk *7* 27 D2
Chesterfield Av *8* 25 D3
Chesterfield Av *15* 24 B1
Chesterfield Cl *15* 24 B1
Chesterfield Copse *15* 24 B1
Chesterfield Gro *15* 24 B1
Chesterfield Pk *15* 24 B1
Chesterfield Vw *15* 24 B1
Chester Rd *6* 44 A1
Chestnut Ct *9* 13 D2
Chestnut Rd *12* 40 A2
Chestnut Rd *Still.* 54 A2
Christ Ch Cath *8* 58 B3
Christchurch Pl *8* 58 B3
Church Av
  (Irishtown) *4* 37 D3
Church Av
  (Rathmines) *6* 44 A3
Church Av *8* 34 B3
Church Av (Glasnevin) *9* 12 A3
Church Av N
  (Drumcondra) *9* 28 B1
Church Ct *15* 24 A1
Church Gdns *6* 44 A2
Churchgate Av *3* 31 C3
Churchill Ter *4* 45 D1
Church La *2*
  off College Grn 59 D3
Church La
  (Rathfarnham) *14* 51 C2
Church La S *8*
  off Kevin St Lwr 36 A3
Church Pk Av *6W* 43 C2
Church Pk Ct *6W* 43 C2
Church Pk Dr *6W* 43 C2
Church Pk Lawn *6W* 43 C2
Church Pk Vw *6W* 43 C2
Church Pk Way *6W* 43 C2
Church Rd *3* 37 C1
Church Rd *13* 18 B2
Church Rd (Finglas) *11* 10 B2
Church St (Finglas) *11* 10 B2
Church St (Howth) *13* 20 B2
Church St E *3* 37 C1
Church St Upr *7* 58 B1
Church Ter *7*
  off Church St 58 B2
Churchtown Av *14* 52 B1
Churchtown Business
  Pk *14* 52 A3
Churchtown Cl *14* 52 B1
Churchtown Dr *14* 52 B1
Churchtown Rd Lwr *14* 52 B1
Churchtown Rd Upr *14* 52 B1
Cian Pk *9* 28 B1
Cill Eanna *5* 15 D3
Citylink Business Pk *12* 40 B1
City Quay *2* 59 F2
Clanawley Rd *5* 30 B1
Clanboy Rd *5* 14 A3
Clanbrassil Cl *8* 43 D1
Clanbrassil St Lwr *8* 35 D3

Clanbrassil St Upr *8* 43 D1
Clancarthy Rd *5* 30 A1
Clancy Av *11* 10 B1
Clancy Rd *11* 11 C1
Clandonagh Rd *5* 14 A3
Clanhugh Rd *5* 30 A1
Clanmahon Rd *5* 14 A3
Clanmaurice Rd *5* 14 A3
Clanmoyle Rd *5* 30 A1
Clanranald Rd *5* 14 A3
Clanree Rd *5* 14 A3
Clanwilliam Pl *2* 37 C3
Clare La *2* 59 E4
Claremont Av *9* 11 D3
Claremont Ct *11* 27 C1
Claremont Dr *11* 11 D2
Claremont Pk (Pairc
  Clearmont) *4* 38 A3
Claremont Rd *4* 38 A3
Claremont Rd *13* 19 C1
Clarence Mangan Rd *8* 35 D3
Clarence St *D.L.* 57 C3
Clarendon Mkt *2*
  off Chatham St 59 D4
Clarendon Row *2*
  off Clarendon St 59 D4
Clarendon St *2* 59 D4
Clare Rd *9* 12 B3
Clare St *2* 59 E4
Clareville Ct *11* 27 D1
Clareville Gro *11* 27 D1
Clareville Pk *11* 27 D1
Clareville Rd *6W* 43 C2
Clarinda Pk N *D.L.* 57 D3
Clarke Ter *8* 35 C3
Classons Br *14* 52 B1
Claude Rd *9* 28 A2
Clifden Rd *10* 32 A2
Cliff Wk (Fingal Way) *13* 21 D2
Clifton Av *Black.* 56 B3
Clifton La *Black.* 56 B3
Clifton Ms *6* 44 A1
Clifton Ter *Black.* 56 B3
Cliftonville Rd *9* 28 A1
Clinches Ct *3* 29 C3
Clogher Rd *12* 42 B1
Cloister Av *Black.* 55 D3
Cloister Gate *Black.* 55 D3
Cloister Grn *Black.* 55 D3
Cloister Gro *Black.* 55 D3
Cloister Pk *Black.* 55 C3
Cloisters, The *6W* 43 C3
Cloisters, The *9* 13 C3
Cloister Sq *Black.* 55 D3
Cloister Way *Black.* 55 D3
Clonard Rd *12* 42 A1
Clonfadda Wd *Boot.* 54 B2
Clonfert Rd *12* 42 B2
Clonlara Rd *4* 38 A2
Clonliffe Av *3* 28 B2
Clonliffe Gdns *3* 28 B2
Clonliffe Rd *3* 28 B2
Clonmacnoise Gro *12* 42 B2
Clonmacnoise Rd *12* 42 B2
Clonmel Rd *11* 11 D1
Clonmel St *2* 36 A3
Clonmore Rd *3* 28 B3
Clonmore Rd *Still.* 54 A3
Clonmore Ter *3* 28 B3
Clonrosse Ct *13*
  off Elton Dr 15 D1
Clonrosse Dr *13* 15 D1
Clonrosse Pk *13*
  off Elton Dr 15 D1
Clonskeagh Br *6* 45 C3
Clonskeagh Dr *14* 45 C3
Clonskeagh Rd *6* 45 C2
Clonskeagh Rd *14* 45 C3
Clonskeagh Sq *14* 45 C3
Clontarf Pk *3* 31 C2
Clontarf Prom *3* 30 A2
Clontarf Rd *3* 29 D2
Clontarf Rd Sta *3* 29 D2
Clonturk Av *9* 28 B1
Clonturk Gdns *9* 28 B1
Clonturk Pk *9* 28 B1
Cloonlara Cres *11*
  off Cloonlara Rd 10 B3
Cloonlara Dr *11*
  off Cloonlara Rd 10 B3
Cloonlara Rd *11* 10 B3
Close, The *6W* 50 A2
Close, The *9* 13 D1

Close, The *Still.* 54 A2
Clover Hill Dr *10* 32 A3
Clover Hill Rd *10* 32 A3
Cloyne Rd *12* 42 B2
Club Rd *22* 40 A2
Clune Rd *11* 10 B1
Clyde La *4* 45 C1
Clyde Rd *4* 45 C1
Coburg Pl *1* 29 C3
Colepark Av *10* 32 A2
Colepark Dr *10* 32 B2
Colepark Grn *10* 32 B2
Colepark Rd *10* 32 A2
Coleraine St *7* 58 B1
College Cres *6W* 50 A1
College Dr *6W* 50 A1
College Grn *2* 59 D3
College La *2* 59 F3
College Pk *6W* 50 A1
College Pk *15* 24 A1
College Rd *15* 24 A1
College St *2* 59 D3
College Vw *1* *24* 48 A3
College Vw *6* 44 B2
Colliers Av *6* 44 B2
Collins Av *9* 13 D3
Collins Av E *5* 14 A3
Collins Av Extension *9* 12 A1
Collins Av W *9* 13 D2
Collins Ct *3* 13 D2
Collins Ct *Black.*
  off Sweetmans Av 55 D2
Collins Dr *11* 11 C1
Collins Grn *11* 11 C1
Collins Pk *9* 13 D3
Collins Pl *11* 11 C1
Collins Row *11* 11 C2
Collins Wd *9* 13 C2
Comeragh Rd *12* 41 D1
Commons St *1* 59 F2
Con Colbert Rd
  (Bothar Coilbeard) *8* 34 A2
Con Colbert Rd
  (Bothar Coilbeard) *10* 33 D2
Connaught St *7* 27 D3
Connaught Ter *6*
  off Rathgar Rd 43 D3
Connolly Av *8* 34 A2
Connolly Gdns *8* 34 A2
Connolly Luas Sta *1* 59 F1
Connolly Sta *1* 59 F1
Conor Clune Rd *7* 25 D1
Conquer Hill Rd *3* 31 C3
Conquer Hill Ter *3* 31 C2
Constitution Hill *7* 58 B1
Convent Av *3* 29 C2
Convent La *14* 51 C3
Convent Lawns *10* 32 A2
Convent Rd *Black.* 55 D2
Convent Rd *D.L.* 57 D3
Convent Vw Cotts *7* 26 A1
Conway Ct *2*
  off Macken St 37 C2
Conyngham Rd *8* 34 A1
Cook St *8* 58 A3
Coolamber Ct *2* *16* 50 A3
Coolamber Pk *16* 50 A3
Coolatree Cl *9* 13 D2
Coolatree Pk *9* 13 D2
Coolatree Rd *9* 13 D2
Cooleen Av *9* 13 C1
Coolevin La *8*
  off Long La 35 D3
Cooley Rd *12* 41 D1
Coolgariff Rd *9* 13 D2
Coolgreena Cl *9* 13 D2
Coolgreena Rd *9* 13 D2
Coolock Av *5* 14 B1
Coolock Cl *5* 14 B1
Coolock Dr *17* 14 B1
Coolock Grn *5* 14 B1
Coolock Gro *5* 14 B1
Coolock Ind Est *17* 15 C1
Coolock Village *5* 14 B2
Coolrua Dr *9* 13 C1
Coombe, The *8* 58 A4
Copeland Av *3* 29 D1
Copeland Gro *3* 29 D1
Cope St *2* 59 D3
Copper All *8* 58 B3
Coppinger Cl *Black.* 55 C3
Coppinger Glade *Black.* 55 C3
Coppinger Row *2*
  off William St S 59 D4

Coppinger Wk *Black.* 55 C3
Coppinger Wd *Black.* 55 C3
Corballis Row *8*
  off Kevin St Upr 58 B4
Cork Hill *2* 58 C3
Cork St *8* 35 C3
Cormac Ter *6W* 51 C1
Corn Ex Pl *2*
  off George's Quay 59 E2
Cornmarket *8* 58 A3
Corporation St *1* 59 E1
Corrib Rd *6W* 42 B3
Corrig Cl *12*
  off Lugaquilla Av 48 B1
Corrybeg *6W* 50 A2
Cottage Pl *1*
  off Portland Pl 28 A2
Coulson Av *6* 43 D3
Court, The *3*
  off Clontarf Rd 30 A2
Court, The *5* 16 A3
Court, The *6W* 50 A2
Court, The *9* 13 C3
Court, The *13* 18 A1
Courtyard, The *14* 51 D2
Cowbooter La *13* 21 C2
Cowley Pl *7* 28 A2
Cow Parlour *8* 35 C3
Cowper Downs *6* 44 A3
Cowper Dr *6* 44 B3
Cowper Gdns *6* 44 B3
Cowper Rd *6* 44 A3
Cowper Sta *6* 44 B3
Cowper St *7* 27 C3
Cowper Village *6* 44 A3
Craigford Av *5* 14 A3
Craigford Dr *5* 14 A3
Craigmore Gdns *Black.* 56 A2
Crampton Bldgs *2*
  off Temple Bar 58 C3
Crampton Ct *2* 58 C3
Crampton Quay *2* 59 D2
Crampton Rd *4* 37 D3
Crane La *2* 58 C3
Crane St *8* 35 C2
Cranfield Pl *4* 37 D3
Cranford Ct *4* 46 A3
Cranmer La *4* 37 C3
Crannagh *6* 45 C3
Crannagh Castle *14* 51 C2
Crannagh Ct *14* 51 C2
Crannagh Gro *14* 51 D2
Crannagh Pk *14* 51 D2
Crannagh Rd *14* 51 C2
Crannagh Way *14* 51 D2
Crawford Av *9* 28 A2
Creighton St *2* 59 F3
Cremona Rd *10* 32 A2
Cremore Av *11* 11 D3
Cremore Cres *11* 11 D3
Cremore Dr *11* 11 D3
Cremore Hts *11*
  off Ballygall Rd E 11 D2
Cremore Lawn *11* 11 D3
Cremore Pk *11* 11 D3
Cremore Rd *11* 11 D3
Cremorne *6* 50 A3
Crescent, The *3* 29 D2
Crescent, The
  (Donnybrook) *4* 45 C2
Crescent, The
  (Beaumont) *9* 13 C2
Crescent, The
  (Whitehall) *9* 13 C3
Crescent, The *13* 18 A1
Crescent Dr *6W* 50 A1
Crescent Gdns *3* 29 C3
Crescent Pl *3* 29 D2
Crescent Vil *9* 28 A1
Crestfield Av *9* 12 B2
Crestfield Cl *9* 12 B2
Crestfield Dr *9* 12 B2
Crestfield Pk *9*
  off Crestfield Cl 12 B2
Crinan Strand *1* 37 C1
Croaghpatrick Rd *7* 26 A2
Crofton Av *D.L.* 57 C2
Crofton Rd *D.L.* 57 C2
Crofton Ter *D.L.* 57 C2
Croftwood Grn *10* 32 A3
Croftwood Rd *10* 32 A3
Croke Pk Ind Est *1* 28 B3
Croker La *8* 35 C2

Cromcastle Av 5 — 14 A1
Cromcastle Dr 5 — 14 A1
Cromcastle Grn 5 — 14 A1
Cromcastle Pk 5 — 14 A1
Cromcastle Rd 5 — 14 A1
Cromwells Fort Rd 12 — 41 C2
Cromwells Quarters 8 — 34 B2
Cross Av Boot. — 55 C1
Cross Av D.L. — 57 C3
Crossbeg Ind Est 24 — 40 A3
Cross Guns Br 11 — 27 D2
Cross Kevin St 8 — 36 A4
Crosslands Ind Est 22 — 40 A3
Crosstrees 3 — 21 C2
Crosthwaite Ter D.L. — 57 D3
Crotty Av 12 — 41 D2
Crown All 2
　off Temple Bar — 58 C3
Crow St 2 — 58 C3
Croydon Gdns 3 — 29 C1
Croydon Grn 3 — 29 C2
Croydon Pk Av 3 — 29 C1
Croydon Ter 3 — 29 C1
Crumlin Pk 12 — 42 A1
Crumlin Rd 12 — 42 A1
Crumlin Shop Cen 12 — 34 B3
Cuala Rd 7 — 27 C2
Cuckoo La 7 — 58 B2
Cuffe La 2 — 36 A3
Cuffe St 2 — 36 A3
Cullenswood Gdns 6 — 44 B2
Cullenswood Pk 6 — 44 B2
Cumberland Rd 2 — 36 B3
Cumberland St D.L. — 57 C3
Cumberland St N 1 — 28 A3
Cumberland St S 2 — 59 F4
Curlew Rd 12 — 41 D1
Curved St 2
　off Eustace St — 58 C3
Curzon St 8 — 36 A3
Custom Ho 1 — 59 E2
Custom Ho Quay 1 — 59 E2
Cymric Rd 4 — 38 A2
Cypress Downs 6W — 50 A2
Cypress Dr 6W — 50 A2
Cypress Garth 6W — 50 A2
Cypress Gro N 6W — 50 A2
Cypress Gro Rd 6W — 50 A2
Cypress Gro S 6W — 50 A2
Cypress Lawn 6W — 50 A2
Cypress Pk 6W — 50 A2
Cypress Rd Still. — 54 A2

D

Dalcassian Downs 11 — 27 D2
Dale Dr Still. — 54 A3
Dale Rd Still. — 54 A3
Dame Ct 2 — 58 C3
Dame La 2 — 58 C3
Dame St 2 — 58 C3
Danes Ct 3 — 31 D2
Danesfort 3 — 30 B2
Daneswell Rd 9 — 28 A1
Dangan Av 12 — 42 A1
Dangan Dr 12 — 42 A3
Dangan Pk 12 — 42 A3
Danieli Dr 5 — 14 B3
Danieli Rd 5 — 14 B3
Daniel St 8 — 35 D3
Dargle Rd 9 — 28 A2
Darleys Ter 8 — 35 C3
Darley St 6 — 43 D1
Darling Est 7 — 25 D1
Dartmouth Ho Ind
　Est 10 — 32 B3
Dartmouth La 6 — 44 B1
Dartmouth Pl 6 — 44 A1
Dartmouth Rd 6 — 44 A1
Dartmouth Sq 6 — 44 B1
Dartmouth Ter 6 — 44 A1
Dartmouth Wk 6
　off Dartmouth Ter — 44 A1
Dartry Cotts 6 — 52 A1
Dartry Pk 6 — 44 A3
Dartry Rd 6 — 44 A3
David Pk 9 — 28 A2
David Rd 9 — 28 A2
Davis Pl 8
　off Thomas Davis
　St S — 58 B4
Davitt Rd 12 — 34 A3
Dawson Ct 2
　off Stephen St — 58 C4

Dawson Ct Black. — 55 C2
Dawson La 2 — 59 E4
Dawson St 2 — 59 D4
Deanstown Av 11 — 9 D2
Deanstown Dr 11 — 10 A2
Deanstown Grn 11 — 10 A2
Deanstown Pk 11 — 10 A2
Deanstown Rd 11 — 10 A2
Dean St 8 — 58 B4
Dean Swift Grn 11 — 11 D2
Dean Swift Rd 11 — 11 D2
Dean Swift Sq 8
　off Swifts All — 58 A4
De Burgh Rd 7 — 34 B1
Decies Rd 10 — 32 A2
De Courcy Sq 9 — 27 D1
Deerpark Av 15 — 24 B1
Deerpark Cl 15 — 24 B1
Deerpark Dr 15 — 24 B1
Deerpark Lawn 15 — 24 B1
Deerpark Rd 15 — 24 B1
Deerpark Rd Still. — 54 A2
Del Val Av 13 — 17 C2
Del Val Ct 13 — 17 C2
Delville Rd 11 — 11 D2
Delvin Rd 7 — 27 C2
Demesne 5 — 30 B1
Denmark St Gt 1 — 28 A3
Denzille La 2 — 59 F4
Denzille Pl 2
　off Denzille La — 59 F4
Dermot O'Hurley Av 4 — 37 D2
Derravaragh Rd 6W — 42 B3
Derry Dr 12 — 42 A2
Derrynane Gdns 4 — 37 D2
Derrynane Par 7 — 28 A2
Derry Pk 12 — 42 A2
Derry Rd 12 — 42 A2
Desmond Av D.L. — 57 C3
Desmond St 8 — 35 D3
Devenish Rd 12 — 42 B2
Deverell Pl 1 — 59 E1
Deverys La 7 — 27 D2
De Vesci Ter D.L. — 57 C3
Devoy Rd 8 — 34 A3
Digges La 2
　off Stephen St — 58 C4
Digges St 2 — 36 A3
Digges St Lwr 2
　off Cuffe La — 36 A3
Dingle Rd 7 — 26 B2
Dispensary La 14 — 51 C3
Distillery Rd 3 — 28 B2
Docklands Innovation
　Pk 3 — 29 D3
Dock Pl S 4
　off Dock St S — 37 D2
Dock St S 4 — 37 D2
Dodderbank 14 — 44 B3
Dodder Dale 14 — 51 C2
Dodder Pk Dr 14 — 51 D1
Dodder Pk Gro 14 — 51 D1
Dodder Pk Rd 14 — 51 D1
Dodder Ter 4 — 37 D2
Doddervale 14 — 52 A1
D'Olier St 2 — 59 D2
Dollymount Av 3 — 31 D2
Dollymount Gro 3 — 31 C2
Dollymount Pk 3 — 31 D2
Dollymount Ri 3 — 31 D2
Dolphin Av 8 — 35 C3
Dolphin Mkt 8
　off Dolphin's Barn St — 35 C3
Dolphin Rd 12 — 34 B3
Dolphin's Barn 8 — 35 C3
Dolphin's Barn St 8 — 35 C3
Dominick La 1 — 58 C1
Dominick Pl 1 — 58 C1
Dominick St D.L. — 57 C3
Dominick St Lwr 1 — 58 C1
Dominick St Upr 7 — 27 D3
Domville Dr 6W — 50 A2
Domville Rd 6W — 50 A2
Donaghmede Av 13 — 16 B1
Donaghmede Dr 13 — 16 B1
Donaghmede Pk 13 — 16 B1
Donaghmede Rd 13 — 16 A1
Donaghmede Shop
　Cen 13 — 16 A1
Donard Rd 12 — 41 D1
Donelan Av 8 — 34 B2
Donnybrook Castle
　Ct 4 — 45 D2

Donnybrook Cl 4 — 45 D3
Donnybrook Grn 4 — 45 D3
Donnybrook Manor 4 — 45 C2
Donnybrook Rd 4 — 45 C2
Donnycarney Rd 9 — 13 D3
Donnycastle 4 — 45 D2
Donore Av 8 — 35 C3
Donore Rd 8 — 35 C3
Donore Ter 8
　off Brown St S — 35 C3
Donovan La 8
　off Clanbrassil
　St Lwr — 35 D3
Doon Av 7 — 27 C3
Doris St 4 — 37 C2
Dornden Pk Boot. — 46 B3
Dorset La 1 — 28 A3
Dorset Pl 1
　off Dorset St Lwr — 28 A3
Dorset St Lwr 1 — 28 A3
Dorset St Upr 1 — 28 A3
Dowkers La 8 — 35 D3
Dowland Rd 12 — 41 D2
Dowling's Ct 2
　off Lombard St E — 59 F2
Dowling's Ct S 2
　off Lombard St E — 59 F2
Downpatrick Rd 12 — 42 B1
Dowth Av 7 — 27 C2
Doyle's La 3 — 31 D2
Drapier Grn 11 — 11 D2
Drapier Rd 11 — 11 D2
Drayton Cl Black. — 56 B3
Drimnagh Rd 12 — 41 D1
Drimnagh Sta 12 — 33 D3
Dromard Rd 12 — 41 D1
Dromawling Rd 9 — 13 D2
Dromdawn Av 9 — 13 C2
Dromeen Av 9 — 13 D2
Dromlee Cres 9 — 13 D2
Dromnanane Pk 9 — 13 D2
Dromnanane Rd 9 — 13 D2
Dromore Rd 12 — 42 A1
Drumalee Av 7
　off Drumalee Rd — 27 C3
Drumalee Ct 7
　off Drumalee Rd — 27 C3
Drumalee Dr 7
　off Drumalee Rd — 27 C3
Drumalee Gro 7
　off Drumalee Rd — 27 C3
Drumalee Pk 7 — 27 C3
Drumalee Rd 7 — 27 C3
Drumcliffe Dr 7 — 26 B2
Drumcliffe Rd 7 — 26 B2
Drumcondra Pk 3 — 28 B2
Drumcondra Rd Lwr 9 — 28 A2
Drumcondra Rd Upr 9 — 28 A1
Drumcondra Sta 3 — 28 B2
Drumfinn Pk 10 — 32 A2
Drumfinn Rd (Bothar
　Drom Finn) 10 — 32 A2
Drummartin Cres 1 14 — 53 D3
Drummartin Rd 14 — 53 D3
Drummartin Ter 14 — 53 D3
Drummond Pl 6
　off Mount
　Drummond Av — 43 D1
Druncondra Br 9 — 28 B1
Drury St 2 — 58 C4
Dublin Ind Est 11 — 11 C3
Dublin Port Tunnel 3 — 29 D3
Dublin Rd 13 — 17 C2
Dufferin Av 8 — 35 D3
Duggan Pl 6
　off Rathmines Rd Upr — 44 A2
Duke La 2 — 59 D4
Duke La Lwr 2
　off Duke St — 59 D3
Duke Row 1
　off North Circular Rd — 28 B3
Duke St 2 — 59 D4
Dunamase Boot. — 55 C1
Dunard Av 7 — 26 B3
Dunard Ct 7 — 26 B2
Dunard Dr 7 — 26 B2
Dunard Pk 7 — 26 B3
Dunard Rd 7 — 26 B3
Dunard Wk 7 — 26 B3
Dunbo Ter 13
　off Church St — 20 B2
Duncarrig 13 — 19 C2

Dundaniel Rd 5 — 13 D1
Dundrum Business
　Pk 14 — 53 C1
Dundrum Rd 14 — 52 B1
Dundrum Shop Cen 14 — 52 B3
Dundrum Sta 14 — 53 C3
Dungar Ter D.L.
　off Northumberland
　Av — 57 D3
Dungriffan Rd 13 — 21 C3
Dun Laoghaire Sta D.L. — 57 D2
Dunleary Hill D.L. — 57 C3
Dunleary Rd D.L. — 57 C3
Dunluce Rd 3 — 30 B1
Dunmanus Rd 7 — 26 B2
Dunne St 1 — 28 B3
Dunree Pk 5 — 15 C1
Dunsandle Ct 15 — 24 A1
Dunsandle Gro 15 — 24 A1
Dunseverick Rd 3 — 30 B1
Dunsink Av 11 — 10 A2
Dunsink Dr 11 — 10 A2
Dunsink Gdns 11 — 10 A2
Dunsink Grn 11 — 10 A2
Dunsink La 15 — 9 C2
Dunsink Pk 11 — 10 A2
Dunsink Rd 11 — 10 B2
Dunsoghly Av 11 — 9 D1
Dunsoghly Dr 11 — 9 D1
Dunsoghly Pk 11 — 9 D1
Dunville Av 6 — 44 A2
Dunville Ter 6
　off Mountpleasant
　Av Upr — 44 A1
Durham Rd 4 — 46 A1
Durrow Rd 12 — 42 B2

E

Eagle Hill Black. — 55 D2
Eagle Hill Av 6W — 43 C3
Eagle Ter 2 16 — 53 C3
Earl Pl 1 — 59 D1
Earls Ct 7 — 26 B2
Earlscourt Ind Est 14 — 52 A3
Earlsfort Mans 2
　off Adelaide Rd — 36 A3
Earlsfort Ter 2 — 36 A3
Earl St N 1 — 59 D1
Earl St S 8 — 58 A4
Eastern Breakwater 1 — 38 B2
East Link 4 — 37 D2
Eastmoreland La 4 — 37 C3
Eastmoreland Pl 4 — 37 C3
East Pt Business Pk 3 — 29 D3
East Rd 3 — 37 D1
East Rd Ind Est 3 — 29 C2
East Wall Rd 3 — 29 C2
Eastwood Cl 11 — 9 D2
Eastwood Cres 11 — 9 D2
Eastwood Pk 11 — 10 A2
Eaton Brae 14 — 52 A1
Eaton Pl Black. — 56 A2
Eaton Rd 6W — 43 C3
Eaton Sq 6W — 43 C3
Eaton Sq Black. — 56 A2
Ebenezer Ter 8 — 35 C3
Eblana Av D.L. — 57 D3
Eblana Vil 2
　off Grand Canal
　St Lwr — 37 C2
Eccles Ct 7
　off Eccles Pl — 28 A3
Eccles Pl 7 — 28 A3
Eccles St 7 — 28 A3
Echlin St 8 — 35 C2
Edenbrook Ct 1 14 — 51 C3
Edenbrook Dr 14 — 50 B3
Edenbrook Pk 14 — 50 B3
Edenmore Av 5 — 15 C2
Edenmore Cres 5 — 15 D2
Edenmore Dr 5 — 15 D2
Edenmore Gdns 5 — 15 C2
Edenmore Grn 5 — 15 D2
Edenmore Gro 5 — 15 D2
Edenmore Pk 5 — 15 C2
Eden Pk Dr 14 — 53 D3
Eden Pk Rd 14 — 53 D3

Eden Quay 1	59	D2
Edenvale Rd 6	44	B2
Effra Rd 6	43	D2
Eglinton Ct 4	45	C2
Eglinton Pk 4	45	C2
Eglinton Rd 4	45	C2
Eglinton Sq 4	45	C2
Eglinton Ter 4	45	C2
Eglinton Ter 14	53	C3
Eldon Ter 8		
off South Circular Rd	35	C3
Elgin Rd 4	45	C1
Elizabeth St 3	28	B2
Elkwood 16	50	A3
Ellenfield Rd 9	13	C2
Ellesmere Av 7	27	C3
Ellis Quay 7	35	C1
Ellis St 7		
off Benburb St	35	C1
Elmcastle Cl 24	48	A2
Elmcastle Ct 24	48	A2
Elmcastle Dr 24	48	A2
Elmcastle Grn 24	48	A2
Elmcastle Pk 24	48	A2
Elmcastle Wk 24	48	A2
Elm Gro Black.	55	D3
Elm Gro Cotts 7		
off Blackhorse Av	26	A2
Elm Mt Av 9	13	D3
Elm Mt Cl 9	13	D3
Elm Mt Ct 9	14	A3
Elm Mt Cres 9	13	D2
Elm Mt Dr 9	13	D3
Elm Mt Gro 9	13	D2
Elm Mt Hts 9	13	D2
Elm Mt Lawn 9	13	D2
Elm Mt Pk 9	13	D2
Elm Mt Ri 9	13	D2
Elm Mt Rd 9	13	D3
Elm Mt Vw 9	13	D2
Elm Pk 4	46	A2
Elmpark Av 6	44	B1
Elmpark Ter 6W	43	C3
Elm Rd 9	13	D3
Elm Rd 12	40	A2
Elms, The 4	46	A3
Elms, The Black.	55	C2
Elmwood Av Lwr 6	44	B1
Elmwood Av Upr 6		
off Elmwood Av Lwr	44	B2
Elton Ct 13		
off Elton Dr	15	D1
Elton Dr 13	15	D1
Elton Pk 13	15	D1
Elton Wk 13		
off Elton Dr	15	D1
Ely Pl 2	36	B3
Ely Pl Upr 2		
off Ely Pl	36	B3
Embassy Lawn 14	45	C3
Emerald Cotts 4	37	C3
Emerald Pl 1		
off Sheriff St Lwr	37	C1
Emerald Sq 8	35	C3
Emerald St 1	37	C1
Emily Pl 1		
off Sheriff St Lwr	59	F1
Emmet Ct 8	33	D3
Emmet Rd 8	33	D3
Emmet Sq Boot.	55	C1
Emmet St 1	28	B3
Emmet St		
(Haroldscross) 6	43	D1
Emor St 8	35	D3
Emorville Av 8	35	D3
Emorville Sq 8		
off South Circular Rd	35	C3
Empress Pl 1	28	B3
Enaville Rd 3	29	C2
Engine All 8	58	A4
Ennafort Av		
(Ascal Dun Eanna) 5	15	C3
Ennafort Ct 5	15	C3
Ennafort Dr		
(Ceide Dun Eanna) 5	15	C3
Ennafort Gro 5	15	C3
Ennafort Pk 5	15	C3
Ennafort Rd 5	15	C3
Ennel Av 5	15	C2
Ennel Dr 5	15	C2
Ennel Pk 5	15	C2
Ennis Gro 4	37	D3
Enniskerry Rd 7	27	D2
Erne Pl 2	37	C2
Erne Pl Little 2	59	F3
Erne St Lwr 2	37	C2
Erne St Upr 2	37	C2
Erne Ter Front 2		
off Erne St Upr	37	C2
Erne Ter Rere 2		
off Erne St Upr	37	C2
Errigal Gdns 12	41	D1
Errigal Rd 12	41	D1
Erris Rd 7	27	C2
Esmond Av 3	29	C2
Esposito Rd 12	41	D2
Essex Quay 8	58	B3
Essex St E 2	58	B3
Essex St W 8	58	C3
Estate Av 4	46	B3
Estate Cotts 4	37	C3
Eugene St 8	35	C3
Eustace St 2	58	C3
Everton Av 7	27	C3
Evora Cres 13	20	B2
Evora Pk 13	20	B2
Evora Ter 13		
off St. Lawrence Rd	20	B2
Ewington La 8	35	C2
Exchange Ct 2		
off Dame St	58	C3
Exchange St Lwr 8	58	B3
Exchange St Upr 8		
off Lord Edward St	58	C3
Exchequer St 2	58	C3

F

Fade St 2	58	C4
Fairbrook Lawn 14	51	C3
Fairfield Av 3	29	C3
Fairfield Pk 6	43	D3
Fairfield Rd		
(Glasnevin) 9	28	A1
Fairlawn Pk 11		
off Fairlawn Rd	10	B2
Fairlawn Rd 11	10	B2
Fairview 3	29	C2
Fairview Av		
(Irishtown) 4	37	D2
Fairview Av Lwr 3	29	C2
Fairview Av Upr 3	29	C2
Fairview Grn 3	29	C2
Fairview Pas 3		
off Fairview Strand	29	C2
Fairview Strand 3	29	C2
Fairview Ter 3	29	C2
Fairways 14	50	B2
Fairways Av 11	11	C2
Fairways Grn 11	11	C2
Fairways Gro 11	11	C2
Fairways Pk 11	11	C2
Faith Av 3	29	C3
Falcarragh Rd 9	12	B1
Farmhill Dr 14	53	C2
Farmhill Pk 14	53	D3
Farmhill Rd 14	53	C3
Farney Pk 4	38	A3
Farnham Cres 11	10	B2
Farnham Dr 11	10	B2
Farrenboley Cotts 14	52	B1
Farrenboley Pk 14	52	B1
Father Kitt Ct 12	42	A2
Father Matthew Br 8	58	B3
Fatima Mans 8	34	B3
Fatima Sta 8	35	C2
Faughart Rd 12	42	B2
Faussagh Av 7	26	B1
Faussagh Rd 7	27	C2
Fenian St 2	59	F4
Ferguson Rd 9	28	A1
Fergus Rd 6W	51	C1
Ferndale Av 11	11	C2
Ferndale Rd 11	11	C2
Fernhill Av 12	49	D1
Fernhill Pk 12	49	D1
Fernhill Rd 12	49	D1
Ferns Rd 12	42	B2
Fernvale Dr 12	49	D1
Ferrard Rd 6	43	D1
Ferrymans Crossing 1	37	C1
Fertullagh Rd 7	27	C2
Field Av 12	41	D2
Fields Ter 6		
off Ranelagh Rd	44	B1
Finches Ind Pk 12	41	C1
Findlater Pl 1		
off Parnell St	28	A3
Findlaters St 7	34	B1
Fingal Pl 7	27	C3
Fingal St 8	35	C3
Finglas Business Pk 11	11	C3
Finglas Pk 11	11	C1
Finglas Pl 11	10	B2
Finglas Rd 11	11	C2
Finglas Rd Old 11	11	D3
Finglas Shop Cen 11	10	B1
Finglaswood Rd 11	10	A1
Finlay Sq 4	54	A2
Finn St 7	27	C3
Finsbury Pk 14	52	B3
Firhouse Rd 16	49	D3
Firhouse Rd 24	49	D3
First Av 1	37	C1
First Av (Inchicore) 10	33	C2
Fishamble St 8	58	B3
Fitzgerald St 6	43	D1
Fitzgibbon La 1	28	B3
Fitzgibbon St 1	28	B3
Fitzmaurice Rd 11	11	D2
Fitzroy Av 3	28	A2
Fitzwilliam Ct 2		
off Pembroke St Upr	36	B3
Fitzwilliam La 2	36	B3
Fitzwilliam Pl 2	36	B3
Fitzwilliam Quay 4	37	D2
Fitzwilliam Sq E 2	36	B3
Fitzwilliam Sq N 2	36	B3
Fitzwilliam Sq S 2	36	B3
Fitzwilliam Sq W 2	36	B3
Fitzwilliam Sq (Ringsend) 4	37	D2
Fitzwilliam St Lwr 2	36	B3
Fitzwilliam St Upr 2	36	B3
Fleet St 2	59	D2
Fleming Pl 4	37	C3
Fleming Rd 9	28	A1
Flemings La 4		
off Haddington Rd	37	C3
Flemingstown Pk 14	52	B2
Fleurville Black.	55	D3
Florence St 8		
off Lennox St	36	A3
Foley St 1	59	E1
Fontenoy St 7	27	D3
Fonthill Abbey 2 14	51	C3
Fonthill Ct 3 14	51	C3
Fonthill Pk 14	51	C3
Fonthill Rd 14	51	C3
Forbes La 8	35	C2
Forbes St 2	37	C2
Forest Av 24	48	A1
Forest Cl 24	48	A1
Forest Dr 24	48	A1
Forest Grn 24	48	A1
Forest Lawn 24	48	A1
Forest Pk 24	48	A1
Fortfield Av 6W	50	B1
Fortfield Ct 6W	50	B1
Fortfield Dr 6W	50	B2
Fortfield Gdns 6	44	A3
Fortfield Gro 6W	50	B2
Fortfield Pk 6W	50	B2
Fortfield Rd 6W	50	B1
Fortfield Ter 6	44	A3
Forth Rd 3	29	D3
Fortview Av 3	31	C3
Fosterbrook Boot.	54	B1
Foster Cotts 7		
off Phibsborough Rd	27	D3
Foster Pl S 2	59	D3
Fosters, The Still.	54	A2
Fosters Av Still.	54	A2
Foster Ter 3	28	B3
Fountain Pl 7	35	C1
Fountain Rd 8	34	B1
Four Cts Sta 7	58	B2
Fourth Av 1	37	C1
Fownes St 2	59	D3
Foxfield Av 5	16	A2
Foxfield Cres 5	16	B2
Foxfield Dr 5	16	B2
Foxfield Grn 5	16	B2
Foxfield Gro 5	16	A2
Foxfield Hts 5	16	A2
Foxfield Lawn 5	16	B2
Foxfield Pk 5	16	B2
Foxfield Rd 5	16	A2
Foxfield St. John 5	16	B2
Foxhill Av 13	15	D1
Foxhill Ct 13	15	D1
Foxhill Cres 13	15	D1
Foxhill Dr 13	15	D1
Foxhill Lawn 13	15	D1
Foxhill Pk 13	15	D1
Foxhill Way 13	15	D1
Foxs La 5	16	B3
Foyle Rd 3	29	C2
Francis St 8	58	A3
Frankfort 14	52	B2
Frankfort Av 6	43	D2
Frankfort Ct 6	43	D3
Frankfort Pk 14	52	B2
Frascati Pk Black.	55	D2
Frascati Rd Black.	55	D2
Frascati Shop Cen Black.	55	D2
Frederick Ct 1		
off Hardwicke St	28	A3
Frederick La 2	59	E4
Frederick La N 1	28	A3
Frederick St N 1	28	A3
Frederick St S 2	59	E4
Frenchmans La 1		
off Gardiner St Lwr	59	E1
Friarsland Av 14	53	C2
Friarsland Rd 14	53	C2
Friary Av 7	58	A2
Friel Av 10	32	A3
Fumbally La 8	35	D3
Furry Pk Ct 5	30	B1
Furry Pk Rd 5	30	B1
Furze Rd 8	24	B2

G

Gaelic St 3	29	C3
Gairdini Sheinleasa 9	12	A1
Galmoy Rd 7	27	C2
Galtymore Cl 12	33	D3
Galtymore Dr 12	34	A3
Galtymore Pk 12	41	D1
Galtymore Rd 12	34	A3
Gandon Cl 6W	43	D1
Garden Croath Black.	55	D3
Garden La 8	58	A4
Gardiner La 1	28	B3
Gardiner Row 1	28	A3
Gardiner's Pl 1	28	A3
Gardiner St Lwr 1	28	B3
Gardiner St Mid 1	28	A3
Gardiner St Upr 1	28	A3
Gardini Lein (Lein Gdns) 5	15	D3
Gardini Phairc An Bhailtini (Villa Pk Gdns) 7	26	A2
Garrynure 6	44	B3
Garryowen Rd 10	32	B2
Gartan Av 9	28	A2
Garville Av 6	43	D3
Garville Av Upr 6	43	D3
Garville Rd 6	43	D3
Geoffrey Keating Rd 8		
off O'Curry Rd	35	D3
George's Av Black.	55	D2
George's Hill 7	58	B2
George's La 7	58	A1
George's Pl 1	28	A3
George's Pl Black.	55	D2
George's Pl D.L.	57	C3
George's Quay 2	59	E2
George's St Lwr D.L.	57	C3
George's St Upr D.L.	57	D3
Georgian Village 15	24	A1
Geraldine St 7	27	D3
Geraldine Ter 6	44	B3
Gerald St 4	37	C2
Gilbert Rd 8	35	D3
Gilford Av 4	46	A1
Gilford Ct 4	46	A1
Gilford Dr 4	46	A1
Gilford Pk 4	46	A1
Gilford Rd 4	46	A1
Glandore Rd 9	13	C3
Glasanaon Ct 11		
off Glasanaon Pk	11	C2
Glasanaon Pk 11	11	C2

Glasanaon Rd 11	11 C1
Glasaree Rd 11	11 C1
Glasilawn Av 11	11 D2
Glasilawn Rd 11	11 C3
Glasmeen Rd 11	11 C3
Glasnamana Pl 11	11 C2
Glasnamana Rd 11	11 C3
Glasnevin Av 11	11 C1
Glasnevin Br 9	27 D1
Glasnevin Business Pk 11	10 A3
Glasnevin Ct 11	11 C3
Glasnevin Downs 11	11 C3
Glasnevin Dr 11	11 D2
Glasnevin Hill 9	12 A3
Glasnevin Pk 11	11 D1
Glasnevin Wds 11	11 C3
Glasson Ct 14	52 B1
Glaunsharoon 4	45 C2
Gleann Na Smol D.L.	56 A3
Glebe Vw 11	10 B1
Gledswood Av 14	53 C1
Gledswood Cl 14	53 C1
Gledswood Dr 14	53 C1
Gledswood Pk 14	53 C1
Glenaan Rd 9	12 B2
Glenabbey Rd Still.	54 A3
Glenanne 12	42 B3
Glenard Av 7	27 C3
Glenarm Av 9	28 B2
Glenarm Sq 9	28 A2
Glenarriff Rd 7	25 D1
Glenart Av Black.	55 C3
Glenaulin 20	24 A3
Glenaulin Dr (Ceide Glennaluinn) 20	32 A1
Glenaulin Pk (Pairc Gleannaluinn) 20	24 A3
Glenavy Pk 6W	42 B3
Glenayle Rd 5	15 D1
Glenayr Rd 6	51 D1
Glenbeigh Pk 7	26 B3
Glenbeigh Rd 7	26 B3
Glenbower Pk 14	52 B3
Glenbrook Pk 14	51 C3
Glenbrook Rd 7	9 D3
Glencarrig 13	19 C1
Glencar Rd 7	26 B3
Glencloy Rd 9	12 B2
Glencorp Rd 9	13 C2
Glendale Pk 12	50 A1
Glendalough Rd 9	28 A1
Glendhu Pk 7	9 D3
Glendhu Rd 7	9 D3
Glendoo Cl 12	
off Lugaquilla Av	48 B1
Glendown Av 6W	49 D1
Glendown Cl 6W	
off Glendown Gro	49 D1
Glendown Ct 6W	49 D1
Glendown Cres 6W	49 D1
Glendown Grn 6W	
off Glendown Gro	49 D1
Glendown Gro 6W	49 D1
Glendown Lawn 6W	50 A1
Glendown Pk 6W	49 D1
Glendown Rd 6W	49 D2
Glendun Rd 9	12 B2
Glenealy Rd 12	43 C1
Glenfarne Rd 5	15 C1
Glengariff Par 7	28 A2
Glenhill Av 11	11 C2
Glenhill Ct 11	11 C2
Glenhill Dr 11	10 B2
Glenhill Gro 11	11 C2
Glenhill Pk 11	10 B2
Glenhill Vil 11	
off Glenhill Pk	10 B2
Glenmalure Pk 8	34 B3
Glenmalure Sq 6	44 B3
Glenmore Rd 7	26 B3
Glenomena Gro Boot.	54 A1
Glenomena Pk Boot.	46 A3
Glenshesk Rd 9	13 C2
Glenties Dr 11	10 A2
Glenties Pk 11	10 A2
Glentow Rd 9	12 B2
Glenvar Pk Boot.	55 C2
Glenview Ind Est 12	34 B3
Glenview Lawn 24	49 C3
Glenview Pk 24	48 B3
Glenville Ind Est Still.	54 A3
Glenwood Rd 5	15 C1
Gloucester La 1	
off Sean McDermott St Lwr	28 B3
Gloucester Pl 1	28 B3
Gloucester Pl Lwr 1	28 B3
Gloucester Pl N 1	28 B3
Gloucester Pl Upr 1	
off Gloucester Pl	28 B3
Gloucester St S 2	59 E2
Glovers All 2	58 C4
Goatstown Av 14	53 C2
Goatstown Rd 14	53 D2
Golden Br 8	33 D2
Goldenbridge Av 8	34 A3
Goldenbridge Gdns 8	34 A3
Goldenbridge Sta 12	34 A3
Goldenbridge Ter 8	
off Connolly Av	34 A3
Golden La 8	58 B4
Goldsmith St 7	27 D3
Gordon Pl 2	
off Richmond St S	36 A3
Gordon St 4	37 C2
Gorsefield Ct 5	15 C2
Gortbeg Av 11	
off Gortbeg Rd	10 B3
Gortbeg Dr 11	10 B3
Gortbeg Pk 11	
off Gortbeg Rd	10 B3
Gortbeg Rd 11	10 B3
Gortmore Av 11	10 B3
Gortmore Dr 11	10 B3
Gortmore Pk 11	
off Gortmore Rd	10 B3
Gortmore Rd 11	10 B3
Government Bldgs 2	59 E4
Gracefield Av 5	15 C3
Gracefield Ct 5	14 B3
Gracefield Rd 5	14 B2
Grace O'Malley Dr 13	20 B2
Grace O'Malley Rd 13	20 B2
Grace Pk Av 3	28 B1
Grace Pk Ct 9	13 C2
Grace Pk Gdns 9	28 B1
Grace Pk Hts 9	13 C3
Grace Pk Meadows 9	13 D3
Grace Pk Rd 9	28 B1
Grace Pk Ter 9	29 C1
Grafton St 2	59 D4
Graham Ct 1	28 A3
Granby La 1	28 A3
Granby Pl 1	58 C1
Granby Row 1	28 A3
Grand Canal Bk 8	35 C2
Grand Canal Bk (Ranelagh) 6	44 A1
Grand Canal Business Cen 8	33 C3
Grand Canal Harbour 8	
off James's St	34 B2
Grand Canal Pl N 8	35 C2
Grand Canal Quay 2	37 C2
Grand Canal St Lwr 2	37 C2
Grand Canal St Upr 4	37 C3
Grand Canal Vw 8	34 A3
Grand Par 6	44 A1
Grange Cl 13	17 C1
Grange Downs 14	51 D3
Grange Dr 13	17 C1
Grangegorman Lwr 7	58 A1
Grangegorman Upr 7	27 C3
Grange Par 13	17 C1
Grange Pk 14	51 C3
Grange Pk Av 5	16 A2
Grange Pk Cl 5	16 A2
Grange Pk Cres 5	16 A2
Grange Pk Dr 5	16 A2
Grange Pk Grn 5	16 A2
Grange Pk Gro 5	16 A2
Grange Pk Par 5	16 A2
Grange Pk Ri 5	16 A2
Grange Pk Rd 5	16 A2
Grange Pk Wk 5	16 A2
Grange Rd 13	16 A1
Grange Rd 14	51 C2
Grange Rd 16	51 C3
Grange Way 13	17 C1
Granite Pl 4	45 D1
Granite Ter 8	
off Inchicore Ter S	33 D2
Grantham Pl 8	36 A3
Grantham St 8	36 A3
Grants Row 2	37 C2
Grattan Br 1	58 C2
Grattan Ct E 2	
off Grattan St	37 C2
Grattan Cres 8	33 D2
Grattan Par 9	28 A2
Grattan Pl 2	
off Grattan St	37 C2
Grattan St 2	37 C2
Gray Sq 8	
off Gray St	58 A4
Gray St 8	58 A4
Great Clarence Pl 2	37 C2
Great Western Av 7	
off North Circular Rd	27 D3
Great Western Sq 7	27 D3
Great Western Vil 7	27 D3
Greek St 7	58 B2
Green, The 9	13 D1
Greenacre Ct 16	49 D3
Greencastle Av 17	14 B1
Greencastle Par 17	15 C1
Greendale Av 5	16 B2
Greendale Rd 5	16 B2
Greendale Shop Cen 5	16 B2
Greenfield Cres 4	45 D3
Greenfield Manor 4	45 D3
Greenfield Pk 4	45 D3
Greenfield Rd 13	18 B1
Greenfield Rd Still.	54 B2
Greenhills Business Cen 24	48 B2
Greenhills Business Pk 24	48 B3
Greenhills Ind Est 12	41 C3
Greenhills Rd 12	40 B3
Greenhills Rd 24	48 B2
Greenlands, The 14	51 D2
Greenlea Av 6W	50 B1
Greenlea Dr 6W	50 B1
Greenlea Gro 6W	50 B1
Greenlea Pk 6W	50 B1
Greenlea Rd 6W	50 B1
Greenmount Av 12	43 D1
Greenmount Ct 12	
off Greenmount Av	43 D1
Greenmount La 12	43 D1
Greenmount Lawns 6	51 C1
Greenmount Rd 6	43 D3
Greenmount Sq 12	
off Greenmount La	43 D1
Greenore Ter 2	
off Grattan St	37 C2
Green Pk 14	52 A1
Green Rd Black.	55 C2
Green St 7	58 B1
Green St E 2	37 D2
Green St Little 7	58 B2
Greentrees Dr 12	49 D1
Greentrees Pk 12	41 D3
Greentrees Rd 12	41 D3
Greenville Av 8	35 D3
Greenville Rd D.L.	56 A3
Greenville Ter 8	35 D3
Greenwich Ct 6	44 A2
Grenville La 1	28 A3
Grenville St 1	28 A3
Greygates Still.	54 B2
Greys La 13	21 C3
Griffith Av 9	12 B3
Griffith Av 11	11 D3
Griffith Br 8	34 A3
Griffith Cl 11	11 C3
Griffith Ct 3	29 C1
Griffith Downs 9	12 B3
Griffith Dr 11	11 C2
Griffith Lawns 9	12 A3
Griffith Par 11	11 C2
Griffith Rd 11	11 C2
Griffith Sq 8	
off Wesley Pl	35 D3
Griffith Sq S 8	
off South Circular Rd	35 C3
Griffith Wk 9	29 C1
Grosvenor Ct 6W	50 A1
Grosvenor Lo 6	43 D2
Grosvenor Pk 6	43 D2
Grosvenor Pl 6	43 D2
Grosvenor Rd 6	43 D2
Grosvenor Sq 6	43 D1
Grosvenor Ter D.L.	57 C3
Grosvenor Vil 6	43 D2
Grotto Av Boot.	55 C1
Grotto Pl Boot.	54 B1
Grove, The 5	16 A3
Grove, The 9	13 C3
Grove Av 6	
off Grove Rd	43 D1
Grove Av (Finglas) 11	11 C1
Grove Av Black.	55 C2
Grove Ho Gdns Black.	55 C3
Grove Lawn Black.	55 C3
Grove Pk 6	43 D1
Grove Pk Av 11	11 C1
Grove Pk Cres 11	11 D1
Grove Pk Dr 11	11 C1
Grove Pk Rd 11	11 C1
Grove Rd (Rathmines) 6	43 D1
Grove Rd (Finglas) 11	11 C1
Grove Wd 11	11 C1
Guild St 1	37 C1
Guinness Enterprise Cen 8	35 C2
Gulistan Cotts 6	35 C2
Gulistan Pl 6	44 A1
Gulistan Ter 6	44 A1
Gurteen Av 10	32 A2
Gurteen Pk 10	32 A2
Gurteen Rd 10	32 A1

H

Haddington Pl 4	37 C3
Haddington Rd 4	37 C3
Haddinton Ter D.L.	57 D3
Haddon Pk 3	
off Seaview Av N	30 A2
Haddon Rd 3	30 A2
Hadleigh Ct 15	8 A3
Hadleigh Grn 15	8 A3
Hadleigh Pk 15	8 A3
Hagans Ct 2	36 B3
Haigh Ter D.L.	57 D3
Halliday Rd 7	35 C1
Halliday Sq 7	35 C1
Halston St 7	58 B1
Hamilton St 8	35 C3
Hammond La 7	58 A2
Hammond St 8	35 D3
Hampstead Av 9	12 A2
Hampstead Ct 9	12 A2
Hampstead Pk 9	12 A3
Hampton Ct 3	31 C1
Hampton Cres Boot.	54 B1
Hampton Grn 7	26 B2
Hampton Pk Boot.	54 B2
Hanbury La 8	58 A3
Hannaville Pk 6W	43 C3
Hanover La 8	58 B4
Hanover Quay 2	37 C2
Hanover Sq W 8	
off Hanover La	58 B4
Hanover St E 2	59 F3
Hanover St W 8	
off Ash St	58 A4
Ha'penny Br 1	59 D2
Harbour Ct 1	
off Marlborough St	59 D2
Harbour Rd 13	20 B1
Harbour Rd D.L.	57 C2
Harbour Ter D.L.	57 C2
Harbour Vw 13	
off St. Lawrence Rd	21 C2
Harcourt Grn 2	36 A3
Harcourt La 2	
off Harcourt Rd	36 A3
Harcourt Rd 2	36 A3
Harcourt Sta 2	36 A3
Harcourt St 2	36 A3
Harcourt Ter 2	36 A3
Harcourt Ter La 2	36 B3
Hardbeck Av 12	41 C2
Hardiman Rd 9	28 A1
Hardwicke Pl 1	28 A3
Hardwicke St 1	28 A3
Harlech Cres 14	53 D2
Harlech Downs 14	53 D2
Harlech Gro 14	53 D2

Harlech Vil 14	53	D2
Harman St 8	35	C3
Harmonstown Rd 5	15	C3
Harmonstown Sta 5	15	C3
Harmony Av 4	45	C2
Harmony Row 2	37	C2
Harold Rd 7	35	C3
Harolds Cross Rd 6W	43	D1
Haroldville Av 8	35	C3
Harrington St 8	36	A3
Harrison Row 6	43	D3
Harry St 2	59	D4
Harty Av 12	41	D2
Harty Ct 12	41	D2
Harty Pl 8	35	D2
Harvard 14	53	D2
Hastings St 4	37	D2
Hatch La 2	36	A3
Hatch Pl 2		
off Hatch La		
Hatch St Lwr 2	36	A3
Hatch St Upr 2	36	A3
Havelock Pl 4		
off Bath Av	37	D3
Havelock Sq E 4	37	D3
Havelock Sq N 4	37	D3
Havelock Sq S 4	37	D3
Havelock Sq W 4	37	D3
Havelock Ter 4		
off Bath Av	37	D3
Haven, The 9	12	A3
Haverty Rd 3	29	D2
Hawkins St 2	59	E2
Hawthorn Av 3	29	C3
Hawthorn Lawn 15	8	A3
Hawthorn Lo 15	8	A3
Hawthorn Manor 1		
Black.	55	D3
Hawthorn Ter 3	29	C3
Hayden Sq 4	54	A2
Haymarket 7	58	A2
Hazelbrook Ct 6W	43	C3
Hazelbrook Dr 6W	42	B3
Hazelbrook Pk 24	48	B2
Hazelbrook Rd 6W	42	B3
Hazelcroft Gdns 11		
off Hazelcroft Rd	10	B2
Hazelcroft Pk 11		
off Hazelcroft Rd	10	B2
Hazelcroft Rd 11	10	B2
Hazeldene 4	45	D2
Hazel Pk 12	42	B3
Hazel Rd 9	13	D3
Hazelwood Ct 5	14	A1
Hazelwood Dr 5	14	A2
Hazelwood Gro 5	14	A2
Hazelwood Pk 5	14	A2
Headford Gro 14	52	A3
Healthfield Rd 6	43	D3
Healy St 1		
off Rutland Pl N	28	B3
Heath, The 6W	50	A2
Heath Cres 7	25	D1
Heathfield Black.	56	B3
Heath Gro 7	26	A1
Heidelberg 14	53	D2
Hellers Copse Black.	55	C3
Hendrick La 7		
off Benburb St	35	C1
Hendrick Pl 7	35	C1
Hendrick St 7	35	C1
Henley Ct 14	52	B2
Henley Pk 14	52	B2
Henley Vil 14	52	B2
Henrietta La 1	27	D3
Henrietta Pl 1	58	B1
Henrietta St 1	58	B1
Henry Pl 1	59	D1
Henry Rd 10	32	A3
Henry St 1	58	C1
Herbert Av 4	46	B3
Herbert Cotts 4	45	D1
Herbert La 2	37	C3
Herberton Dr 12	34	B3
Herberton Pk 8	34	B3
Herberton Rd 8	34	B3
Herberton Rd 12	34	B3
Herbert Pk 4	45	C1
Herbert Pl 2	37	C3
Herbert Rd 4	37	D3
Herbert St 2	36	B3
Heuston Luas Sta 8	35	C1
Heuston Sta 8	34	B1
Hewardine Ter 1		
off Killarney	28	B3
Heytesbury La 4	45	C1
Heytesbury Pl 8		
off Long La	35	C1
Heytesbury St 8	36	A3
Hibernian Av 3	29	C3
Hibernian Ind Est 24	48	A3
Highfield Ct 6	43	D3
Highfield Gro 6	44	A3
Highfield Pk 14	52	B2
Highfield Rd 6	43	D3
High Pk 9	13	C3
High St 8	58	B3
Hill, The Black.	57	C3
Hill, The Still.	55	C3
Hillcrest 6W	50	A3
Hillcrest Pk 11	11	D1
Hillsbrook Av 12	41	D3
Hillsbrook Cres 12	41	D3
Hillsbrook Dr 12	42	A3
Hillsbrook Gro 12	41	D3
Hillside Dr 14	51	D2
Hillside Vw 5	17	C2
Hill St 1	28	A3
Hilltop Shop Cen 5	15	D2
Hoeys Ct 2		
off Castle St	58	B3
Hogan Av 2	37	C2
Hogan Pl 2	37	C2
Holles Row 2	59	F4
Holles St 2	59	F4
Hollybank Av 6	44	B2
Hollybank Rd 9	28	A1
Hollybrook Ct 3		
off Hollybrook Rd	30	A2
Hollybrook Ct Dr 3	30	A2
Hollybrook Gro 3	29	D2
Hollybrook Pk 3	30	A2
Hollybrook Rd 3	30	A2
Holly Rd 9	29	D1
Hollywood Dr 14	53	D3
Hollywood Pk 14	53	D3
Holycross Av 3	28	B2
Holyrood Pk 4		
off Sandymount Av	46	A1
Holywell Av 13	16	A1
Holywell Cres 13	16	A1
Holywell Rd 13	16	A1
Home Fm Pk 9	28	B1
Home Fm Rd 9	12	A3
Homeville 6	44	A2
Hope Av 3	29	C3
Hope St 4	37	C2
Hopkins Sq 4	54	A2
Horseman's Row 1		
off Parnell St	28	A3
Horton Ct 6W	51	C1
Hotel Yd 1	58	C2
Howard St 4	37	C2
Howth Junct 5	16	B1
Howth Rd 3	29	D2
Howth Rd 5	16	B1
Howth Rd (Howth) 13	19	D1
Howth Sta 13	20	B1
Howth Vw Pk 13	16	A1
H.S. Reilly Br 11	10	A3
Huband Br 4	37	C3
Huband Rd 12	41	C1
Hughes Rd E 12	41	D2
Hughes Rd N 12	41	D2
Hughes Rd S 12	41	D2
Hume Cen 10	32	A3
Hume St 2	36	B3
Huxley Cres 8	35	C3
Hyacinth St 3	29	C3
Hyde Pk 6W	50	B2
Hyde Pk Av Black.	55	C2
Hyde Pk Gdns Black.	55	C2
Hyde Sq 4	54	A1

I

I.D.A. Ind Cen 7	27	C3
Idrone Ter Black.	55	D2
ILAC Cen 1	58	C1
Imaal Rd 7	27	C2
Inagh Rd 10	32	A2
Inchicore Par 8	33	D2
Inchicore Rd 8	34	A2
Inchicore Sq 8	33	D2
Inchicore Ter N 8	33	D2
Inchicore Ter S 8	33	D2
Infirmary Rd 7	34	B1
Ingram Rd 8	35	D3
Innisfallen Par 7	28	A2
Innishmaan Rd 9	12	B2
Innismore 12	41	D2
Inns Quay 7	58	B2
Invermore Gro 13		
off Carraroe Rd	16	A1
Inverness Rd 3	29	C2
Inver Rd 7	26	B2
Iona Cres 9	28	A1
Iona Dr 9	28	A2
Iona Pk 9	28	A2
Iona Rd 9	27	D2
Iona Vil 9	28	A1
Iris Gro Still.	54	A2
Irishtown Rd 4	37	D2
Irvine Cres 3		
off Church Rd	37	C1
Irvine Ter 3	37	C1
Irwin Ct 8	34	B2
Irwin St 8	34	B2
Island St 8	35	C1
Island Vw 5	17	C2
Island Vil 2		
off Hogan Av	37	C2
Isolda Rd 4	38	A2
Ivar St 7	35	C1
Iveagh Bldgs 8		
off Kevin St Upr	35	D3
Iveagh Gdns 12	42	A1
Iveleary Rd 9	12	B2
Iveragh Ct 4	37	D3
Iveragh Rd 9	12	B2

J

James Joyce Ct 13	17	C2
James Larkin Rd 3	17	C2
James Larkin Rd 5	16	A3
James McCormack		
Gdns 13	18	A1
James Pl E 2	36	B3
James's Gate 8		
off James's St	34	B2
James's Sta 8	34	B2
James's St 8	34	B2
James's St E 2	36	B3
James St N 3	29	C3
Jamestown Av 8	33	C3
Jamestown Business		
Pk 11	10	B1
Jamestown Ind Est 8	33	C3
Jamestown Rd		
(Inchicore) 8	33	C3
Jamestown Rd		
(Finglas) 11	10	B1
Jamestown Sq 10	33	C3
Janelle Shop Cen 11	10	B2
Jane Ville D.L.		
off Tivoli Rd	57	C3
Jerome Connor Pl 7		
off Sullivan St	34	B1
Jervis La Lwr 1	58	C2
Jervis La Upr 1	58	C1
Jervis Sta 1	58	C2
Jervis St 1	58	C1
Jetty Rd 1	38	B1
John Dillon St 8	58	B3
John F. Kennedy Av 12	40	A1
John F. Kennedy Dr 12	40	B1
John F. Kennedy		
Ind Est 12	40	A1
John F. Kennedy Pk 12	40	A1
John F. Kennedy Rd 12	40	A1
John McCormack		
Av 12	41	D2
Johns La W 8	58	A3
Johnsons Ct 2		
off Grafton St	59	D4
Johnsons Pl 2		
off King St S	59	D4
Johnstown Pk 11	11	D2
John St S 8	35	C2
John St W 8	58	A3
Jones's Rd 3	28	B2
Josephine Av 7		
off Leo St	28	A3
Joshua La 2		
off Dawson St	59	D4
Joyce Rd 9	28	A1
Joy St 4		
off Barrow St	37	C2

K

KCR Ind Est 12	42	B3
Keadeen Av 12	48	B1
Kearns Pl 8	34	B2
Keeper Rd 12	34	B3
Kells Rd 12	42	B2
Kelly's Av D.L.	57	C3
Kellys Row 1	28	A3
Kempton Av 7	25	D1
Kempton Ct 7	25	D1
Kempton Grn 7	25	C1
Kempton Gro 7	25	D1
Kempton Heath 7	25	D1
Kempton Lawn 7	25	D1
Kempton Pk 7	25	D1
Kempton Ri 7	25	D1
Kempton Vw 7	25	D1
Kempton Way 7	25	D1
Kenilworth La 6	43	D2
Kenilworth Pk 6W	43	C2
Kenilworth Rd 6	43	D2
Kenilworth Sq E 6	43	D2
Kenilworth Sq N 6	43	D2
Kenilworth Sq S 6	43	D2
Kenilworth Sq W 6	43	D2
Kenmare Par 1		
off Dorset St Lwr	28	A2
Kennington Cres 6W	49	C2
Kennington Cl 6W	49	C2
Kennington Lawn 6W	49	C2
Kennington Rd 6W	49	C2
Keogh Sq 8	33	D2
Kerlogue Rd 4	38	A2
Kevanagh Av 10	32	A3
Kevin St Lwr 8	36	A3
Kevin St Upr 8	58	B4
Kickam Rd 8	34	A2
Kilakea Cl 12		
off Tibradden Dr	48	B1
Kilakea Dr 12		
off Tibradden Dr	48	B1
Kilbarrack Av 5	17	C2
Kilbarrack Gdns 5	17	C2
Kilbarrack Gro 5	16	B2
Kilbarrack Ind Est 5	16	B1
Kilbarrack Par 5	16	B1
Kilbarrack Rd 5	16	A1
Kilbarrack Shop Cen 5	16	A1
Kilbarrack Sta 5	16	A2
Kilbarrack Way 5	16	B1
Kilbarron Av 5	13	D1
Kilbarron Dr 5	13	D1
Kilbarron Pk 5	13	D1
Kilbarron Rd 5	13	D1
Kilbride Rd 5	30	B1
Kildare Pk 12	42	A1
Kildare Rd 12	42	B1
Kildare St 2	59	E4
Kildonan Av 11	10	A1
Kildonan Dr 11	10	A1
Kildonan Rd 11	10	A1
Kilfenora Rd 12	42	B2
Kilkieran Ct 7	26	B1
Kilkieran Rd 7	26	B1
Killala Rd 7	26	B2
Killan Rd 3	37	C1
Killarney Av 1	28	B3
Killarney Par 7	28	A2
Killarney St 1	28	B3
Killeen Rd 6	44	A2
Killeen Rd 10	40	A1
Killeen Rd 12	40	A1
Killester Av 5	30	B1
Killester Ct 5	14	B3
Killester Pk 5	14	B3
Killester Sta 5	30	B1
Kilmacud Pk Still.	53	D3
Kilmacud Rd Upr 14	53	D3
Kilmainham Br 8	34	A2
Kilmainham La 8	34	A2
Kilmashogue Cl 12		
off Kilmashogue Dr	48	B1
Kilmashogue Dr 12	48	B1
Kilmashogue Gro 12	48	B1
Kilmore Av 14	14	A1
Kilmore Cl 5	14	A1
Kilmore Cres 5	14	A1

Kilmore Dr 5	14	A1
Kilmore Rd 5	14	A2
Kilmorony Cl 13	16	A1
Kilnamanagh Rd 12	41	C2
Kilnamarragh Shop		
Cen 24	48	A2
Kilohan Gro 12	49	C1
Kilrock Rd 13	21	C2
Kilshane Rd 11	9	D2
Kilvere 14	50	B2
Kilworth Rd 12	33	D3
Kimmage Ct 6W	42	B3
Kimmage Gro 6W	43	C3
Kimmage Rd Lwr 6W	43	C2
Kimmage Rd W 12	42	A3
Kinahan St 1	34	B1
Kincora Av 3	30	A2
Kincora Ct 3	31	C2
Kincora Dr 3	30	B2
Kincora Gro 3	30	B2
Kincora Pk 3	30	B2
Kincora Rd 3	30	B2
Kingram La 2	36	B3
Kings Av 3	29	C3
Kings Hall 20	32	B1
Kings Inns St 1	58	C1
Kingsland Par 8	44	A1
Kingsland Pk Av 8	36	A3
King St N 7	58	B1
King St S 2	59	D4
Kingswood Sta 24	48	A1
Kinvara Av 7	25	D1
Kinvara Dr 7	25	D1
Kinvara Gro 7	25	D1
Kinvara Pk 7	25	D1
Kinvara Rd 7	25	D1
Kippure Av 12	48	B1
Kippure Pk 11	10	A3
Kirkwood 4	46	A1
Kirwan St 7	35	C1
Kirwan St Cotts 7		
off Kirwan St	27	C3
Kitestown Rd 13	21	C3
Knapton D.L.		
off Vesey Pl	57	C3
Knapton Lawn D.L.	57	C3
Knapton Rd D.L.	57	C3
Knights Br 3	30	B2
Knockcullen 16	50	A3
Knockcullen Dr 16	50	A3
Knockcullen Lawn 16	50	A3
Knockcullen Pk 16	50	A3
Knocklyon Av 16	49	D3
Knocklyon Dr 16	50	A3
Knocklyon Ms 16	49	D3
Knockmaroon Hill 20	24	A3
Knockmaroon Rd 15	24	A3
Knocknarea Av 12	42	A1
Knocknarea Rd 12	41	D1
Knocknashee 14	53	D3
Kor Riada 20	32	B1
Kor Dev Pk 12	40	B1
Kyber Rd 8	25	D3
Kyle-Clare Rd 4	38	A2
Kylemore Av 10	32	A3
Kylemore Dr 10	32	B3
Kylemore Pk Ind Est 10	32	B3
Kylemore Pk N 10	32	A3
Kylemore Pk S 10	32	B3
Kylemore Pk W 10	32	B3
Kylemore Rd 10	32	B2
Kylemore Rd 12	32	B2
Kylemore Rd 20	32	A1
Kylemore Sta 12	40	B1

L

Laburnum Rd 14	45	C3
Lad La 2	36	B3
Lagan Rd 11	10	B3
Lakelands, The 14	51	C2
Lakelands Pk 6W	51	C1
Lally Rd 10	33	C2
Lambay Rd 9	12	A3
Lambourne Village 3	30	B2
Lambs Ct 8		
off James's St	34	B2
Landen Rd 10	32	B3
Landscape Av 14	52	A2
Landscape Cres 14	52	A2
Landscape Gdns 14	52	A2
Landscape Pk 14	52	A2
Landscape Rd 14	52	A2
Landys Ind Est 16	50	A3

Langrishe Pl 1		
off Summerhill	28	B3
Lansdowne Gdns 4		
off Shelbourne Rd	37	D3
Lansdowne Hall 4		
off Tritonville Rd	37	D3
Lansdowne La 4	37	D3
Lansdowne Pk 4	37	C3
Lansdowne Pk 16	50	A3
Lansdowne Rd 4	37	C3
Lansdowne Rd		
Stadium 4	37	D3
Lansdowne Rd Sta 4	37	D3
Lansdowne Ter 4		
off Serpentine Av	45	D1
Lansdowne Valley		
Cres 12		
off Kilworth Rd	41	D1
Lansdowne Valley		
Rd 12	41	C1
Lansdowne Village 4	37	D3
Lansdown Valley Pk 12	33	D3
Laracor Gdns 13	16	A1
Laragh Cl 13	16	A1
Laragh Gro 13		
off Laragh Cl	16	A1
Larchfield 14	52	B2
Larchfield Pk 14	53	C2
Larchfield Rd 14	53	C2
Larch Gro 6	44	B2
Larkfield Av 6W	43	C2
Larkfield Gdns 6W	43	C2
Larkfield Gro 6W	43	C3
Larkfield Pk 6W	43	C3
Larkhill Rd 9	12	A2
La Touche Dr 12	33	C3
La Touche Rd 12	41	C1
Lauders La 13	18	B1
Laurel Av 14	52	B3
Laurel Dr 14	52	B3
Laurel Rd 14	52	B3
Laurels, The 6W	43	C3
Laurels, The 14	52	B3
Laurelton 6	51	D1
Laurence Brook 20	32	B1
Lavarna Gro 6W	50	B1
Lavarna Rd 6W	42	B3
Lavista Av (Killester) 5	30	B1
La Vista Av 13	19	C3
Lawn, The 11	10	B1
Lea Cres 4	46	A1
Leahys Ter 4	38	A3
Lea Rd 4	46	A1
Le Bas Ter 6		
off Leinster Rd W	43	D2
Le Broquay Av 10	32	A3
Lee Rd 11	27	C1
Leeson Ct 2	36	B3
Leeson La 2	36	B3
Leeson Pk 6	44	B1
Leeson Pk Av 6	44	B1
Leeson Pl 2	36	B3
Leeson St Br 2	36	B3
Leeson St Lwr 2	36	B3
Leeson St Upr 4	44	B1
Leeson Village 6	44	B1
Le Fanu Dr 10	32	A3
Le Fanu Rd 10	32	A2
Leicester Av 6	43	D2
Leighlin Rd 12	42	B2
Lein Gdns		
(Gardini Lein) 5	15	D3
Lein Pk 5	15	C2
Lein Rd 5	15	C2
Leinster Av 3	29	C3
Leinster La 2		
off Leinster St S	59	E4
Leinster Lawn 14	53	C1
Leinster Mkt 2		
off D'Olier St	59	D1
Leinster Pl 6	43	D2
Leinster Rd 6	43	D2
Leinster Rd W 6	43	D2
Leinster Sq 6	44	A2
Leinster St E 3	29	C3
Leinster St N 7	27	D2
Leinster St S 2	59	E4
Leitrim Pl 4		
off Grand Canal		
St Upr	37	C3
Leix Rd 7	27	C2
Leland Pl 1	37	C1

Lemon St 2	59	D4
Lennox Pl 8	44	A1
Lennox St 8	36	A3
Lentisk Lawn 13	16	A1
Leo Av 7		
off Leo St	28	A3
Leo St 7	28	A3
Leslies Bldgs 7	27	D3
Leukos Rd 4	38	A2
Le Vere Ter 6	43	D1
Liberty La 8	36	A3
Library Rd D.L.	57	C3
Liffey Dockyard 1	37	D1
Liffey St 10	33	C2
Liffey St Lwr 1	58	C2
Liffey St Upr 1	58	C2
Liffey St W 7		
off Benburb St	35	C1
Limekiln Av 12	49	C1
Limekiln Cl 12	49	D1
Limekiln Dr 12	49	D1
Limekiln Gro 12	41	D3
Limekiln La 12	49	D1
Limekiln Pk 12	49	D1
Limekiln Rd 12	49	C1
Lime St 2	37	C2
Lincoln La 7	58	A2
Lincoln Pl 2	59	E4
Linden Black.	55	C3
Linden Gro Black.	55	D3
Linden Vale Black.	55	D3
Lindsay Rd 9	27	D2
Linenhall Par 7	58	B1
Linenhall Ter 7	58	B1
Lisburn St 7	58	B1
Liscannor Rd 7	26	B1
Lisle Rd 12	41	D2
Lismore Rd 12	42	B2
Lissadel Av 12	34	A3
Lissadel Ct 12	42	A1
Lissadel Dr 12	42	A1
Lissadel Rd 12	42	A1
Lissenfield 6	44	A1
Litten La 1	59	D2
Little Britain St 7	58	B1
Little Strand St 7	58	B2
Loftus La 1	58	C1
Lombard Ct 2	59	F2
Lombard St E 2	59	F3
Lombard St W 8	35	D3
Lomond Av 3	29	C2
London Br 4	37	D3
Londonbridge Dr 4		
off Londonbridge Rd	37	D3
Londonbridge Rd 4	37	D3
Longdale Ter 9	12	A1
Longford La 8		
off Longford St Gt	58	C4
Longford Pl Black.		
Longford St Gt 8	58	C4
Longford St Little 2	58	C4
Longford Ter Black.	56	B3
Long La 7	28	A3
Long La (Tenter Flds) 8	35	D3
Long La Gro 8	35	D3
Long Mile Rd 12	40	B2
Longs Pl 8	35	C2
Longwood Av 8	35	D3
Longwood Pk 14	51	D3
Lorcan Av 9	13	C1
Lorcan Cres 9	13	C1
Lorcan Dr 9	13	C1
Lorcan Grn 9	13	C1
Lorcan Gro 9	13	C1
Lorcan O'Toole Pk 12	42	A3
Lorcan Pk 9	13	C1
Lorcan Rd 9	13	C1
Lorcan Vil 9	13	C1
Lord Edward St 2	58	B3
Lord's Wk 8	26	A3
Loreto Av 14	51	D3
Loreto Ct 14	51	D3
Loreto Cres 14	51	D3
Loreto Pk 14	51	D3
Loreto Rd 8	35	C3
Loreto Row 14	51	D3
Loreto Ter 14	51	D3
Lorne Ter 8		
off Brookfield Rd	34	B2
Lotts 1	59	D2

Lough Conn Av 10	32	A1
Lough Conn Dr 10	32	A1
Lough Conn Rd		
(Bothar Loch Con) 10	32	A1
Lough Conn Ter 10	32	A1
Lough Derg Rd 5	15	D2
Lourdes Rd 8	35	C3
Louvain 14	53	D2
Louvain Glade 14	53	D2
Love La E 2	37	C3
Lower Dodder Rd 14	51	D1
Lower Glen Rd 15	24	A3
Lower Kilmacud Rd 14	53	D3
Lower Kilmacud Rd		
Still.	54	A3
Luby Rd 8	34	A2
Lucan Rd 20	24	A3
Lugaquilla Av 12	48	B1
Luke St 2	59	E2
Lullymore Ter 8	35	C3
Lurgan St 7	58	B1
Lynchs La 10	32	B2
Lynchs Pl 7	27	D3
Lyndon Gate	26	A2

M

M50 Business Pk 24	48	A1
Mabbot La 1	59	E1
Mabel St 3	28	B2
Macartney Br 2	36	B3
McAuley Av 5	15	C2
McAuley Dr 5	15	C2
McAuley Pk 5	15	C2
McAuley Rd 5	15	C2
McCabe Vil Boot.	54	B1
McCarthy's Bldgs 7		
off Cabra Rd	27	D2
McDowell Av 8	34	B2
McKee Dr 7	26	B3
McKee Pk 7	26	B3
McKee Rd 11	10	B1
Macken St 2	37	C2
Macken Vil 2	37	C2
Mackies Pl 2	36	B3
McMahon St 8	35	D3
McMorrough Rd 6W	43	C3
Madeleine Ter 8	33	D2
Madison Rd 8	34	B3
Magennis Pl 2	59	F3
Magennis Sq 2		
off Pearse St	59	F3
Magenta Hall 9	13	C1
Mageough Home 6	44	A3
Mahers Pl 2		
off Macken St	37	C2
Maiden Row 20	32	B1
Main Rd 24	48	B3
Main Rd Tallaght 24	48	B3
Main St (Raheny) 5	15	D3
Main St (Finglas) 11	10	B1
Main St (Howth) 13	21	C2
Main St (Dundrum) 14	52	B3
Main St		
(Rathfarnham) 14	51	D3
Main St 20	32	B1
Main St 24	48	A3
Main St Black.	55	D2
Malachi Rd 7	35	C1
Malahide Rd 3	29	D2
Malahide Rd 5	14	A3
Malahide Rd 17	15	C1
Mallin Av 8	35	C3
Malone Gdns 4	37	D2
Malpas Pl 8		
off Malpas St	35	D3
Malpas St 8	35	D3
Malpas Ter 8		
off Malpas St	35	D3
Mander's Ter 6		
off Ranelagh Rd	44	B1
Mangerton Rd 12	41	C1
Mannix Rd 9	28	A1
Manor Av 6W	50	B1
Manor Pl 7	35	C1
Manor St 7	27	C3
Mansion Ho 2	59	D4
Maolbuille Rd 11	12	A2

Maple Dr 6W 43 C3
Maple Rd 14 45 C3
Maples, The 14 53 C1
Maples, The D.L. 56 A3
Maquay Br 4 37 C3
Maretimo Gdns E Black. 56 A2
Maretimo Gdns W Black. off Newtown Av 56 A2
Maretimo Pl Black. off Newtown Av 56 A2
Maretimo Rd Black. off Newtown Av 56 A2
Maretimo Vil Black. off Newtown Av 55 D2
Margaret Pl 4 37 D2
Marguerite Rd 9 28 A1
Marian Cres 14 50 B3
Marian Dr 14 50 B2
Marian Gro 14 50 B3
Marian Pk 13 17 C1
Marian Pk (Rathfarnham) 14 50 B3
Marian Rd 14 50 B3
Marine Dr 4 38 A3
Marine Rd D.L. 57 D3
Mariners Cove 13 21 C3
Mariner's Port 1 37 C1
Marine Ter D.L. 57 D3
Marino Av 3 29 D1
Marino Grn 3 29 D1
Marino Mart 3 29 D2
Marino Pk 3 29 C2
Marino Pk Av 3 29 C2
Marion Vil 8 35 C2
Market St S 8 35 C2
Marks All W 8 58 B4
Marks La 2 59 F3
Mark St 2 59 F3
Marlborough Ms 7 26 B3
Marlborough Pl 1 59 D1
Marlborough Rd (Donnybrook) 4 44 B2
Marlborough Rd 7 26 B3
Marlborough St 1 59 D1
Marne Vil 7 27 D3
Marrowbone La 8 35 C3
Marrowbone La Cl 8 35 C2
Marshalsea La 8 35 C2
Martello Av D.L. 57 D3
Martello Ms 4 46 B2
Martello Ter Boot. 55 C1
Martello Vw 4 38 A3
Martello Wd 4 46 B1
Martin Savage Pk 15 9 C3
Martin Savage Rd 7 25 D2
Martins Row 20 24 B3
Martin St 8 44 A1
Maryfield Av 5 14 A2
Maryfield Coll 9 13 C3
Maryfield Cres 5 14 A2
Maryfield Dr 5 14 A2
Mary's Abbey 7 58 B2
Mary's La 7 58 B2
Mary St 1 58 C2
Mary St Little 7 58 B2
Maryville Rd 5 15 C3
Mask Av (Ascal Measc) 5 14 B2
Mask Cres 5 14 B2
Mask Dr 5 14 B2
Mask Grn 5 14 B2
Mask Rd 5 14 B2
Mastersons La 2 off Charlemont St 36 A3
Mather Rd N Still. 54 A2
Mather Rd S Still. 54 A2
Maunsell Pl 7 off Mountjoy St 28 A3
Maxwell Rd 6 44 A2
Maxwell St 8 35 C3
Mayfield 6 51 D1
Mayfield Rd (Terenure) 6W 43 C3
Mayfield Rd (Kilmainham) 8 34 B3
May La 7 58 A2
Mayola Ct 14 52 B2
Mayor St Lwr 1 37 C1
Mayor St Upr 1 37 D1
May St 3 28 B2
Maywood Av 5 16 A3
Maywood Cl 5 16 A3
Maywood Cres 5 16 A3
Maywood Dr 5 16 A3
Maywood Gro 5 16 A3
Maywood La 5 16 A3
Maywood Pk 5 16 A3
Maywood Rd 5 16 A3
Meades Ter 2 37 C2
Meadowbank 6 51 D1
Meadowbrook Av 13 17 D1
Meadowbrook Lawn 13 17 D1
Meadowbrook Pk 13 17 D1
Meadow Pk Av 14 52 A3
Meadows, The 5 15 C3
Meath Pl 8 58 A4
Meath Sq 8 off Gray St 58 A4
Meath St 8 58 A3
Meehan Sq 4 54 A1
Meetinghouse La 7 off Mary's Abbey 58 C2
Mellifont Av D.L. 57 D3
Mellowes Av 11 10 A1
Mellowes Ct 11 10 B1
Mellowes Cres 11 10 B1
Mellowes Pk 11 10 A1
Mellowes Rd 11 10 A1
Mellows Br 8 35 C1
Melrose Av 3 29 C2
Melvin Rd 6W 43 C3
Memorial Rd 1 59 E2
Mercer St Lwr 2 58 C4
Mercer St Upr 2 36 A3
Merchamp 3 31 C2
Merchants Quay 8 58 A3
Merchants Rd 3 37 D1
Merlyn Dr 4 46 A2
Merlyn Pk 4 46 A2
Merlyn Rd 4 46 A2
Merrion Cres Boot. 46 B3
Merrion Gro Boot. 54 B1
Merrion Pk Boot. 54 B2
Merrion Pl 2 59 E4
Merrion Rd 4 45 D1
Merrion Row 2 36 B3
Merrion Shop Cen 4 46 A2
Merrion Sq E 2 59 F4
Merrion Sq N 2 59 F4
Merrion Sq S 2 59 F4
Merrion Sq W 2 59 E4
Merrion Strand 4 46 B2
Merrion St Lwr 2 off Clare St 59 F4
Merrion St Upr 2 36 B3
Merrion Vw Av 4 46 A2
Merrion Village 4 46 A2
Merrywell Ind Est 22 40 A3
Merton Av 8 35 C3
Merton Cres 6 44 B3
Merton Dr 6 44 B2
Merton Rd 6 44 B3
Merton Wk 6 44 B3
Merville Av 3 29 C2
Mespil Rd 4 36 B3
Mews, The 3 30 B2
Mews, The (Dollymount) 3 31 D2
Middle Third 5 30 B1
Military Rd (Rathmines) 6 44 A1
Military Rd (Kilmainham) 8 34 B2
Military Rd (Phoenix Pk) 8 33 C1
Millbourne Av 9 28 A1
Millbrook Av 13 15 D1
Millbrook Ct 8 34 B2
Millbrook Dr 13 16 A1
Millbrook Gro 13 15 D1
Millbrook Rd 13 15 D1
Millbrook Village 6 off Prospect La 45 C3
Millennium Br 1 58 C2
Millgate Dr 12 49 D1
Mill La 8 off Newmarket 35 D3
Mill La 15 9 C3
Millmount Av 9 28 A1
Millmount Gro 14 52 B1
Millmount Pl 9 28 B1
Millmount Ter (Drumcondra) 9 off Millmount Av 28 B1
Millmount Ter (Dundrum) 14 off Millmount Gro 52 B1
Millmount Vil 9 28 A1
Mill St 8 35 D3
Milltown Av 6 44 B3
Milltown Br Rd 14 44 B3
Milltown Dr 14 52 A2
Milltown Gro 14 52 A2
Milltown Hill 6 off Milltown Rd 44 B3
Milltown Path 6 44 B3
Milltown Rd 6 44 B3
Milltown Sta 6 44 B3
Millwood Pk 5 15 D1
Millwood Vil 5 15 D1
Misery Hill 2 37 C2
Moatfield Av 5 15 C1
Moatfield Pk 5 15 C1
Moatfield Rd 5 15 C1
Moeran Rd 12 41 D2
Moira Rd 7 35 C1
Moland Pl 1 off Talbot St 59 E1
Molesworth Pl 2 off Molesworth St 59 E4
Molesworth St 2 59 D4
Molyneux Yd 8 58 A3
Monasterboice Rd 12 42 A1
Monck Pl 7 27 D3
Monkstown Cres Black. 56 B3
Monkstown Gate Black. 57 C3
Monkstown Rd Black. 56 A2
Monkstown Valley Black. 56 B3
Montague Ct 2 off Protestant Row 36 A3
Montague La 2 36 A3
Montague Pl 2 off Montague La 36 A3
Montague St 2 36 A3
Montpelier Dr 7 34 B1
Montpelier Gdns 7 34 B1
Montpelier Hill 7 34 B1
Montpelier Par Black. 56 A3
Montpelier Pk 7 35 C1
Montpelier Pl Black. 35 C1
Montrose Av 5 13 D2
Montrose Cl 5 13 D2
Montrose Ct 5 13 D2
Montrose Cres 5 14 A1
Montrose Dr 5 13 D1
Montrose Gro 5 13 D2
Montrose Pk 5 13 D2
Moore La 1 59 D1
Moore St 1 59 D1
Morehampton La 4 45 C1
Morehampton Rd 4 45 C1
Morehampton Sq 4 44 B1
Morehampton Ter 4 45 C1
Morgan Pl 7 off Inns Quay 58 B2
Morning Star Av 7 58 A1
Morning Star Rd 8 35 C3
Mornington Gro 5 14 B2
Mornington Rd 6 44 B2
Morrogh Ter 3 29 C1
Moss St 2 59 E2
Mountain Vw Av 6 off Harolds Cross Rd 43 D2
Mountain Vw Cotts 6 44 B2
Mountain Vw Dr 14 52 A3
Mountain Vw Pk 14 52 A3
Mountain Vw Rd 6 44 B2
Mount Albion Rd 14 52 A3
Mount Albion Ter 1 14 52 A3
Mount Annville 14 54 A3
Mount Annville Lawn 14 53 D3
Mount Annville Pk 14 54 A3
Mount Annville Rd 14 53 D3
Mount Annville Wd 14 54 A3
Mount Argus Cl 6W 43 C2
Mount Argus Ct 6W 43 C2
Mount Argus Cres 6W 43 C2
Mount Argus Grn 6W 43 C2
Mount Argus Gro 6W 43 C2
Mount Argus Pk 6W 43 C2
Mount Argus Rd 6W 43 C2
Mount Argus Ter 6W 43 C2
Mount Argus Vw 6W 43 C2
Mount Argus Way 6W 43 C2
Mount Brown 8 34 B2
Mount Carmel Av 14 53 C2
Mount Carmel Rd 14 53 C2
Mount Dillon Ct 5 14 B2
Mountdown Dr 12 49 D1
Mountdown Pk 12 49 D1
Mountdown Rd 12 49 D1
Mount Drummond Av 6 43 D1
Mount Drummond Sq 6 43 D1
Mount Eden Rd 4 45 C2
Mount Harold Ter 6 43 D2
Mountjoy Cotts 7 28 A2
Mountjoy Par 1 off North Circular Rd 28 B3
Mountjoy Pl 1 28 B3
Mountjoy Prison Cotts 7 off Cowley Pl 28 A2
Mountjoy Sq E 1 28 B3
Mountjoy Sq N 1 28 A3
Mountjoy Sq S 1 28 A3
Mountjoy Sq W 1 28 A3
Mountjoy St 7 27 D3
Mountjoy St Mid 7 27 D3
Mount Merrion Av Black. 54 B2
Mount Olive Gro 5 16 A1
Mount Olive Pk 5 16 A1
Mount Olive Rd 5 16 A1
Mountpleasant Av Lwr 6 44 A1
Mountpleasant Av Upr 6 44 A1
Mountpleasant Bldgs 6 44 A1
Mountpleasant Par 6 off Mountpleasant Pl 44 A1
Mountpleasant Pl 6 44 A1
Mountpleasant Sq 6 44 A1
Mount Prospect Av 3 31 C2
Mount Prospect Dr 3 31 C1
Mount Prospect Gro 3 31 D1
Mount Prospect Lawns 3 31 C2
Mount Prospect Pk 3 31 C2
Mount Sandford 6 45 C2
Mount Shannon Rd 8 34 B3
Mount St Cres 2 37 C3
Mount St Lwr 2 37 C2
Mount St Upr 2 36 B3
Mount Tallant Av 6W 43 C3
Mount Tallant Ter 6 off Harolds Cross Rd 43 D1
Mount Temple Rd 7 35 C1
Mount Town Rd Upr D.L. 57 C3
Mourne Rd 12 34 B3
Moyclare Av 13 17 D1
Moyclare Cl 13 17 D1
Moyclare Dr 13 17 D1
Moyclare Gdns 13 18 A1
Moyclare Pk 13 17 D1
Moyclare Rd 13 17 D1
Moy Elta Rd 3 29 C3
Moyle Rd 11 26 B1
Moyne Rd 6 44 B2
Moynihan Ct 24 48 B3
Muckross Av 12 41 D3
Muckross Cres 12 41 D3
Muckross Dr 12 42 A3
Muckross Grn 12 42 A3
Muckross Gro 12 41 D3
Muckross Par 7 off Killarney Par 28 A2
Muckross Pk 12 41 D3
Muirfield Dr 12 41 C1
Mulcahy Keane Est 12 41 C3
Mulgrave St D.L. 57 D3
Mulroy Rd 7 27 C1
Mulvey Pk 14 53 C2
Munster St 7 27 D2
Murrays Cotts 10 off Sarsfield Rd 33 D2
Murtagh Rd 7 35 C1
Museum Sta 7 35 C1
Muskerry Rd 10 32 B2
Myra Cotts 8 34 A2

N

Naas Rd 12	40	A2
Naas Rd Business Pk 12	41	C1
Naas Rd Ind Pk 12	41	C1
Nanikin Av 5	15	C3
Nash St 8	33	C3
Nashville Pk 13	21	C2
Nashville Rd 13	21	C2
Nassau Pl 2	59	E4
Nassau St 2	59	D3
Navan Rd 8	25	D1
Navan Rd 15	8	A3
Neagh Rd 6W	43	C3
Nelson St 7	28	A3
Nephin Rd 7	26	A2
Nerneys Ct 1	28	A3
Neville Rd 6	44	A3
New Bride St 8	36	A3
Newbridge Av 4	37	D3
Newbridge Dr 4	37	D3
Newbrook Av 13	16	B1
Newbrook Rd 13	16	B1
New Ch St 7	58	A2
Newcomen Av 3	29	C3
Newcomen Br 3	29	C3
Newcomen Ct 3 off North Strand Rd	29	C3
New Gra Rd 7	27	C2
Newgrove Av 4	38	A3
New Ireland Rd 8	34	B3
New Lisburn St 7 off Coleraine St	58	B1
Newmarket 8	35	D3
Newmarket St 8	35	D3
Newport St 8	35	C2
New Rd (Inchicore) 8	33	C3
New Rd 13	21	C3
New Row S 8	35	D3
New Row Sq 8	58	B4
New St Gdns 8	35	D3
New St S 8	35	D3
Newtown Av Black.	56	A2
Newtown Cotts 17	15	C1
Newtown Dr 13	15	C1
Newtown Pk 24	48	B3
Newtownpark Av Black.	55	D3
Newtown Vil Black.	56	A2
New Wapping St 1	37	C1
Niall St 7	27	C3
Nicholas Av 7 off Church St	58	B1
Nicholas Pl 8 off Patrick St	58	B4
Nicholas St 8	58	B4
Nore Rd 11	26	B1
Norfolk Mkt 1 off Parnell St	28	A3
Norfolk Rd 7	27	D2
Norseman Pl 7	35	C1
North Av Still.	54	A2
Northbrook Av 4	44	B1
Northbrook Av Lwr 4 off North Strand Rd	29	C3
Northbrook Av Upr 3	29	C3
Northbrook La 6	44	B1
Northbrook Rd 6	44	A1
Northbrook Ter 3	29	C3
Northbrook Vil 6 off Northbrook Rd	44	A1
Northbrook Wk 6	44	B1
North Circular Rd 1	28	A3
North Circular Rd 7	28	A2
Northcote Av 8	57	C3
Northcote Pl D.L.	57	C3
North Dublin Docklands 1	38	A1
North Gt Clarence St 1	28	B3
North Gt Georges St 1	28	A3
Northland Dr 11	11	C3
Northland Gro 11	11	C3
North Quay Extension 1	37	D1
North Rd 15	25	C1
North Rd Number 1 1	38	A1
North Strand Rd 1	29	C3
North Strand Rd 3	29	C3
Northumberland Av D.L.	57	D3
Northumberland Pk D.L.	57	D3
Northumberland Pl D.L. off Northumberland Av	57	D3
Northumberland Rd 4	37	C3
North Wall Quay 1	37	C1
Nortons Av 7	27	D3
Norwood Pk 6	44	B2
Nottingham St 3	29	C3
Nugent Rd 14	52	A3
Nutgrove Av (Ascal An Charrain Chno) 14	51	D3
Nutgrove Cres 14	52	A3
Nutgrove Enterprise Pk 14	52	A3
Nutgrove Office Pk 14	52	A3
Nutgrove Pk 14	53	C1
Nutgrove Shop Cen 14	52	A3
Nutgrove Way 14	52	A3
Nutley Av 4	45	D2
Nutley La 4	46	A3
Nutley Pk 4	46	A3
Nutley Rd 4	45	D2
Nutley Sq 4	45	D2

O

Oak Apple Grn 6	43	D3
Oakdown Rd 14	52	A3
Oakfield Pl 8	35	D3
Oaklands Cres 4	44	A3
Oaklands Dr 4	45	D1
Oaklands Dr 6	44	A3
Oaklands Pk 4	45	D1
Oaklands Ter 4 off Serpentine Av	45	D1
Oaklands Ter 6	43	D3
Oak Lawn Castle.	8	A3
Oakley Gro Black.	55	D3
Oakley Pk 3	31	C2
Oakley Pk Black.	55	D3
Oakley Rd 6	44	B1
Oak Lo 15	24	A1
Oak Pk Av 9	13	C1
Oak Pk Cl 9	13	C1
Oak Rd 9	29	D1
Oaks, The 3	31	D2
Oaks, The 14	52	B3
Oakwood Av 11	11	C1
Obelisk Gro Black.	55	D3
Obelisk Wk Black.	55	D3
O'Brien Rd 12	41	D2
O'Brien's Pl N 9	28	A1
O'Brien's Ter 9 off Prospect Rd	27	D2
Observatory La 6 off Rathmines Rd Lwr	44	A1
O'Carolan Rd 8	35	D3
O'Connell Av 7	27	D3
O'Connell Br 1	59	D2
O'Connell Gdns 4	37	D3
O'Connell St Lwr 1	59	D1
O'Connell St Upr 1	59	D1
O'Curry Av 8	35	D3
O'Curry Rd 8	35	D3
O'Daly Rd 9	12	A3
Odd Lamp Rd 8	25	D2
O'Devaney Gdns 7	34	B1
O'Donoghue St 8	33	C3
O'Donovan Rd 8	35	D3
O'Donovan Rossa Br 8 off Winetavern St	58	B3
O'Dwyer Rd 12	41	D2
Offaly Rd 7	27	C2
Offington Av 13	19	C1
Offington Ct 13	19	C1
Offington Dr 13	19	C2
Offington Lawn 13	19	C2
Offington Pk 13	19	C1
O'Hogan Rd 10	33	C2
Olaf Rd 7	35	C1
Old Br Rd 16	50	A2
Old Cabra Rd 7	26	B2
Old Camden St 2 off Harcourt Rd	36	A3
Old Castle Av 13	19	C3
Old Co Glen 12	42	B1
Old Co Rd 12	42	A1
Old Dublin Rd Still.	54	B3
Old Dunleary D.L.	57	C3
Old Fm, The 14	53	D3
Old Kilmainham 8	34	A2
Old Kilmainham Village 8	34	B2
Old Malahide Rd 5	14	B1
Old Mill Ct 8	35	D3
Old Mountpleasant 6 off Mountpleasant Pl	44	A1
Old Naas Rd 12	40	B1
Old Orchard 14	50	A3
Old Rectory Pk 14	53	C3
Old Sawmills Ind Est 12	41	C3
Oldtown Av 9	12	A1
Oldtown Pk 9	12	A1
Oldtown Rd 9	12	A1
O'Leary Rd 8	34	A3
Olivemount Gro 14	53	C1
Olivemount Rd 14	53	C1
Oliver Bond St 8	58	A3
Oliver Plunkett Av (Irishtown) 4	37	D2
Olney Cres 6W	51	C1
Omni Pk 9	12	B1
Omni Pk Shop Cen 9	12	B1
O'Moore Rd 10	33	C2
O'Neachtain Rd 9	28	A1
O'Neill's Bldgs 8	36	A3
Ontario Ter 6	44	A1
Ophaly Ct 14	53	C2
O'Quinn Av 8	34	B2
O'Rahilly Par 1 off Moore St	59	D1
Orchard, The 3	29	C2
Orchard, The 5	14	B3
Orchard, The 6W	42	B3
Orchard Cotts 2 Black.	55	D3
Orchard La 6	44	A1
Orchard Rd 3	29	C2
Orchard Rd 5	16	B3
Orchard Rd 6	44	A3
Orchardstown 14	50	B3
Orchardstown Av 14	50	B3
Orchardstown Dr 14	50	A3
Orchardstown Pk 14	50	A3
Orchardstown Vil 14	50	B3
Ordnance Survey Rd 8	24	B2
O'Reilly's Av 8	34	B2
Oriel Pl 1	29	C3
Oriel St Lwr 1	37	C1
Oriel St Upr 1	37	C1
Ormeau St 4 off Gordon St	37	C2
Ormond Mkt Sq 7 off Ormond Quay Upr	58	B2
Ormond Quay Lwr 1	58	C2
Ormond Quay Upr 7	58	B2
Ormond Rd N 9	28	B1
Ormond Rd S (Rathmines) 6	44	A2
Ormond Sq 7	58	B2
Ormond St 8	35	C3
Orpen Cl Black.	55	C3
Orpen Dale Black.	55	C3
Orwell Gdns 14	52	A1
Orwell Pk 6	52	A1
Orwell Pk Av 6W	49	D2
Orwell Pk Cl 6W	49	D2
Orwell Pk Cres 6W	49	D2
Orwell Pk Dale 6W	49	D2
Orwell Pk Dr 6W	49	D2
Orwell Pk Glade 6W	49	D2
Orwell Pk Glen 6W	49	D2
Orwell Pk Grn 6W	49	D2
Orwell Pk Gro 6W	49	D2
Orwell Pk Hts 6W	49	D2
Orwell Pk Lawns 6W	49	D2
Orwell Pk Ri 6W	49	D2
Orwell Pk Vw 6W	49	D2
Orwell Pk Way 6W	49	D2
Orwell Rd 6	43	D3
Orwell Rd 6W	49	D2
Orwell Rd 14	52	A1
Orwell Shop Cen 6W	49	D2
Orwell Wds 6	52	A1
Oscar Sq 8	35	D3
Osprey Av 6W	49	C1
Osprey Dr 6W	49	C1
Osprey Lawn 6W	49	D1
Osprey Pk 6W	49	C1
Osprey Rd 6W	49	D2
Ossory Rd 3	29	C3
Ossory Sq 8	35	D3
Ostman Pl 7	35	C1
O'Sullivan Av 3	28	B2
Oswald Rd 4	38	A3

Oulton Rd 3	30	B2
Our Ladys Cl 8	35	C2
Our Lady's Rd 8	35	C3
Ovoca Rd 8	35	D3
Owendore Av 14	51	C2
Owendore Cres 14	51	C2
Owens Av 8	34	B2
Owenstown Pk 4	54	A2
Oxford Rd 6	44	A1
Oxford Ter 3 off Church Rd	37	C1
Oxford Ter 6 off Oxford Rd	44	A1
Oxmantown La 7 off Blackhall Pl	35	C1
Oxmantown Rd 7	27	C3
Oxmantown Rd Lwr 7 off Arbour Hill	35	C1

P

Pacelli Av 13	17	C2
Packenham D.L.	57	C3
Paddock, The 7	25	C1
Pairc Baile Munna 11	11	D1
Pairc Clearmont (Claremont Pk) 4	38	A3
Pairc Gleannaluinn (Glenaulin Pk) 20	24	A3
Pakenham Rd Black.	56	B3
Pakerton D.L. off Sloperton	57	C3
Palace St 2 off Dame St	58	C3
Palmerston Gdns 6	44	A3
Palmerston Gro 6	45	C3
Palmerston La 6	44	A3
Palmerston Pk 6	44	A3
Palmerston Pl 7	27	D3
Palmerston Rd 6	44	A2
Palmerston Vil 6	44	A3
Palms, The 14	53	D2
Paradise Pl 7	28	A3
Park, The 9	13	D2
Park Av 4	46	A1
Park Av 16	51	C3
Park Cres 8	26	A2
Park Cres 12	42	A3
Park Dr 6	44	B2
Parkgate Pl Business Cen 8	34	B1
Parkgate St 8	34	B1
Parkhill Way 24	48	A2
Parklands, The 14	51	C2
Park La 4	46	A1
Park La 20	32	B1
Park La E 2	59	E3
Park Lawn 3	31	D1
Parkmore Dr 6W	50	B1
Parkmore Ind Est 22	40	B2
Park Pl 8 off South Circular Rd	34	A1
Park Rd 7	25	D1
Park Rd D.L.	57	D3
Park Shop Cen 7	27	C3
Park St 10	33	C2
Park Ter 8	58	A4
Parkvale 13	17	C3
Parkview 7	26	B3
Park Vw 15	24	B1
Parkview Av (Haroldscross) 6	43	D2
Park Vw Av (Rathmines) 6	44	A2
Park Vil 15	8	A3
Park Vil Black.	55	D3
Parkway Business Cen 24	40	A3
Park W Ind Pk 10	32	A3
Parliament Row 2 off Fleet St	59	D2
Parliament St 2	58	C3
Parnell Av 12 off Parnell Rd	43	D1
Parnell Ct 12	43	D1
Parnell Pl 1	28	A3
Parnell Rd 12	35	C3
Parnell Sq E 1	28	A3

Entry	Ref
Parnell Sq N 1	28 A3
Parnell Sq W 1	28 A3
Parnell St 1	58 C1
Partridge Ter 8	33 C3
Patrician Vil Black.	55 C3
Patricks Row Black.	
off Carysfort Av	55 D2
Patrick St 8	58 B4
Patrick St D.L.	57 D3
Patrickswell Pl 11	10 B2
Patriotic Ter 8	
off Brookfield Rd	34 B2
Paul St 7	58 A2
Pea Fld Boot.	55 C2
Pearse Gro 2	
off Great Clarence Pl	37 C2
Pearse Ho 2	59 F3
Pearse Sq 2	37 C2
Pearse Sta 2	59 F3
Pearse St 2	59 E3
Pecks La 15	8 A3
Pembroke Cotts (Donnybrook) 4	45 C2
Pembroke Cotts (Ringsend) 4	37 D2
Pembroke Cotts (Dundrum) 14	53 C3
Pembroke Gdns 4	37 C3
Pembroke La 4	36 B3
Pembroke La 4	37 C3
Pembroke Pk 4	45 C1
Pembroke Pl 2	
off Pembroke St Upr	36 B3
Pembroke Rd 4	37 C3
Pembroke Row 2	36 B3
Pembroke St 4	37 D2
Pembroke St Lwr 2	36 B3
Pembroke St Upr 2	36 B3
Penrose St 4	37 C2
Percy French Rd 12	41 D2
Percy La 4	37 C3
Percy Pl 4	37 C3
Peter Row 8	58 C4
Petersons Ct 2	59 F2
Peters Pl 2	36 A3
Peter St 8	58 C4
Petrie Rd 8	35 D3
Phibsborough 7	27 D2
Phibsborough Av 7	27 D3
Phibsborough 7	27 D3
Phibsborough Rd 7	27 D3
Philipsburgh Av 3	29 C2
Philipsburgh Ter 3	29 C1
Philomena Ter 4	37 D2
Phoenix Av 15	8 A3
Phoenix Ct 7	
off Cavalry Row	35 C1
Phoenix Ct 15	8 A3
Phoenix Dr 15	8 A3
Phoenix Gdns 15	8 A3
Phoenix Manor 7	26 B3
Phoenix Pl 15	
off Phoenix Av	8 A3
Phoenix St 7	58 A2
Phoenix St 10	33 C2
Phoenix Ter Boot.	55 C1
Pigeon Ho Rd 4	37 D2
Pig La 1	28 B3
Piles Bldgs 8	
off Golden La	58 B4
Piles Ter 2	
off Sandwith St Upr	59 F3
Pimlico 8	58 A4
Pimlico Sq 8	
off The Coombe	58 A4
Pim St 8	35 C2
Pinebrook Av 5	14 A3
Pinebrook Cres 5	
off Pinebrook Av	14 A2
Pinebrook Gro 5	
off Pinebrook Rd	14 A3
Pinebrook Ri 5	14 A3
Pinebrook Rd 5	14 A3
Pine Gro 16	50 A3
Pine Haven Boot.	55 C1
Pine Hurst 7	26 B2
Pine Rd 4	38 A2
Pines, The 5	14 B3
Pinewood Av 11	11 D1
Pinewood Cres 11	11 D1
Pinewood Dr 11	11 D1
Pinewood Grn 11	11 D1
Pinewood Gro 11	11 D1
Pinewood Pk 14	50 B3
Pinewood Vil 11	11 D1
Pleasants La 8	36 A3
Pleasants Pl 8	36 A3
Pleasants St 8	36 A3
Plunkett Rd 11	10 A1
Poddle Pk 12	42 B3
Polo Rd 8	26 A3
Poolbeg St 2	59 E2
Poole St 8	35 C2
Poplar Row 3	29 C2
Poplars, The D.L.	56 A3
Portland Cl 1	28 B3
Portland Pl 1	28 A2
Portland Row 1	28 B3
Portland St N 1	28 B3
Portmahon Dr 8	34 B3
Portobello Br 6	44 A1
Portobello Harbour 8	44 A1
Portobello Pl 8	44 A1
Portobello Rd 8	43 D1
Portobello Sq 8	
off Clanbrassil St Upr	43 D1
Portside Business Cen 3	29 D3
Port Side Ct 3	29 C3
Potato Mkt 7	
off Green St Little	58 B2
Powers Ct 2	
off Warrington Pl	37 C3
Powers Sq 8	
off John Dillon St	58 B4
Prebend St 7	58 B1
Preston St 1	28 B3
Price's La 2	59 F3
Prices La 6	44 A1
Priestfield Cotts 8	35 C3
Priestfield Dr 8	
off South Circular Rd	35 C3
Priestfield Ter 8	
off South Circular Rd	35 C3
Primrose Av 7	27 D3
Primrose Hill D.L.	57 C3
Primrose St 7	27 D3
Prince Arthur Ter 6	44 A2
Prince of Wales Ter 4	45 D1
Princes St N 1	59 D2
Princes St S 2	59 F2
Princeton 14	53 D2
Priory, The 7	26 A1
Priory Av Black.	55 C2
Priory Dr Black.	54 B3
Priory E 7	26 A1
Priory Gro Black.	54 B3
Priory Hall Black.	54 B3
Priory N 7	26 A1
Priory Rd 6W	43 C2
Priory W 7	26 A1
Probys La 1	58 C2
Proby Sq Black.	55 D3
Promenade Rd 3	30 A3
Prospect Av 9	27 D1
Prospect Cem 11	27 D1
Prospect La 6	45 C3
Prospect Rd 9	27 D2
Prospect Sq 9	27 D1
Prospect Ter (Sandymount) 4	
off Beach Rd	38 A3
Prospect Way 9	27 D1
Protestant Row 2	36 A3
Prouds La 2	59 D4
Prussia St 7	27 C3
Purser Gdns 6	44 A2

Q

Entry	Ref
Quarry Dr 12	41 D3
Quarry Rd (Cabra) 7	27 C2
Queens Pk D.L.	56 A3
Queens Rd D.L.	57 D3
Queen St 7	58 A2
Quinns La 2	36 B3

R

Entry	Ref
Rafters Av 12	42 A1
Rafters La 12	42 A1
Rafters Rd 12	42 A1
Raglan La 4	45 C1
Raglan Rd 4	45 C1
Raheen Dr 10	32 A3
Raheen Pk 10	32 A3
Raheny Pk 5	16 A3
Raheny Rd 5	15 D2
Raheny Sta 5	15 D3
Railway Av 8	
off Tyrconnell Rd	33 D3
Railway Av (Inchicore) 8	33 C3
Railway Av 13	18 A1
Railway Cotts 4	
off Serpentine Av	45 D1
Railway St 1	28 B3
Railway Ter 2	
off Grattan St	37 C2
Rainsford Av 8	35 C2
Rainsford St 8	35 C2
Raleigh Sq 12	42 A1
Ramillies Rd 10	32 B2
Ramleh Cl 6	45 C3
Ramleh Pk 6	45 C3
Ramleh Vil 6	44 B3
Ranelagh Av 6	44 B1
Ranelagh Rd 6	44 B1
Ranelagh Sta 6	44 B1
Raphoe Rd 12	42 A1
Rathdown Av 6W	51 C1
Rathdown Ct 6W	43 C3
Rathdown Cres 6W	51 C1
Rathdown Dr 6W	51 C1
Rathdown Pk 6W	51 C1
Rathdown Rd 7	27 D3
Rathdown Sq 7	27 C3
Rathdown Vil 6W	51 C1
Rathdrum Rd 12	43 C1
Rathfarnham Gate 14	51 C2
Rathfarnham Mill 14	51 C2
Rathfarnham Pk 14	51 C1
Rathfarnham Rd 6W	51 C1
Rathfarnham Rd 14	51 C1
Rathfarnham Shop Cen 14	50 B2
Rathfarnham Wd 14	51 D2
Rathgar Av 6	43 D2
Rathgar Pk 6	43 D3
Rathgar Rd 6	43 D3
Rathland Rd (Bothar Raitleann) 12	42 B3
Rathlin Rd 9	12 A3
Rathmines Av 6	44 A2
Rathmines Rd Lwr 6	44 A1
Rathmines Rd Upr 6	44 A2
Rathmore Pk 5	16 A3
Rath Row 2	59 E2
Rathvale Av 13	15 C1
Rathvale Dr 13	15 C1
Rathvale Gro 13	
off Rathvale Av	15 C1
Rathvale Pk 13	15 C1
Rathvilly Dr 11	10 A2
Rathvilly Pk 11	10 A2
Rathvilly Rd 11	10 A2
Ratoath Av (Ascal Ratabhachta) 11	9 D2
Ratoath Dr 11	9 D1
Ratoath Est 11	26 A1
Ratoath Pk 7	26 B2
Ratoath Rd 11	9 D2
Ratra Rd 7	25 D1
Ravensdale Cl 12	42 B3
Ravensdale Pk 12	42 B3
Ravensdale Rd 3	29 D3
Raymond St 8	35 D3
Red Brick Ter 3 Black.	55 D3
Redcourt Oaks 3	31 D2
Red Cow Business Pk 22	40 A2
Red Cow La 7	58 A1
Redesdale Cres Still.	54 A3
Redesdale Rd Still.	54 A3
Redmonds Hill 2	36 A3
Redwood Av 24	48 A2
Redwood Cl 24	
off Redwood Av	48 A2
Redwood Ct 14	52 A2
Redwood Gro Boot.	55 C2
Redwood Hts 24	
off Redwood Pk	48 A2
Redwood Pk 24	48 A2
Redwood Ri 24	
off Redwood Pk	48 A2
Redwood Vw 24	
off Redwood Av	48 A2
Reginald Sq 8	58 A4
Reginald St 8	58 A4
Rehoboth Av 8	35 C3
Rehoboth Pl 8	35 C3
Reillys Av 8	
off Dolphin's Barn St	35 C3
Reuben Av 8	34 B3
Reuben St 8	35 C3
Rialto Br 8	34 B3
Rialto Bldgs 8	
off Rialto Cotts	34 B3
Rialto Cotts 8	34 B3
Rialto Dr 8	34 B3
Rialto St 8	34 B3
Ribh Av 5	15 C3
Ribh Rd 5	15 C3
Richelieu Pk 4	46 A2
Richmond Av Black.	56 B3
Richmond Av N 3	29 C2
Richmond Av S 6	44 B3
Richmond Cotts 1	28 B3
Richmond Cotts (Inchicore) 8	34 A2
Richmond Cotts N 1	
off Richmond Cotts	28 B3
Richmond Ct 6	52 B1
Richmond Cres 1	28 B3
Richmond Est 3	29 C2
Richmond Grn Black.	56 B3
Richmond Gro Black.	56 B3
Richmond Hill 6	44 A1
Richmond Hill Black.	56 B3
Richmond La 1	
off Russell St	28 B3
Richmond Ms 6	44 A1
Richmond Par 1	28 B3
Richmond Pk Black.	56 B3
Richmond Pl 6	44 A1
Richmond Pl S 2	
off Richmond St S	44 A1
Richmond Rd 3	28 B1
Richmond Row 8	44 A1
Richmond Row S 2	
off Richmond St S	36 A3
Richmond St N 1	28 B3
Richmond St S 2	36 A3
Richview Office Pk 14	45 C3
Richview Pk 6	44 B3
Ringsend Br 4	37 D2
Ringsend Pk 4	37 D2
Ringsend Rd 4	37 C2
Ring St 8	33 C3
Ring Ter 8	33 D3
Rise, The (Drumcondra) 9	12 A3
Rise, The Still.	54 B2
River Gdns 9	12 A3
River Rd 11	9 D3
River Rd 15	9 D3
Riversdale Av 6	51 D1
Riversdale Gro 6W	42 B3
Riversdale Ind Est 12	40 B1
Riverside Cotts 6W	50 B2
Riverside Dr 14	51 D2
Riverside Wk 4	45 C3
Riverston Abbey 7	26 A1
Riverview Ct 20	32 B1
Road Number 1 1	38 A1
Road Number 2 1	38 A1
Road Number 3 1	38 A1
Robert Emmet Br 12	43 D1
Robert Pl 3	
off Clonliffe Rd	28 B2
Robert St 3	
off Clonliffe Rd	28 B2
Robert St 8	35 C2
Robinhood Business Pk 22	40 A2
Robinhood Ind Est 22	40 B2
Robinhood Rd 22	40 B2
Robinsons Ct 8	58 A4
Rockfield Av 12	49 D1
Rockfield Dr 12	42 A3

Rockford Pk *D.L.* 56 A3
Rock Hill *Black.* 55 D2
Rock Rd *Boot.* 46 B3
Rockville Cres *D.L.* 56 A3
Rockville Dr *D.L.* 56 A3
Rockville Pk *D.L.* 56 A3
Rockville Rd *D.L.* 56 A3
Roebuck Av *Still.* 54 B2
Roebuck Castle *14* 53 D1
Roebuck Downs *14* 53 C2
Roebuck Dr *12* 41 D3
Roebuck Hall *14* 53 D2
Roebuck Rd *14* 53 C1
Roger's La *2* 36 B3
Roncalli Rd *13* 17 C2
Roosevelt Cotts *7* 26 A2
Rope Wk Pl *4* 37 D2
Rory O'More Br *8* 35 C1
Rosary Gdns E *D.L.* 57 C3
Rosary Gdns W *D.L.* 57 C3
Rosary Rd *8* 35 C3
Rosary Ter *4* 37 D2
Rosbeg Ct *13* 17 C2
Rose Glen Av *5* 16 B2
Rose Glen Rd *5* 16 A2
Rosemount *14* 52 B2
Rosemount Av *5* 14 B3
Rosemount Ct *5* 53 C3
Rosemount Ct *Boot.* 54 B1
Rosemount Cres *5* 53 C1
Rosemount Pk *14* 53 C2
Rosemount Rd *7* 27 D3
Rosemount Ter *Boot.* 54 B1
Rosevale Ct *5*
  off Brookwood Glen 15 C3
Rosevale Mans *5*
Rosmeen Gdns *D.L.* 57 D3
Rossmore Av *6W* 49 D2
Rossmore Av *10* 32 A2
Rossmore Cl *6W* 49 D3
Rossmore Cres *6W* 49 D2
Rossmore Dr *6W* 49 D2
Rossmore Dr *10* 32 A1
Rossmore Gro *6W* 49 D2
Rossmore Lawns *6W* 49 D2
Rossmore Pk *6W* 49 D3
Rossmore Rd *6W* 49 D2
Rossmore Rd *10* 32 A1
Ross Rd *8* 58 B4
Ross St *7* 26 B3
Rostrevor Rd *6* 51 D1
Rostrevor Ter *6* 51 D1
Rothe Abbey *8* 34 A3
Rowanbyrn *D.L.* 56 A3
Rowan Hall *6*
  off Prospect La 45 C3
Rowan Pk *Black.* 56 A3
Royal Canal Bk *7* 27 D3
Royal Canal Ter *7* 27 D3
Royal Liver Retail Pk *12* 40 B1
Royal Ter *3*
  off Inverness Rd 29 C2
Royse Rd *7* 27 D2
Royston *12* 42 A3
Rugby Rd *6* 44 A1
Rugby Vil *6*
  off Rugby Rd 44 A1
Rushbrook Av *6W* 49 C2
Rushbrook Ct *6W* 49 D2
Rushbrook Dr *6W* 49 D2
Rushbrook Gro *6W* 49 D2
Rushbrook Pk *6W* 49 D2
Rushbrook Vw *6W* 49 C2
Rushbrook Way *6W* 49 D2
Russell Av *3* 28 A2
Russell Av E *3* 29 C3
Russell St *1* 28 B3
Rutland Av *12* 43 C1
Rutland Gro *12* 43 C1
Rutland Pl *3*
  off Clontarf Rd 30 B3
Rutland Pl N *1* 28 B3
Rutland Pl W *1* 28 B3
Rutland St Lwr *1* 28 B3
Rutledges Ter *8* 35 C3
Ryders Row *1*
  off Parnell St 58 C1

S
Sackville Av *3* 28 B3
Sackville Gdns *3* 28 B3
Sackville La *1*
  off O'Connell St Lwr 59 D1

Sackville Pl *1* 59 D2
St. Agnes Pk *12* 42 A2
St. Agnes Rd *12* 42 A2
St. Aidan's Dr *14* 53 D2
St. Aidan's Pk *3* 29 D2
St. Aidan's Pk Av *3* 29 D2
St. Aidan's Pk Rd *3* 29 D2
St. Alban's Pk *4* 46 B2
St. Alban's Rd *8* 35 D3
St. Alphonsus Av *9* 28 B2
St. Alphonsus Rd *9* 28 A2
St. Andoens Ter *8*
  off Cook St 58 A3
St. Andrew's La *2*
  off Trinity St 59 D3
St. Andrew's St *2* 59 D3
St. Annes *2* 42 A3
St. Anne's Av *5* 15 D3
St. Anne's Dr *5* 15 D3
St. Annes Rd *8* 35 C3
St. Anne's Rd N *9* 28 A2
St. Anne's Sq *Black.* 55 D2
St. Anne's Ter *5* 15 D3
St. Anthony's Cres *12* 41 C3
St. Anthony's Pl *1*
  off Temple St N 28 A3
St. Anthony's Rd *8* 34 A3
St. Aongus Cres *24* 48 B2
St. Aongus Grn *24* 48 B2
St. Aongus Gro *24* 48 B2
St. Aongus Lawn *24* 48 B2
St. Aongus Rd *24* 48 B2
St. Assam's Av *5* 16 A3
St. Assam's Dr *5* 16 A3
St. Assam's Pk *5* 16 A2
St. Assam's Rd E *5* 16 A3
St. Assam's Rd W *5* 16 A3
St. Attracta Rd *7* 27 C2
St. Audoens Ter *8*
  off School Ho La W 58 B3
St. Augustine St *8* 58 A3
St. Barnabas Gdns *3* 29 C3
St. Brendan's Av *5* 14 B2
St. Brendan's Cotts *4* 37 D2
St. Brendan's Cres *12* 49 C1
St. Brendan's Dr *5* 14 B2
St. Brendan's Pk *5* 15 C2
St. Brendan's Ter *5* 14 B1
St. Brendan's Ter *D.L.*
  off Library Rd 57 C3
St. Bricin's Pk *7* 35 C1
St. Bridget's Av *3* 29 C3
St. Bridget's Dr *12* 41 C3
St. Brigid's Ct *5*
  off St. Brigid's Dr 14 B3
St. Brigid's Cres *5* 14 B2
St. Brigid's Dr *5* 14 B3
St. Brigids Flats *14* 45 C3
St. Brigids Gdns *1* 37 C1
St. Brigids Grn *5* 14 B3
St. Brigids Gro *5* 14 B3
St. Brigids Lawn *5* 14 B3
St. Brigid's Rd *5* 14 B3
St. Brigid's Rd Lwr *9* 28 A2
St. Brigid's Rd Upr *9* 28 A2
St. Brigids Shop Mall *5* 14 B2
St. Broc's Cotts *4* 45 C2
St. Canice's Pk *11* 11 D2
St. Canice's Rd *11* 11 D2
St. Catherine's Av *8* 35 C3
St. Catherine's La W *8* 58 A3
St. Clare's Av *6*
  off Harolds Cross Rd 43 D1
St. Clare's Ter *6*
  off Mount
  Drummond Av 43 D1
St. Clement's Rd *9* 28 A2
St. Columbanus Av *14* 52 B1
St. Columbanus Pl *14* 52 B1
St. Columbanus Rd *14* 52 B1
St. Columba's Rd *12* 41 C3
St. Columba's Rd Lwr *9* 28 A2
St. Columba's Rd Upr *9* 28 A2
St. Conleth's Rd *12* 41 C3
St. Davids *5* 14 A3
St. Davids Pk *5* 14 A3
St. David's Ter *7*
  off Blackhorse Av 26 B3
St. David's Ter
  (Glasnevin) *9* 12 A3
St. Davids Wd *5* 14 A3
St. Declan Rd *3* 29 C1
St. Declan Ter *3* 29 D1

St. Donagh's Cres *13* 16 A1
St. Donagh's Pk *13* 16 B1
St. Donagh's Rd *13* 16 A1
St. Eithne Rd *7* 27 C2
St. Elizabeth's Ct *7*
  off North Circular Rd 27 C3
St. Enda's Dr *14* 51 C3
St. Enda's Pk *14* 51 C3
St. Enda's Rd *6* 43 C3
St. Finbar's Cl *12* 49 C1
St. Finbar's Rd *7* 26 B1
St. Fintan Rd *7* 27 C2
St. Fintan's Cres *13* 19 C3
St. Fintan's Gro *13* 19 C3
St. Fintan's Pk *13* 19 C3
St. Fintan's Rd *13* 19 C3
St. Fintan Ter *7* 27 C1
St. Gabriels Ct *3* 31 D2
St. Gabriel's Rd *3* 31 D2
St. Gall Gdns N *14* 52 B1
St. Gall Gdns S *14* 52 B1
St. George's Av *3* 28 B2
St. Gerard's Rd *12* 41 C3
St. Helena's Dr *11* 10 B2
St. Helena's Rd *11* 10 B2
St. Helen's Rd *Boot.* 54 B1
St. Helens Wd *Boot.* 54 B1
St. Ignatius Av *7* 28 A2
St. Ignatius Rd *7* 28 A2
St. Ita's Rd *9* 28 A1
St. James Pl *8* 33 D2
St. James's Av *3* 28 B2
St. James's Rd *8* 35 C2
St. James's Pl *8*
  off Tyrconnell Rd 33 D3
St. James's Rd *12* 41 C3
St. James's Ter *8* 33 D3
St. James's Wk *8* 34 B3
St. Jarlath Rd *7* 27 C2
St. Johns *4* 46 A2
St. John's Av *8*
  off John St S 58 A4
St. John's Ct *3* 30 A1
St. Johns Ct *5* 14 A1
St. John's Pk *D.L.* 57 C3
St. John's Rd *4* 46 A1
St. John's Rd W *8* 34 A2
St. John St *8*
  off Blackpitts 35 D3
St. Johns Wd *3* 30 B2
St. Joseph's Av *3* 28 B2
St. Joseph's Av *9* 28 A2
St. Josephs Ct *7* 27 C3
St. Josephs Gro *14* 53 C3
St. Joseph's Par *7* 28 A3
St. Joseph's Pl *7*
  off Dorset St Upr 28 A3
St. Joseph's Rd *7* 27 C3
St. Joseph's Rd *12* 41 C3
St. Joseph's Sq *3*
  off Vernon Av 31 C2
St. Joseph's St *7*
  off Synnott Pl 28 A3
St. Joseph's Ter *1*
  off North Circular Rd 28 B3
St. Joseph's Ter *3* 29 C2
St. Kevins Ct *6* 43 D3
St. Kevins Gdns *6* 44 A3
St. Kevin's Par *8* 35 D3
St. Kevins Pk
  (Rathgar) *6* 44 A3
St. Kevin's Rd *8* 43 D1
St. Killian's Av *12* 40 B3
St. Laurence Gro *20* 32 B1
St. Laurence Rd *20* 32 B1
St. Laurence's Mans *1* 37 C1
St. Laurences Pk *Still.* 54 B3
St. Laurence St N *1*
  off Sheriff St Lwr 59 F1
St. Lawrence Gro *3* 30 A2
St. Lawrence Pl *1*
  off Sheriff St Lwr 59 F1
St. Lawrence Rd
  (Clontarf) *3* 30 A2
St. Lawrence Rd
  (Howth) *13* 20 B2
St. Lawrences Ct *3* 30 A2
St. Lawrence St *1*
  off Sheriff St Lwr 59 F1
St. Lawrence Ter *13* 21 C2
St. Luke's Cres *14* 52 B1
St. Magdalene Ter *4* 37 D2
St. Malachy's Dr *12* 41 C3

St. Malachy's Rd *9* 28 A1
St. Margaret's Av 16 B2
St. Margaret's Av N *1*
  off North Circular Rd 28 B3
St. Margaret's Ter *8* 35 C3
St. Martin's Dr *12* 42 B3
St. Martin's Pk *12* 42 B2
St. Mary's Av
  (Rathfarnham) *14* 51 C2
St. Mary's Av N *7* 28 A3
St. Mary's Av W *10* 33 D2
St. Mary's Cres *12* 41 D1
St. Mary's Dr *12* 41 D1
St. Mary's La *4* 37 C3
St. Mary's Pk *12* 41 D2
St. Mary's Pk *15* 9 D2
St. Mary's Pl *13*
  off Main St 21 C2
St. Mary's Pl N *7* 28 A3
St. Mary's Rd *3* 29 C3
St. Mary's Rd *12* 41 D2
St. Mary's Rd N *13*
  off Main St 21 C2
St. Mary's Rd N *3* 29 C3
St. Mary's Rd S *4* 37 C3
St. Mary's St *D.L.* 57 C3
St. Mary's Ter *7* 28 A3
St. Mel's Av *12* 49 C1
St. Michael's Est *8* 34 A3
St. Michael's Hill *8* 58 B3
St. Michael's La *8*
  off High St 58 B3
St. Michael's Rd *9* 28 A1
St. Michael's St *7* 35 D3
St. Michan's St *8* 58 B2
St. Michan's St *7*
  off High St 58 B3
St. Mobhi Boithirin *9* 12 A3
St. Mobhi Ct *9* 12 A3
St. Mobhi Dr *9* 28 A1
St. Mobhi Gro *9* 28 A1
St. Mobhi Rd *9* 28 A1
St. Mobhis Br *9* 28 A1
St. Nessan's Ter *13*
  off Tuckett's La 20 B2
St. Nicholas Pl *8* 58 B4
St. Pappin Grn *11* 11 D2
St. Pappin Rd *11* 11 D2
St. Patrick Av *3*
  off North Strand Rd 29 C3
St. Patrick's Cl *8* 58 B4
St. Patrick's Cotts *14* 51 C3
St. Patrick's Par *9* 28 A2
St. Patrick's Rd *9* 28 A2
St. Patrick's Rd *12* 41 C3
St. Patrick's Ter *1*
  off Russell St 28 B3
St. Patrick's Ter *3*
  off North Strand Rd 29 C3
St. Patrick's Ter *8* 33 D2
St. Patrick's Vil *4* 37 D2
St. Peters Av *7* 27 D2
St. Peters Cl *7* 27 D3
St. Peter's Cres *12* 41 D3
St. Peter's Dr *12* 41 D3
St. Peter's Rd *7* 27 D2
St. Peter's Rd *12* 41 C3
St. Peter's Ter *13* 20 B2
St. Philomena's Rd *11* 27 D2
St. Stephen's Grn *2* 36 B3
St. Stephen's Grn N *2* 59 D4
St. Stephen's Grn Pk *2* 36 A3
St. Stephen's Grn
  Shop Cen *2* 59 D4
St. Stephen's Grn S *2* 36 A3
St. Stephen's Grn
  Sta *2* 59 D4
St. Stephen's Grn W *2* 36 A3
St. Teresa's La *12* 42 A3
St. Teresa's Pl *9*
  off Prospect Av 27 D1
St. Teresa's Rd *9* 27 D1
St. Teresa's Rd
  (Crumlin) *12* 42 A3
St. Theresa Gdns *8* 35 C3
St. Thomas' Mead *Still.* 54 B2
St. Thomas' Rd
  (Tenter Flds) *8* 35 D3
St. Thomas' Rd *Still.* 54 A2

St. Thomas's Av 7
  off Constitution Hill 58 B1
St. Vincent's Pk Black. 56 A2
St. Vincent St N 7 27 D3
St. Vincent St S
  (Tenter Flds) 8 35 D3
St. Vincent St W 8 33 D2
Salamanca 14 53 D2
Sallymount Av 6 44 B1
Sallymount Gdns 6 44 B1
Sally's Br 8 43 C1
Salthill & Monkstown
  Sta Black. 56 B2
Salzburg 14 53 D2
Sampsons La 1 58 C1
Sandford Av
  (Donnybrook) 4 45 C2
Sandford Av 8 35 C3
Sandford Cl 6 44 B2
Sandford Gdns 4 45 C2
Sandford Gdns 8
  off Donore Av 35 C3
Sandford Rd 6 44 B2
Sandford Ter 6 44 B2
Sandon Cove 3 30 B2
Sandwith Pl 2 59 F3
Sandwith St Lwr 2 59 F3
Sandwith St Upr 2 59 F3
Sandymount Av 4 45 D1
Sandymount Castle
  Dr 4 46 A1
Sandymount Castle
  Rd 4 46 A1
Sandymount Grn 4 38 A3
Sandymount Rd 4 38 A3
Sandymount Sta 4 46 A1
Sans Souci Pk Boot. 54 B1
Santa Sabina Manor 13 19 C2
Santry Hall Ind Est 9 12 B1
Sarah Pl 8 34 A1
Sarsfield Quay 7 35 C1
Sarsfield Rd 8 33 D2
Sarsfield Rd 10 33 C2
Sarsfield St 7 27 D3
Sarto Lawn 13 17 C1
Sarto Pk 13 17 C1
Sarto Ri 13 17 C2
Sarto Rd 13 17 C2
Saul Rd 12 42 B1
School Av 5 14 B3
Schoolhouse La 2 59 D4
School Ho La W 8 58 B3
School St 8 35 C2
Seabury 4 46 B1
Seacliff Av 13 17 D1
Seacliff Dr 13 17 C1
Seacliff Rd 13 17 C1
Seacourt 3 31 C2
Seafield Av 3 31 C2
Seafield Av Black. 56 B3
Seafield Cl Boot. 54 A1
Seafield Ct 13 18 A1
Seafield Cres Boot. 54 B1
Seafield Down 3 31 D2
Seafield Dr Boot. 54 A1
Seafield Gro 3 31 D2
Seafield Pk Boot. 54 B1
Seafield Rd Boot. 54 A1
Seafield Rd E 3 31 C2
Seafield Rd W 3 30 B2
Seafort Av 4 38 A3
Seafort Cotts 4
  off Seafort Av 38 A3
Seafort Gdns 4 38 A3
Seafort Vil 4
  off Seafort Av 38 A3
Seagrange Rd 13 17 C1
Seamus Ennis Rd 11 10 B1
Sean Heuston Br 8 34 B1
Sean McDermott St
  Lwr 1 28 B3
Sean McDermott St
  Upr 1 59 D1
Sean More Rd 4 38 A3
Sean O'Casey La 1 28 B3
Seapark 3 31 C2
Seapark Dr 3 31 C2

Seapark Rd 3 31 C2
Seapoint Av Black. 56 A2
Seapoint Sta Black. 56 A2
Seaview Av 3 29 C3
Seaview Av N 3 30 A2
Sea Vw Ter 4 45 D2
Seaview Ter 13 21 C1
Second Av 1 37 C1
Selskar Ter 6 44 A1
Serpentine Av 4 45 D1
Serpentine Pk 4 37 D3
Serpentine Rd 4 37 D3
Serpentine Ter 4 45 D1
Seven Oaks 9 12 B3
Seville Pl 1 29 C3
Seville Ter 1 28 B3
Shamrock Cotts 1
  off Shamrock Pl 29 C3
Shamrock Pl 1 29 C3
Shamrock St 7
  off Primrose St 27 D3
Shamrock Ter 1 29 C3
Shamrock Vil 6W 43 D2
Shanard Av 9 12 A1
Shanard Rd 9 12 A1
Shanboley Rd 9 13 C1
Shandon Cres 7 27 D2
Shandon Dr 7 27 D2
Shandon Gdns 7 27 C1
Shandon Pk 7 27 D2
Shandon Pk Black. 56 A2
Shandon Rd 7 27 D2
Shangan Av 9 12 B1
Shangan Gdns 9 12 B1
Shangangh Rd 9 28 A2
Shangan Grn 9 12 B1
Shangan Pk 9 12 B1
Shangan Rd 9 12 A1
Shanglas Rd 9 13 C1
Shanid Rd 6W 43 C3
Shanliss Av 9 12 B1
Shanliss Dr 9 12 B1
Shanliss Gro 9 12 B1
Shanliss Rd 9 12 B1
Shanliss Wk 9 12 B1
Shanliss Way 9 12 B1
Shannon Ter 8 34 B2
Shanowen Av 9 12 A2
Shanowen Cres 9 12 B1
Shanowen Dr 9 12 B1
Shanowen Gro 9 12 A1
Shanowen Pk 9 12 A1
Shanowen Rd Ind Est 9 12 B2
Shanrath Rd 9 13 C1
Shantalla Av 9 13 C2
Shantalla Dr 9 13 C2
Shantalla Pk 9 13 C2
Shantalla Rd 9 13 C2
Shanvarna Rd 9 13 C1
Shaws La 4 37 D3
Shaw St 2 59 E3
Shelbourne Av 4 37 D3
Shelbourne La 4 37 C3
Shelbourne Rd 4 37 D3
Shellysbanks Rd 4 38 B3
Shelmalier Rd 3 29 C3
Shelmartin Av 3 29 C2
Shelmartin Ter 3 29 C1
Shelton Dr 12 42 A3
Shelton Gdns 12 42 A3
Shelton Gro 12 42 A3
Shelton Pk 12 42 A3
Sheriff St Lwr 1 59 F1
Sheriff St Upr 1 37 D1
Sherkin Gdns 9 12 B3
Sherrard Av 1 28 A2
Sherrard St Lwr 1 28 A3
Sherrard St Upr 1 28 A3
Shielmartin Dr 13 19 C3
Shielmartin Pk 13 22 A2
Shielmartin Rd 13 22 A2
Ship St Gt 8 58 C3
Ship St Little 8 58 B3
Shrewsbury 4 46 A1
Shrewsbury Pk 4 46 A1
Shrewsbury Rd 4 45 D2
Sibthorpe La 6 44 B1
Sigurd Rd 7 27 C3
Silloge Av 11 11 D1
Silloge Gdns 11 12 A1
Silloge Rd 11 12 A1

Silver Birches 14 53 C3
Silverwood Dr 6W
  off Templeville Dr 50 A2
Silverwood Dr 14 50 B3
Silverwood Rd 14 50 B3
Simmon's Ct 4
  off Simmonscourt
  Castle 45 D1
Simmonscourt Av 4 45 D2
Simmonscourt Castle 4 45 D1
Simmonscourt Rd 4 45 D1
Simmonscourt Ter 4 45 D2
Simonscourt Sq 4 45 D1
Simonscourt Vw 4 45 D1
Sion Hill Boot. 55 C1
Sion Hill Av 6W 43 C2
Sion Hill Ct 9 13 C3
Sion Hill Rd 9 13 C3
Sir John Rogersons
  Quay 2 37 C1
Sitric Rd 7 35 C1
Skellys La 5 13 D2
Skippers All 8 58 B3
Skreen Rd 7 26 A2
Slademore Cl 13 15 D1
Slademore Dr 13 15 D1
Slade Row 7 35 C1
Slane Rd 12 42 B1
Slaney Cl 11 27 C1
Slaney Rd 11 27 C1
Slemish Rd 7 26 A2
Slievebloom Pk 12 41 D1
Slievebloom Rd 12 41 D1
Slievemore Rd 12 42 A1
Slievenamon Rd 12 34 A3
Slieve Rua Dr Still. 54 A3
Sloperton 2 D.L. 57 C3
Slopes, The D.L. 57 C3
Smithfield 7 58 A2
Smithfield Sta 7 58 A2
Smiths Vil D.L. 57 C3
Somerset St 4
  off Doris St 37 D2
Somerville Av 12 41 D2
Somerville Grn 12 41 D2
Somerville Pk 12 41 D2
Sommerville 14 52 B2
Sorbonne 14 53 D2
South Av Still. 54 A3
South Bk Rd 4 38 A2
South Circular Rd 8 34 A1
Southdene Black. 56 B3
South Docks Rd 4 37 D2
Southern Cross Av 8 34 A2
South Gt Georges St 2 58 C4
South Hill 6 44 A3
South Hill 13 19 C3
South Hill Av Boot. 54 B2
South Hill Pk Boot. 54 B2
South Lotts Rd 4 37 D3
South Rd Number 4 1
  off Alexandra Rd 38 B1
Southwood Pk Boot. 55 C2
Spade Enterprise
  Cen 7 35 C1
Spafield Ter 4 45 D1
Spa Rd
  (Kilmainham) 8 33 D2
Spa Rd (Phoenix Pk) 8 26 A3
Spawell Rd Br 16 50 A3
Spencer Dock 1 37 C1
Spencer St 8
  off South Circular Rd 35 C3
Spencer St N 3 29 C3
Sperrin Rd 12 33 D3
Spire Vw Ct 6 43 D2
Spire Vw La 6 43 D2
Spitalfields 8 58 A4
Springdale Rd 5 15 C1
Springfield 7 26 A2
Springfield Av 6W 50 B2
Springfield Cres 6W 50 B2
Springfield Dr 6W 50 B2
Springfield Pk 6W 50 B2
Springfield Rd 6W 50 B2
Spring Gdn La 2 59 E3
Spring Gdn St 3 29 C3
Square, The 4 37 D2
Square, The 6W 43 C2
Stable La 2
  off Harcourt St 36 A3
Stable La 4
  off Londonbridge Rd 37 D2

Stables, The Boot. 54 B1
Stamer St 8 36 A3
Stanford Grn 12 41 D2
Stanhope Cen 7 27 D3
Stanhope Grn 7 35 C1
Stannaway Av 12 42 A2
Stannaway Dr 12 42 B2
Stannaway Rd 12 42 A2
Station Rd 5 15 D3
Station Rd 13 18 A1
Steelpes, The 10 33 C2
Steevens La 8 35 C2
Stella Av 9 12 A3
Stephens La 2 37 C3
Stephens Pl 2
  off Stephens La 37 C3
Stephens Rd 8 34 A3
Stephen St 2 58 C4
Stephen St Upr 8 58 C4
Stiles Ct, The 3
  off The Stiles Rd 30 A2
Stiles Rd, The 3 30 A2
Stillorgan Pk Black. 55 C3
Stillorgan Pk Av Black. 55 C3
Stillorgan Rd 4 45 D2
Stillorgan Rd Still. 54 B2
Stillorgan Shop Cen
  Still. 55 C3
Stirling Pk 14 52 A1
Stirrup La 7
  off Beresford St 58 B1
Stockton Ct 15 8 A3
Stockton Dr 15 24 A1
Stockton Grn 15 24 A1
Stockton Gro 15 24 A1
Stockton Lawn 15 8 A3
Stockton Pk 15 24 A1
Stonepark Abbey 14 51 D3
Stonepark Ct 14 51 D3
Stonepark Dr 14 51 D3
Stonepark Grn 14 51 D3
Stonepark Orchard 14 51 D3
Stoneview Pl D.L. 57 C3
Stoneybatter 7 35 C1
Stoney Rd 3
  off East Wall Rd 29 C3
Stoney Rd
  (Dundrum) 14 53 C3
Store St 1 59 E1
Stormanstown Rd 11 11 D2
Stradbrook Gdns Black. 56 A3
Stradbrook Lawn D.L. 56 A3
Stradbrook Pk D.L. 56 A3
Stradbrook Rd D.L. 56 A3
Strand Rd
  (Sandymount) 4 38 A3
Strand Rd 13 19 C2
Strand St 4 37 D2
Strand St Gt 1 58 C2
Strandville Av E 3 30 A2
Strandville Av N 3 29 C3
Strandville Ho 3 30 A2
Strangford Gdns 3 29 C3
Strangford Rd E 3 29 C3
Streamville Rd 13 16 A1
Suffolk St 2 59 D3
Suir Rd 8 34 A2
Suir Rd Sta 12 34 A3
Sullivan St 7 34 B1
Summerhill 1 28 B3
Summerhill Par 1 28 B3
Summerhill Par D.L. 57 D3
Summerhill Pl 1 28 B3
Summerhill Rd D.L. 57 D3
Summer Pl 1 28 B3
Summer St N 1 28 B3
Summer St S 8 35 C2
Summerville 3 30 B2
Summerville Pk 6 44 A3
Sunbury Gdns 6 44 A3
Sundrive Pk 12 42 B1
Sundrive Rd 12 42 B1
Sundrive Shop Cen 12 43 C2
Sunnybank Ter 14 52 B3
Sunshine Ind Est 12 42 A1
Superquinn Shop
  Cen 12 41 C2
Susan Ter 8 35 D3
Susanville Rd 3 28 B2
Sussex Rd 4 44 B1
Sussex St D.L. 57 D3
Sussex Ter Lwr 4
  off Mespil Rd 36 B3

Sussex Ter Upr *4*
 off *Leeson St Upr* — 36 B3
Sutton Ct *13* — 17 D1
Sutton Cross Shop
 Cen *13* — 18 B1
Sutton Downs *13* — 17 D2
Sutton Gro *13* — 17 D1
Sutton Lawns *13* — 17 D1
Sutton Pk *13* — 17 D1
Sutton Sta *13* — 18 A1
Swan Pl *4*
 off *Morehampton Rd* — 45 C1
Swan Shop Cen *6* — 44 A2
Swans Nest Av *5* — 16 B1
Swans Nest Ct *5* — 16 B1
Swans Nest Rd *5* — 16 A1
Swanville Pl *6* — 44 A2
Swanward Business
 Cen *24* — 40 A3
Swanward Ct *12* — 43 C1
Swan Yd *2*
 off *Harry St* — 59 D4
Sweeneys Ter *8*
 off *Mill St* — 35 D3
Sweetmans Av *Black.* — 55 D2
Sweetmount Av *14* — 52 B3
Sweetmount Dr *14* — 52 B3
Sweetmount Pk *14* — 52 B3
Swifts All *8* — 58 A4
Swifts Row *7*
 off *Ormond Quay
 Upr* — 58 B2
Swilly Rd *7* — 26 B2
Swords Rd *9* — 12 B3
Swords St *7* — 27 C3
Sybil Hill Av *5* — 15 C3
Sybil Hill Rd *5* — 15 C3
Sycamore Cres *Still.* — 54 B2
Sycamore Dr *24* — 48 A1
Sycamore Pk *24* — 48 A1
Sycamore Rd *12* — 40 A2
Sycamore Rd *Still.* — 54 B2
Sycamore St *2* — 58 C3
Sydenham Ms *D.L.* — 57 D3
Sydenham Rd
 (Sandymount) *4* — 45 D1
Sydenham Rd
 (Dundrum) *14* — 53 C3
Sydenham Vil *14* — 53 C3
Sydney Av *Black.* — 55 D2
Sydney Par Av *4* — 46 A2
Sydney Par Sta *4* — 46 A2
Sydney Ter *Black.* — 55 D2
Sykes La *6* — 43 D3
Synge La *8* — 36 A3
Synge Pl *8* — 36 A3
Synge St *8* — 36 A3
Synnott Pl *7* — 28 A3
Synnott Row *7* — 28 A2

T

Tailor's Mkt *8* — 58 B3
Talbot La *1*
 off *Talbot St*
Talbot Lo *Black.* — 55 C3
Talbot Mem Br *1* — 59 E2
Talbot Pl *1* — 59 E1
Talbot St *1* — 59 D1
Tallaght Enterprise
 Cen *24* — 48 A3
Tallaght Rd *24* — 49 C3
Tallagt Rd *6W* — 48 A1
Tamarisk Av *24* — 48 A1
Tamarisk Cl *24*
 off *Tamarisk Way* — 48 A1
Tamarisk Ct *24* — 48 A2
Tamarisk Dale *24*
 off *Tamarisk Dr* — 48 A1
Tamarisk Dr *24* — 48 A1
Tamarisk Gro *24*
 off *Tamarisk Pk* — 48 A2
Tamarisk Hts *24* — 48 A2
Tamarisk Lawn *24* — 48 A2
Tamarisk Pk *24* — 48 A2
Tamarisk Vw *24*
 off *Tamarisk Pk* — 48 A2
Tamarisk Wk *24*
 off *Tamarisk Dr* — 48 A1
Tamarisk Way *24* — 48 A1
Taney Av *14* — 53 C3
Taney Ct *14* — 53 C3
Taney Cres *14* — 53 C3
Taney Dr *14* — 53 C3

Taney Gro *14* — 53 D3
Taney Lawn *14* — 53 C3
Taney Manor *14* — 53 C3
Taney Pk *14* — 53 C3
Taney Ri *14* — 53 C3
Taney Rd *14* — 53 C3
Tara Hill Cres *14* — 51 C3
Tara Hill Gro *14* — 51 C3
Tara Hill Rd *14* — 51 C3
Tara Lawn *13* — 16 A1
Tara St *2* — 59 E2
Tara St Sta *2* — 59 E2
Taylors La *8* — 35 C2
Temple Bar *2* — 58 C3
Temple Cotts *7* — 27 D3
Temple Ct *7* — 35 C1
Temple Cres *Black.* — 56 A2
Temple Gdns *6* — 44 A3
Temple Hill *Black.* — 56 A2
Temple La N *1* — 28 A3
Temple La S *2* — 58 C3
Temple Manor Av *12* — 49 C1
Temple Manor Cl *12* — 49 C1
Temple Manor Ct *12* — 49 C1
Temple Manor Dr *12* — 49 C1
Temple Manor Gro *12* — 49 C1
Temple Manor Way *12* — 49 C1
Templemore Av *6* — 43 D3
Templeogue Lo *6W* — 49 D2
Templeogue Rd *6W* — 50 B2
Templeogue Wd *6W* — 50 A2
Temple Pk *6* — 44 B3
Temple Pk Av *Black.* — 56 A2
Temple Pl *6* — 44 B1
Temple Rd *6* — 44 A3
Temple Rd *Black.* — 55 D2
Temple Sq *6* — 44 A3
Temple St N *1* — 28 A3
Temple St W *7* — 35 C1
Temple Vil *6*
 off *Palmerston Rd* — 44 A2
Templeville Av *6W* — 50 A2
Templeville Dr *6W* — 50 B2
Templeville Pk *6W* — 50 B2
Templeville Rd *6W* — 49 D1
Terenure Pk *6W* — 43 C3
Terenure Pl *6W* — 51 C1
Terenure Rd E *6* — 43 C3
Terenure Rd N *6W* — 43 C3
Terenure Rd W *6W* — 42 B3
Terminal Rd N *1* — 39 C1
Thatch Rd, The *9* — 13 C2
Third Av *1* — 37 C1
Third Av *8*
 off *Dolphin's Barn* — 35 C3
Thomas Ct *8* — 35 C2
Thomas Davis St S *8* — 58 B4
Thomas Davis St W *8* — 33 D3
Thomas La *1*
 off *O'Connell St Upr* — 59 D1
Thomas Moore Rd *12* — 41 C2
Thomas St E *8* — 37 D2
Thomas St W *8* — 35 C2
Thomond Rd *10* — 32 B2
Thormanby Lawns *13* — 21 C2
Thormanby Lo *13* — 21 D3
Thormanby Rd *13* — 21 C2
Thormanby Wds *13* — 21 C3
Thorncastle St *4* — 37 D2
Thorncliffe *14* — 52 B1
Thorncliffe Pk *14* — 52 A1
Thorndale Av *9*
 off *Elm Mt Rd* — 14 A3
Thorndale Ct *9* — 13 C2
Thorndale Cres *9*
 off *Elm Mt Rd* — 14 A3
Thorndale Dr *5* — 12 A3
Thorndale Gro *5* — 12 A3
Thorndale Lawns *9*
 off *Elm Mt Rd* — 14 A3
Thorndale Pk *9*
 off *Elm Mt Rd* — 14 A3
Thornhill Rd *Still.* — 54 A3
Thornville Av *5* — 16 B2
Thornville Dr *5* — 16 B2
Thornville Pk *5* — 16 B2
Thornville Rd *5* — 16 B2
Thor Pl *7* — 35 C1
Three Rock Cl *12* — 48 B1
Thundercut All *7*
 off *Smithfield* — 58 A1
Tibradden Cl *12*
 off *Tibradden Dr* — 48 B1

Tibradden Dr *12* — 48 B1
Tibradden Gro *12*
 off *Tibradden Dr* — 48 B1
Timber Quay *1* — 38 A1
Tinkler's Path *8* — 24 B2
Tivoli Av *6W* — 43 D2
Tivoli Rd *D.L.* — 57 C3
Tivoli Ter E *D.L.* — 57 C3
Tivoli Ter N *D.L.* — 57 C3
Tivoli Ter S *D.L.* — 57 C3
Tolka Cotts *11* — 11 C3
Tolka Est Rd *11* — 11 C3
Tolka Quay *1* — 37 D1
Tolka Quay Rd *1* — 38 B1
Tolka Rd *3* — 28 B2
Tolka Vale *11* — 11 C3
Tolka Valley Business
 Pk *11* — 10 B3
Tolka Valley Ind Est *11* — 10 B3
Tolka Valley Rd *11* — 10 A3
Tolka Vw Ter *11* — 11 C3
Tom Clarke Ho *3* — 29 C2
Tom Kelly Rd *2* — 44 A1
Tonduff Ct *12*
 off *Lugaquilla Av* — 48 B1
Tonguefield Rd *12* — 42 B2
Tonlegee Av *5* — 15 D1
Tonlegee Dr *5* — 15 C1
Tonlegee Rd *5* — 15 C1
Torlogh Gdns *3* — 29 C2
Torlogh Par *3* — 29 C1
Tourmakeady Rd *9* — 43 D3
Tower Av *6* — 43 D3
Tower Rd *15* — 24 A2
Tower Vw Cotts *11* — 27 D1
Townsend St *2* — 59 E2
Trafalgar La *Black.* — 56 A2
Trafalgar Ter *Black.* — 56 A2
Tram Ter *3* — 31 C3
Tramway Cotts *7* — 27 D2
Tramway Ct *13* — 18 A1
Tramway Ter *4* — 46 A1
Tramway Vil *6W* — 43 C3
Tranquility Gro *5* — 14 A1
Treepark Av *24* — 48 A2
Treepark Cl *24* — 48 A2
Treepark Dr *24* — 48 A2
Treepark Rd *24* — 48 A2
Trees Av *Still.* — 54 B3
Trees Rd Lwr *Still.* — 54 B3
Trees Rd Upr *Still.* — 54 A3
Trevor Ter *2*
 off *Grattan St* — 37 C2
Trimbleston *14* — 53 D2
Trimleston Av *Boot.* — 46 B3
Trimleston Dr *Boot.* — 46 B3
Trimleston Gdns *Boot.* — 46 B3
Trimleston Pk *Boot.* — 46 B3
Trimleston Rd *Boot.* — 54 B1
Trim Rd *5* — 13 D1
Trinity Coll Enterprise
 Cen *2* — 37 C2
Trinity St *2* — 59 D3
Trinity Ter *3* — 29 C2
Tritonville Av *4* — 38 A3
Tritonville Cl *4* — 37 D3
Tritonville Cres *4* — 38 A3
Tritonville Rd *4* — 37 D3
Tryconnell Pk *8* — 33 D2
Tuckett's La *13* — 20 B2
Tudor Rd *6* — 44 B3
Turnberry *13* — 17 D1
Turrets, The *4* — 37 D3
Turrets Flats *6*
 off *Rathmines Rd Upr* — 44 A2
Tuscany Downs *5* — 15 D2
Tuscany Pk *13* — 17 D1
Tymon La *24* — 49 C2
Tymon N Av *24* — 48 B2
Tymon N Gdns *24* — 48 B3
Tymon N Gro *24* — 48 B3
Tymon N Lawn *24* — 48 B3
Tymon N Pk *24* — 48 B3
Tymon N Rd *24* — 48 B2
Tymonville Av *24* — 48 B2
Tymonville Ct *24* — 48 A2
Tymonville Cres *24* — 48 A2
Tymonville Dr *24* — 48 B2
Tymonville Gro *24* — 48 B2
Tymonville Pk *24* — 48 B2
Tymonville Rd *24* — 48 B2

95

Tyrconnell Rd *8* — 33 D3
Tyrconnell St *8* — 33 D3
Tyrconnell Vil *8*
 off *Grattan Cres* — 33 D2
Tyrone Pl *8* — 33 D3

U

Ulster St *7* — 27 D2
Ulster Ter *1* *Still.* — 55 C3
Upper Cliff Rd *13* — 21 C2
Uppercross Rd *8* — 34 B3
Upper Glen Rd *15* — 24 B3
Ushers Island *8* — 35 C1
Ushers Quay *8* — 58 A2
Usher St *8* — 58 A3

V

Valentia Par *7* — 28 A2
Valentia Rd *9* — 12 A3
Valeview Cres *11* — 10 A2
Valeview Dr *11* — 10 A2
Valeview Gdns *11* — 10 A2
Valley Pk Av *11* — 9 D2
Valley Pk Dr *11* — 9 D3
Valley Pk Rd *11* — 9 D3
Vauxhall Av *8* — 35 C3
Vavasour Sq *4* — 37 D3
Venetian Hall *5* — 14 B3
Ventry Dr *7* — 26 B1
Ventry Pk *7* — 26 B1
Ventry Rd *7* — 26 B1
Verbena Av *13* — 17 C2
Verbena Gro *13* — 17 C1
Verbena Lawns *13* — 17 C1
Verbena Pk *13* — 17 C1
Vergemount *6*
 off *Clonskeagh Rd* — 45 C3
Vergemount Hall *6* — 45 C3
Vergemount Pk *6* — 45 C3
Vernon Av (Clontarf) *3* — 31 C2
Vernon Av *6*
 off *Frankfort Av* — 43 D2
Vernon Ct *3* — 31 C3
Vernon Dr *3* — 31 C1
Vernon Gdn *3* — 31 C2
Vernon Gro *3* — 31 C2
Vernon Gro (Rathgar) *6* — 44 A3
Vernon Heath *3* — 31 C1
Vernon Par *3*
 off *Clontarf Rd* — 30 A2
Vernon Pk *3* — 31 C2
Vernon Ri *3* — 31 C1
Vernon St *8* — 35 D3
Vernon Ter *6*
 off *Frankfort Av* — 44 A3
Veronica Ter *4* — 37 D2
Verschoyle Ct *2*
 off *Verschoyle Pl* — 37 C3
Verschoyle Pl *2* — 37 C3
Vesey Ms *D.L.* — 57 C3
Vesey Pl *D.L.* — 57 C3
Vicar St *8* — 58 A3
Victoria Av *4* — 45 C2
Victoria Br *2* — 37 C2
Victoria Quay *8* — 35 C1
Victoria Rd (Clontarf) *3* — 30 A2
Victoria Rd
 (Terenure) *6* — 51 D1
Victoria St *8* — 35 D3
Victoria Ter *3*
 off *Clontarf Rd* — 31 C3
Victoria Ter *14* — 52 B3
Victoria Vil *3* — 29 D2
Victoria Vil (Rathgar) *6* — 43 D3
Viking Pl *7*
 off *Arbour Hill* — 35 C1
Viking Rd *7* — 35 C1
Village, The *5* — 16 A3
Village, The *9* — 12 B3
Village Ct *14* — 51 C2
Village Grn *24* — 48 A3
Villa Pk Av (Ascal Pairc
 An Bhailtini) *7* — 26 A2
Villa Pk Dr (Ceide Pairc
 An Bhailtini) *7* — 26 A2
Villa Pk Gdns (Gardini
 Pairc An Bhailtini) *7* — 26 A2

Villa Pk Rd (Bothar Pairc
 An Bhailtini) 7 26 A2
Villiers Rd 6 44 A3
Vincent Ter 9 28 A1
Violet Hill Dr 11 11 C3
Violet Hill Pk 11 11 C3
Violet Hill Rd 11 11 C3
Virginia Dr 11
 off Virginia Pk 10 A2
Virginia Pk 11 10 A2

W

Wad Br 9 12 A2
Wadelai Grn 11 12 A2
Wadelai Rd 11 11 D2
Wade's Av 5 15 D3
Wainsfort Av 6W 50 A1
Wainsfort Cres 6W 50 A1
Wainsfort Dr 6W 42 A3
Wainsfort Gdns 6W
 off Wainsfort Cres 50 A1
Wainsfort Gro 6W 50 B1
Wainsfort Pk 6W 50 A1
Wainsfort Rd 6W 50 A1
Waldemar Ter 14 52 B3
Waldrons Br 6 52 A1
Walk, The 6W 50 A2
Walkinstown Av 12 41 C2
Walkinstown Cres 12 41 C2
Walkinstown Cross 12 41 C2
Walkinstown Dr 12 41 C2
Walkinstown Grn 12 41 C2
Walkinstown Mall 12 41 C2
Walkinstown Par 12 41 C2
Walkinstown Rd 12 41 C2
Walkinstown Rd
 (Bothar Chille
 Na Manac) 12 41 C2
Wallace Rd 12 41 D2
Walnut Av 9 12 B3
Walnut Ct 9 12 B3
Walnut Lawn 9 12 B3
Walnut Pk 9 12 B3
Walnut Ri 9 12 B3
Walsh Rd 9 12 A3
Waltham Ter Black. 55 C2
Walworth Rd 8
 off Victoria St 43 D1
Wards Hill 8 35 D3
Warners La 6 36 B3
Warren Grn 13 18 A1
Warrenmount 8 35 D3
Warrenmount Pl 8 35 D3
Warrenpoint 3 30 A2
Warren St 8 44 A1
Warrington La 2
 off Warrington Pl 37 C3
Warrington Pl 2 37 C3
Warwick Ter 6
 off Sallymount Av 44 B1
Wasdale Gro 6 51 D1
Wasdale Pk 6 51 C1
Washington La 14 50 B3
Washington Pk 14 50 B2
Washington St 8 35 D3
Watercourse 6W 49 D2
Waterfall Av 3 28 B2
Waterfall Rd 5 15 D3
Waterloo Av 3 29 C3
Waterloo La 4 44 B1
Waterloo Rd 4 45 C1
Watermill Av 5 15 D3
Watermill Dr 5 15 D3
Watermill Lawn 5 16 A3
Watermill Pk 5 15 D3
Watermill Rd (Bothar
 An Easa) 5 15 D3
Watling St 8 35 C2
Waverley Av 3 29 C2
Waverley Business
 Pk 12 40 B1
Waverley Ter 6
 off Kenilworth Rd 43 D2
Weaver La 7
 off Phibsborough Rd 27 D3
Weavers Sq 8 35 D3
Weaver's St 8 58 A4

Wellesley Pl 1
 off North Circular Rd 28 B3
Wellington La 4 45 C1
Wellington La 6W 49 D2
Wellington Pk 6W 49 D1
Wellington Pl
 (Donnybrook) 4 45 C1
Wellington Pl N 7 27 D3
Wellington Quay 2 58 C3
Wellington Rd 4 45 C1
Wellington Rd 6W 49 D2
Wellington Rd 8 34 A1
Wellington St D.L. 57 C3
Wellington St Lwr 7 28 A3
Wellington St Upr 7 27 D3
Wellmount Av 11 10 A2
Wellmount Ct 11 10 A2
Wellmount Cres 11 10 A2
Wellmount Dr 11 10 A2
Wellmount Grn 11 10 A2
Wellmount Par 11 10 A2
Wellmount Pk 11 10 A2
Wellmount Rd 11 10 A2
Wellpark Av 9 12 B3
Wentworth Ter 2
 off Hogan Pl 37 C2
Werburgh St 8 58 B3
Wesley Pl 8 35 D3
Wesley Rd 6 43 D3
Westbourne Rd 6W 51 C1
Westbrook 12 42 A3
Westbrook Rd 14 52 B2
Westcourt 8
 off Basin St Upr 35 C2
Westcourt La 8 35 C2
Western Ind Est 12 40 A2
Western Parkway
 Business Cen 12 40 B3
Western Parkway
 Business Pk 12 40 B3
Western Rd 8 35 C3
Western Way 7 27 D3
Westfield Rd 6W 43 C2
Westgate Business
 Pk 24 40 A3
Westhampton Pl 6W 43 C3
Westland Ct 2
 off Cumberland St S 59 F4
Westland Row 2 59 F3
Westlink Ind Est 10 32 B3
Westmoreland Pk 6 44 B1
Westmoreland St 2 59 D3
Weston Av 14 52 B3
Weston Cl 14 52 B3
Weston Gro 14 52 B3
Weston Pk 14 52 B3
Weston Rd 14 52 B3
Weston Ter 14 52 B3
West Pk 5 15 C2
West Pk Dr 11 11 D3
Westpoint Ct Business
 Pk 12 40 B1
West Rd 3 29 C3
West Row 1 58 C1
West Ter 8 33 D2
Westwood Av 11 9 D2
Westwood Rd 11 9 D2
Wexford St 2 36 A3
Wharton Ter 6
 off Harolds Cross Rd 43 D1
Whitebank Rd 4 38 B2
Whitebarn Rd 14 52 A2
Whitebeam Av 14 45 C3
Whitebeam Rd 14 45 C3
Whitechurch
 Abbey 7 14 51 C3
Whitechurch Pines 14 51 C3
Whitechurch Rd 14 51 C3
Whitechurch Rd 16 51 C3
Whitechurch
 Stream 5 14 51 C3
Whitefriar Pl 8
 off Aungier St 58 C4
Whitefriar St 8 58 C4
Whitehall Cl 6W 49 D1
Whitehall Gdns 12 42 A3
Whitehall Pk 12 49 D1
Whitehall Rd
 (Rathfarnham) 14 52 A3
Whitehall Rd E 12 49 D1
Whitehall Rd W 12 49 D1
White Oak 14 53 C1
Whites La N 7 27 D3

Whites Rd 15 24 A2
Whitethorn Av 5 14 A2
Whitethorn Cl 5 13 D2
Whitethorn Cres 5 14 A2
Whitethorn Gro 5 14 A2
Whitethorn La 4
 off Thorncastle St 37 D2
Whitethorn Pk 5 14 A2
Whitethorn Ri 5 14 A2
Whitethorn Rd 5 13 D2
Whitethorn Rd 14 45 C3
Whitton Rd 6 43 C3
Whitworth Av 3
 off Whitworth Pl 28 A2
Whitworth Pl 3 28 A2
Whitworth Rd 1
 off Seville Pl 29 C3
Whitworth Rd 9 27 D2
Wicklow La 2
 off Wicklow St 59 D3
Wicklow St 2 59 D3
Wigan Rd 9 28 A2
Wilderwood Gro 6W 49 D2
Wilfield 4 46 A1
Wilfield Rd 4 46 A1
Wilfrid Rd 6W 43 D2
Willbrook Gro 14 51 C3
Willbrook Lawn 14 51 C3
Willbrook Pk 14 51 C3
Willbrook Rd 14 51 C3
Willbrook St 14 51 C3
Willfield Pk 4 46 A1
William's La 1
 off Princes St N 59 D2
William's Pk 6 44 A1
William's Pl S 8 35 D3
William's Pl Upr 1 28 A2
William's Row 1
 off Abbey St Mid 59 D2
William St N 1 28 B3
William St S 2 59 D4
Willington Av 6W 49 D1
Willington Cl 6W 49 D1
Willington Cres 6W 49 D1
Willington Dr 6W 49 D2
Willington Grn 6W 49 D1
Willington Gro 6W 49 D2
Willington Pk 6W
 off Willington Gro 49 D2
Willow Bk D.L. 57 C3
Willowbank Pk 14 50 B3
Willow Business Pk 12 40 A1
Willowfield 4 46 A1
Willowfield Av 14 53 D2
Willowfield Pk 14 53 D2
Willow Ms 4 46 B2
Willow Pk Av 11 11 D1
Willow Pk Cl 11 11 D1
Willow Pk Cres 11 11 C1
Willow Pk Dr 11 11 D1
Willow Pk Gro 11 11 D1
Willow Pk Lawn 11 11 D1
Willow Pk Rd 11 11 D1
Willow Pl Boot. 55 C1
Willows, The 11 27 C1
Willows, The D.L. 56 A3
Willow Ter Boot.
 off Rock Rd 55 C1
Wilson Cres Still. 54 A2
Wilson Rd Still. 54 A2
Wilsons Pl
 off Grants Row 37 C2
Wilton Pl 2 36 B3
Wilton Ter 2 36 B3
Windele Rd 9 28 A1
Windgate Ri 13 23 D2
Windgate Rd 13 21 C3
Windmill Av 12 42 A2
Windmill Cres 12 42 A1
Windmill La 2 59 F2
Windmill Pk 12 42 A2
Windmill Rd 12 42 A2
Windsor Av 3 29 C2
Windsor Pl 2 36 B3
Windsor Rd 6 44 A2
Windsor Ter 8 43 D1
Windsor Ter D.L. 67 D3
Windsor Vil 2 29 C2
Windy Arbour Sta 14 52 B2
Winetavern St 8 58 B3
Winton Av 9 43 D3
Winton Rd 6 44 B1
Wolfe Tone Av D.L. 57 C3

Wolfe Tone Quay 7 35 C1
Wolfe Tone St 1 58 C2
Wolseley St 8 35 D3
Woodbank Av 11 9 D2
Woodbank Dr 11 9 D2
Woodbine Av Boot. 46 A3
Woodbine Cl 5 15 D1
Woodbine Dr 5 15 D2
Woodbine Pk 5 15 D2
Woodbine Pk Boot. 46 B3
Woodbine Rd 5 16 A1
Woodbine Rd Boot. 46 A3
Woodbrook Pk 16 50 A3
Woodcliff Hts 13 21 C3
Woodfield Av 10 33 D2
Woodfield Pl 10
 off Woodfield Av 33 D2
Woodhaven 14 44 B3
Woodlands 6 51 D2
Woodlands, The 14 51 D2
Woodlands Av Still. 54 B3
Woodlands Dr Still. 54 B3
Woodlands Pk Black. 54 B3
Woodland Vil 6 44 B1
Woodlawn Cres 14 52 B2
Woodlawn Gro 14 52 B2
Woodlawn Pk 14 52 B2
Woodlawn Ter 14 52 B3
Wood Quay 8 58 B3
Woodside 3 31 C1
Woodside 14 51 D2
Woodside Dr 14 51 D2
Woodside Gro 14 51 D2
Woodstock Gdns 6 44 B2
Wood St 8 58 C4
Woodview Black. 55 C2
Woodview Cl 13 16 A1
Woodview Cotts 14 51 C2
Woodview Pk 13 16 A1
Woodville Rd 9
 off Botanic Av 28 A1
Wynberg Pk D.L. 56 A3
Wynnefield Rd 6 44 A2
Wynnsward Dr 14 53 C1
Wynnsward Pk 14 53 C1

X

Xavier Av 3 29 C3

Y

Yale 14 53 D2
Yankee Ter Black. 55 D3
Yellow Rd 9 13 C2
Yewland Ter 6W 43 C3
York Av 6 44 A2
York Rd 4 37 D2
York Rd 6 44 A2
York Rd D.L. 57 C3
York St 2 58 C4
York Ter D.L. 57 C3

Z

Zion Rd 6 51 D1
Zoo Rd 8 34 B1